The Sound
of the Harvest

A BRIDGEPOINT BOOK

BridgePoint,
an imprint of
Baker Books,
is your connection
for the best in
serious reading
that integrates
the passion of
the heart with
the scholarship
of the mind.

The Sound of the Harvest

Music's Mission in Church and Culture

J. Nathan Corbitt

A BridgePoint Book

Baker Books

A Division of Baker Book House Co
Grand Rapids, Michigan 49516

solway

© 1998 by J. Nathan Corbitt

Published by Baker Books
a division of Baker Book House Company
P.O. Box 6287, Grand Rapids, MI 49516-6287

and

Solway
an imprint of Paternoster Press
P.O. Box 300, Carlisle, Cumbria CA3 0QS
United Kingdom

Printed in the United States of America

Library of Congress Cataloging-in-Publication Data

Corbitt, J. Nathan.
    The sound of the harvest : music in global Christianity / J. Nathan Corbitt.
        p. cm.
    "A BridgePoint book."
    Includes bibliographical references and index.
    ISBN 0-8010-5829-5 (pbk.)
    1. Music in churches. 2. Music in Christian education. I. Title.
ML3001.C785   1998
264'.2—dc21   98-28640

British Library of Congress Cataloging in Publication data are on file at the British Library.

U.K. ISBN: 1-900507-88-9

For information about academic books, resources for Christian leaders, and all new releases available from Baker Book House, visit our web site:
http://www.bakerbooks.com

Contents

Preface

What does God's singing sound like? I had to ask the first time I read Zephaniah 3:17, "The Lord your God is with you, he is mighty to save. He will take great delight in you, he will quiet you with his love, he will rejoice over you with singing." Is there some cosmic song permeating the air we breathe? In 1719, when Isaac Watts penned the hymn "Joy to the World," he surely contemplated how "heaven and nature sing."

Does the sprout sing when it breaks free of its pod? Do you wonder, if so, whether a bean sprout has a different song than a cabbage? Does the earth roll and rock when a thousand shoots break from its grasp and reach for the sky, singing in cacophonous melody? Yes, all nature sings of the glory of God, from the noisy clapping of the sea and babbling brooks, to colorful, sprouting plants (Ps. 98). God's song is manifested in the hearts of humans as well.

Like a vast and fruitful garden music bears its melodies in every space where humans seek to break free of physical and spiritual captivity. A common grace of divine creation, all people sing, play, dance, and chant their joys of freedom, as well as their sorrows and longings. Reflecting the earthground of culture, they express their hopes and aspirations, and praise their gods. As diverse as God's fearfully and wonderfully made creation (Ps. 139:14), music is always crosscultural. Its meanings are so bound to the people and cultures who

7

make it, we often fail to see our commonness because of our strangeness. God's song of a redemptive call and purpose are found in every place.

Some of us choose to live in terrariums and never know this beauty because we sing with ethnocentric tongues as opposed to those of celestial angels. Dominant cultures spread their music like the pervasive kudzu vine. Carried on the floods of digital technology, the gentle songs of remote cultures and ancient hymns are washed away to the gutters of history like musical deadwood because we perceive them to be irrelevant to our experience or too difficult to learn.

Yet, as a plant is born, bears fruit, and dies, music also exhibits a life cycle. Bound to the context of its original cultural garden, which is ever changing and dynamic, music finds not an immediate death, but a fading relevance to the people who call it their own. New music is born with a cross-pollinated and grafted heritage from tradition and eventually finds its way into the marketplace of the city street. It is from the streets of our lives that we both share and borrow our musical experience.

With this pervasive music, is there something different, unique, even holy about the music of people who call themselves Christian? Do Christians have a special song to sing? If so, how do we know what is the best of Christian music? In 1984 I met a woman who changed my view of God's singing. By many human standards her music wasn't beautiful, but it was God's singing in the new life of a believer—the sound of a spiritual harvest. From that time, I have reevaluated my concepts of beauty and Christian music ministry.

Recently I gave a lecture at Eastern College entitled, "God don't make no bad music!" It was intended to be provocative and several people took the bait. In the halls I received comments ranging from, "No, God don't make no bad music, but people sure do," to, "Is this program about the music of the ghetto?" God's singing is about the song he has placed in the hearts of his creation from farmland, suburbs, ghetto, village, and even cyberspace. The Christian's calling is to tend that musical garden in the kingdom with eyes of the Father, who cares as much for human hearts as the diverse bodies that encase them and live in the markets and city streets.

Writing a book about this vast subject runs the risk of being so general it appears trite and irrelevant. At the same time, trying to include examples from literally thousands of Christian communities is an impossibility. As a "big picture" person, I have tried to provide a comprehensive, educational, and entertaining look at the holistic ministry of music in global Christianity. I also tend toward polemic explanations. The world is not so dichotomistic, but I find that contrasting ideas is a useful method for stimulating thought and conversation. Many colleagues, friends, students, and teachers have served as helpful sources of information, encouragement, and criticism.

Initial suggestions were made by Paul Warnock, John Benham, David Brown, Paul Aday, William Wan, Joseph Lee, Harry Eskew, Jeff Deiselberg who stretched my metaphor into the street, Frank Fortunato, and Rosalie Vrijhoff. Lila Balisky contributed detailed suggestions that served as a focusing guide. I thank Orville Boyd Jenkins for his meticulous preediting. Michael Hawn and Vernon Charter for their supportive comments and excellent feedback on the entire manuscript many of which I included in the final revisions. Thanks to Ron Matthews, Joe Modica, Doug Smith, Lynn Bransma, Ken Perkins, Nate Coleman, Jeff Sharpe, Joy Berger, Michael Heinese, Heewon Chang, Teresa Nevola, Manaseh G. Mutsoli, Ezekiel Birya, Esther Kahindi Baya, Edwin Wanyama, Daniel and Sari Pascoe in the United States and Mexico, Rev. Dr. and Mrs. Imotemjen Aier for their hospitality in India, Thang Cin Sum and his family in Myanmar, the friendly people in Vietnam, John and Mary Oostdyk for introducing me to the Netherlands, Jeff and Annie Dieselberg and Matt and Lori Mann in Thailand, James and Sara Wiegner in Costa Rica, Roberta King in Kenya, and many friends who hosted me on my journeys and stimulated my thinking. Thanks to my cousin Daniel Johnson, whose ability to communicate has helped me understand the needs and gifts of the "deaf" community.

I am especially grateful to the students of Eastern College. First, "The Angels of Harmony" have been an inspiration with their infectious singing and Christian spirit, which exhibits a truly accepting love of their own differences. Their director, Dr. Vivian Nix-Early, shares a similar vision for kingdom community in our contemporary world. Working with director/pianist Bill Reeves they have created a picture in more than sound that is truly worth a thousand words. Erin Anderson, a senior intercultural communications/dance major who served as my research assistant and first reader. As a student, Erin read the work from her perspective and constantly brought my circular and random thinking style into focus, constantly saying, "where are you going with this?" Finally I am thankful for a loving and supportive family throughout my life, both nuclear and extended. But mostly Vickie, my wife, who while completing her MBA managed to read, discuss, and share, and my children Heather, Zach, and Laura who always asked how things were going.

Introduction*

The rotund African pastor barged into my office in Nairobi with all the authority of a Kikuyu chief. Flashing a sharkskin suit and silk tie as if cloaked in a leopard skin and brandishing an ivory knobkerry, Reverend Thuku dictated instructions for summoning choirs. "We are going to visit the president at his country estate," he commanded. "Christians from all over the country will meet on New Year's Day, and we want the best music. MUSIC IS OUR FACE!" A commanding grin illuminated his regal countenance.

"Well, which face is it?" I wanted to retort, but held my tongue. Not that he was two-faced or that he talked out of both sides of his mouth, as I had heard some complain. He, and the organization he represented, had many faces. With some jealousy, I quickly unfolded my mental map. He represented an organization with twenty-five language groups, of which he spoke at least seven. He was a highland coffee farmer, and yet had traveled around the world. He seemed to be at home equally in the village mud church, the town storefront gathering, the city evangelistic rally, or his own high church worship. He could dance to the thundering *kiroho* (spiritual) drums of Kikuyu Christian heart music, belt his beloved pentatonic

*The introduction is based on my article, "The Face of Music," which appeared in *EM News* 6, no. 2 (1997).

11

"Amazing Grace," and tolerate the new electric guitars youth introduced into his massive stone cathedral—albeit there was controversy among the membership. Reverend Thuku had many musical faces and he naturally understood the role music played in his ministry.

This was before the days of "multiculturalism" and "global competency." Reverend Thuku was the archetype of a growing African and world population. A product of what Ali Mazrui called the "marketplace of ideas" in the triple heritage of Africa, he was a blended man who didn't fit monolithic categories. Reverend Thuku was a person of the future and music was part of his identity. Yet music was more than mere identity. As an expression of cultural values and application of biblical command, it was a tool for ministry that served his diverse congregations in search of kingdom community. I was curious: How could he have so many musical faces and, at the same time, be so focused in his ministry?

The Face of Music

During the process of writing this book, I coordinated a singing tour to South Africa and Kenya with Eastern College's gospel choir, the Angels of Harmony. Initiated twenty-five years ago from a Wednesday prayer meeting of a small group of African American students, it has grown to over seventy members. The style is unmistakable—melismatic passages are belted straight out into a congregation who cannot contain their emotion within confining pews. Call-and-response singing beckons people into the aisles, dancing, jumping, clapping, and singing. Some are so filled with the Spirit they run about the sanctuary, hands in the air, shouting to the Maker who they envision seated just below the ceiling. To be an Angel of Harmony on the Eastern College campus is to be *identified* with the African American Christian community.

If you could see this choir, however, you might experience some cognitive dissonance and have to create new ethnic music categories. The Angels of Harmony is a virtual rainbow of ethnic faces—Anglos, Latinos, Asians, Africans, and African Americans have chosen this style to express their musical and spiritual identities. There are seventy "Reverend Thukus" revealing their faces.

Their musical faces are *multiple* in that no one member would define himself or herself by a single musical style. Each group member enjoys other kinds of music. Their identities are *contextual* in that during a performance they all are Angels, but in other contexts each of the members may take on another identity. One is a music major and performs a Brahms lied with vocal polish and refinement, while another appreciates the complexity of the Indian sitar. All of them express *dynamic identity*, one that is in the process of growth and change.

James Banks, multicultural education authority, proposed that we are continually developing an ethnic identity. There are six stages in ethnic development, ranging from ethnic psychological captivity to global competency (Banks, 1988). Applying these stages to musical identity is one way of understanding changes taking place around the globe.

Ethnic groups who are *psychologically captive* often believe what others say about their group. They give up their own musical identity in favor of a more powerful group. Many African people bowed to paternalistic missionaries who told them their music was not godly or reverent. They sang hymns, not because of the beauty or theology, but because they believed their own had little value. In the same way, I refused to sing country and blue grass during my seminary days because these styles were not "artful" in the eyes of some of my instructors. In the case of Cambodia, there was little choice for decision; traditional musicians were eradicated along with many intellectuals in a successful cultural manipulation during the 1970s.

At some point, marginalized groups may develop *identity clarification*, where they begin to rediscover and take pride in their music and culture. We have seen this worldwide with a growth in cultural festivals and dance troupes. Among the African American community we have witnessed the growth of Kwanza and an African "roots" rediscovery. Native Americans proudly gather for celebrations, and Mexican Americans seek to understand the Mayans, Aztecs, Toltecs, and Mexicas.

Many ethnic groups are *encapsulated*. U.S. American Christians can particularly relate to this. It has been said that the most segregated hour in America is the Sunday morning worship. Our history of segregation and discrimination lingers in the sanctuary. However, music of this dimension has to do with a suitable language (verbal, symbolic, and musical) of expression that reflects cultural values.

Monolinguality restricts one's ability to be anything other than encapsulated. During my research among the Mijikenda of the coast of Kenya, I understood why many women of the rural *kaya* never accepted the Christian faith. They literally could not communicate in a musical language other than their *kiringongo* heart style. It was not until the church began to express musical praise in that style and language that they began to understand the implications of the gospel. Their encapsulation was not intentional; for the most part, it was circumstantial. However, once they became *bicultural* (speaking two or more languages and interacting with other ethnic groups and cultures), their monolingual styles were no longer totally satisfactory in expressing their changing identity—for whatever reason. And now we begin to see the face of Reverend Thuku.

Reverend Thuku had a *national identity*. Not only did he appreciate his own ethnic heritage and its music, but he had the vision and concern for other identities within the country of Kenya. He was Kenyan, at its best. He was multilingual and could move between different ethnic groups. Which face did he show to the president? All of them. English hymns of an international language, Swahili choruses of Kenyan nationality, and ethnic choir songs all graced the celebration. Each style reflected cultural values based on a converging church history.

The Culture of Music

At the Angels of Harmony rehearsal, I recognized opposing value systems based on heritage, history, and cultural worldview. Christopher Small (1977), in his *Music, Society, and Education,* was probably the first to show architectural differences between the music of the West and many non-Western traditions. Referring to Western music as "music of the concert hall"—framed music—he developed a convincing argument for the spectator nature of Western classical tradition, as opposed to the participatory nature of many non-Western musics.

Square Music

As I looked at the "White faces" in the choir, I identified with their "square" musical heritage. Each Sunday in the Southern United States I entered a rectangular building with hard bench pews all neatly placed in rows. The service started exactly at eleven and ended by twelve, or my preacher father heard complaints. The order of the service was exact, even for an evangelical Baptist church. It was as much a ritual as a Roman Catholic liturgy. *Book music* prevailed, as written notation dictated the hymns. Special music was framed within a boxed location in the sanctuary. This square music, which reinforced square (linear) values, was packed in the bags of nineteenth-century missionaries, along with other cultural symbols, to accompany the gospel of Christ into distant lands.

If I now look at the printed music of a hymn (e.g., "What a Friend We Have in Jesus") several cultural values are present. There is a desire for uniformity and precision, which reflects most strongly the influence of the Industrial Revolution. Each copy of the hymn is identical. Linear time is reflected in the barred music of 4/4 time. A specific pitch and key are demanded at the beginning of the hymn. There is, for the most part, a beginning and an ending. The linear text reinforces a cognitive style encouraged as soon as childhood education begins. The values of capitalism and private ownership are also present. The hymn is copyrighted, for a renewable sixty-four years, and both the composer's and author's names appear on the page.

In performance, there is a sense of an *expectancy of the predictable;* the climax of the piece is prescribed. This climax may be notated with a fermata, a climbing melodic pattern, or final cadence. Much like the music of the concert hall, people spectate for music of worship. They sit and listen to organ prelude, offertory, and "choir special." Reverence is shown through respectful silence until, and if, a polite applause completes the performance. This culture would collide with another more expressive one.

15

Round Music

I can also identify with the historical origins of the "Black" faces. Somewhere in an African village a young Christian arises on Sunday morning. From out of his round hut he walks into the circular village center. The previous night the community participated in singing and dancing in circles with *body and soul* music. This is round music, the face—and heart—of African culture.

The *expectancy of the unexpected* permeates round music. Participants know something is going to happen, they just don't know when. There is an air of excitement and expectation of a climax within the "performance." Community or collectivist values prevail in this music making. There is no individual ownership of the music; the song belongs to the community. It is not, by and large, bought and sold, but shared by all who collectively participate. At the same time, with the exceptions of historical griots, individual grandstanding or solo performance is discouraged because of the potential detriment to community values. As the seasons of the year and cycles of life move from the present into the past of a community of "living dead," conversational music in call and response welcomes everyone into a dialogue of community. Time is not finite and framed within twenty-four bars of exact pitches and beats. The event takes precedence. There is freedom for emotional expression within the circle of a well-defined community. This was the heart of Reverend Thuku.

These cultural music systems still exist in some encapsulated communities. However, in what Octavio Paz (Paz, 1985) called the "land of the superimposed pyramid" (referring to the continual introduction and dominance of new societies in the history of Mexico), music changes faces as societies interact. The cultural ecology takes on new and different shapes while struggling to maintain an equilibrium of life, identity, and purpose.

The Function of Music

By and large, music has roots born in the monocultural garden of the heart. In ages past, a rural community renewed itself through

16

the cycles of i.
the heart of the c
let gave promise of .
danced as the comr
Throughout the year
toward righteous living,
uals, storytellers educate.
the sick. Music weaved a
harvest time.

Likewise, the new birth of a believer
munity to celebrate in song, prayer, an
itual harvests perpetually rang through i.
centers around the world. These spiritual .
through many countries. Since the turn of the ce...
of the modern missionary movement, testimony and gos,
of the harvest have sprouted to give a Christian identity to new birt.
in many lands. In every village, tribe, and country diverse peoples
spontaneously sing of the spiritual harvest within their lives and
communities. The outburst of song can match the wealth of music
from the Wesleyan movement in England or the Great Awakenings
in America.

The contemporary and urbanized population will not be denied
their spiritual expression. Born of the same Spirit and manifested
in the beat of the streets, it follows the winds of globalization and
market economies. Contemporary Christian music and rap have
more in common than one might think. Bonded in a glue of rhythm
and blues, each calls for liberation and justice from the contexts of
suburbia and inner city, class and race.

Without question music has played and will continue to play a
significant role in the life of the church. Rich in tradition and founded
in biblical example, we sing and play songs of praise within the sanctuary of public worship. Most commonly, music plays a priestly role,
carrying spiritual movement from within our hearts outward to
physical expression. At other times, music is a proclaimer, herald-
ing the good news in melodious tidings. We are familiar with these
two functions, worship and evangelism. Yet underutilized and waiting for recognition are other valuable functions of education, healing, prophetic utterance, and more. Christian communities outside

... discover the fu...

... ...cal

...ristian community. These include worship, prophecy (a call to justice), proclamation, healing, education, and theology. In the second part, "Music for the Kingdom," I give principles for the practical concerns of the musician, pastor, lay leader, and interested parishioner. You will gain understanding and encouragement to use music effectively in mission, ministry, and service through song.

In Chapter One, "Kingdom Music," I outline basic theoretical concerns that will serve as the basis for the entire book. We will look at the nature of music, a definition of God's kingdom, and the important role of music in ministry. Chapter Two, "Music as Priest," discusses music's first and most visible function, the unifying role it fulfills in the worship of Christian community. Worship is the apex event in the celebration and "sacrament" of the church. The ritual (drama) of the worship event is central to the Christian community. Like an officiating Old Testament priest, music unifies expressive congregations in the kingdom of God on earth through common song and uncommon singing. Derived from biblical models and traditional rites of passage, kingdom citizens are led to pray, celebrate, and give thanks through text, music, and movement. Music's first role, then, is that of officiating priest.

Congregations follow basic principles for creating unity in worship. In today's world of diverse cultures, contemporary Christians are challenged to incorporate cultural differences. Examples are drawn from the huge metachurch in Asia, the "seeker services" of the megachurch in American cities, urban African congregations, and rural villages in nonindustrialized countries. At our places of worship we can discover new songs that reflect the unified heart of diverse peoples. Using biblical and cultural examples, we will seek to answer basic questions about music in worship. What ceremonies are unique to Christian worship? How do congregations create unity through music amidst diversity?

In Chapter Three, "Music as Prophet," we learn that prophets are signposts and lighthouses who direct us to truth and righteousness. Music as indirect communication provides a convenient avenue for modern-day prophets to warn, cajole, penetrate, and prophesy. Music camouflages their voices as they battle for truth in untruthful and unrighteous places. Musicians call for political reform and forewarn a second coming.

There is a role for the prophet in the life of the church. Used by the marginalized, downtrodden, and poor, music as prophet cries for justice and freedom from earthly oppression.

Verbal proclamation of the gospel is essential to Christianity. In Chapter Four, "Music as Proclaimer," we find that music is a powerful medium of communication. Covering such basics as definitions of proclamation and the gospel, case studies are used to describe how music proclaims an ageless gospel in an age of change. Not only are we interested in how music communicates, but we look at the sociological, theological, and musical needs of our different audiences.

In Chapter Five, "Music as Healer," we discover how music is used in healing around the world. From the time David played the harp to soothe Saul's ailing soul, music has demonstrated its healing power. In remote African villages, Christians chant incantations in the name of Jesus to cast out demons. Emerging in the United States is the field of music therapy, which opens new venues for music as a balm of healing.

19

Music is active theology. In Chapter Six, "Music as Preacher," we look at how the words and texts chosen by the singer reflect active theological beliefs. Text is the principal consideration in most church music. If one cannot judge a book by its cover, one cannot judge a song by its musical sound. To many, the text of a song far outweighs its music. To others, it is the sound. The prime theological question that all songs answer is: What is the good life, and how does one attain it? Musicians, pastors, and lay leaders must gain the critical listening skills to evaluate the music of the church.

In Chapter Seven, "Music as Teacher," we will explore how music is used in education and training in different cultures. God commanded Moses to write a musical history and teach the Israelites an unforgettable music message. Oral societies inculcate values, transmit messages, and teach wisdom through song, drama, and dance. The Christian church has also taken this music responsibility seriously. Hymnal committees carefully review the teaching of hymns. Children learn stories, sing songs, and act dramas of the Christian faith.

How then do we teach, promote, encourage, and make music for the church? What practical steps can pastors, music leaders, and cross-cultural missionaries take to achieve an effective music ministry? In this second part, "Music for the Kingdom," we look at the when, where, and how of kingdom music.

Chapter Eight, "The Voice," provides criteria for evaluating music across cultures. Is it the voice or the heart that really matters? We will consider how vocal sound is produced and what constitutes a singing style. We will also discuss the concept of "good" music and establish basic biblical principles for evaluating music.

Chapter Nine, "The Song," discusses the primary forms of music found in the Christian church, including their historical development. Each geography and culture has produced music. Early missionary hymns were later modified and flowered into African, Latin American, and Asian hymns. Spontaneous song burst from Spirit-filled believers. Contemporary writing schools and choir festivals foster new songs as they are pollinated from place to place in a paperless culture. Contemporary Christian music flourishes in the United States and is spreading globally. Is there a universal song? What are hymns, songs, and spiritual songs? Which songs should be used in new churches? How should music be selected for diverse congregations? Whose responsibility is it to write new music for the church?

Instruments are not denied their place in the church. In Chapter Ten we consider the "devil's ribs," or the guitar, and other instruments that are now widely accepted around the world. Some consider the organ the "sacred" church instrument. Others prohibit instruments based on their "secular" association. Has the computer and electronic synthesizer become Satan's hand in creating a spectating congregation? This chapter surveys the many instruments used in church worship and some biblical criteria for their incorporation.

Chapter Eleven, "Musicians," discusses the cultural concept of what defines a person as a "musician" and what qualities are critical for leadership. In the Western world, technique is important. In the developing world, building community through song is important. Biblical principles from the calling of David illustrate the inherent gifts for music leadership along with some natural pitfalls of pride, greed, and lust. Guidelines are offered for selecting music leadership and achieving effective leadership in church music programs. How do people know they have a gift of music? How do congregations incorporate musicians and their gifts in ministry? Do musicians have faults that inhibit the ministry? What dangers await the effective musician? How are musicians trained?

Song leader, hymn writer, choir organizer, singer, and instrumentalist, the Christian musician takes his or her role seriously. From all walks of life and with many aspirations, musicians reflect the traditions of the past and lead the church into the future. Training is sometimes limited and rewards are few, but the joys of music are central to the life of the Christian community.

Part 1

Music
in the
Kingdom

Kingdom Music

Is there something different, unique, even holy about the music of people who call themselves Christian? Do Christians have a special song to sing? If so, how do we know what is the best of Christian music? My intent in this chapter is to provide a theoretical and theological framework for subsequent chapters as we look at music in the lives of those who call themselves followers of Christ.

This book is more than a book about music. Rather, it is a book about people who make music. Ideally, you would hear a song and see the people who make the music, in order to place it in a cultural context. Since we cannot do that through the printed page, I have chosen to use stories because they can bring abstract ideas to life. So following a brief introduction, I present anecdotes to set the stage for discussion. In "The Sound of the Harvest . . ." I relate stories from the past in primarily rural contexts. In ". . . And the Beat of the Street" I share stories from the present context in primarily urban settings.

Christians and their communities, whether meeting in a village church, urban theater or cathedral, suburban house or the cyberspace of the Internet, give witness to a redemptive history in the kingdom of God while living in earthly cultures they call home. It is exactly this life which creates such tension for those Stanley Hauerwas (1989) calls "resident aliens," those believers who live in worldly cultures yet follow spiritual rules under an eternal Lord.

Pick a city anywhere in the world and walk the streets on Saturday night and Sunday morning—Loiza, Puerto Rico; Limon, Costa Rica; Nairobi, Kenya; Southampton, New Jersey; Yangoon, Myanmar; or Calcutta, India. What do you hear? Music, pouring into the streets in torrents of pulsating rhythms, screaming guitars and blaring trumpets mingling with, and sometimes covering, solemn chant, stately hymn, and exuberant chorus. If you walk into the stores and row houses, you see and hear music downloaded off the Internet from anywhere in the world.

Because of technology, music has broken free of cultural norms and symbolic magnets and, like water, finds its own way into every cultural garden. Particularly in the age of what William Knoke (1996) has called "the placeless society," where everything is everywhere all the time through the marvels of cyberspace, musical styles that once gave identity to specific peoples have now been placed in an open global market. A young international generation, suspended culturally rootless in a virtual world, is no longer bound by the walls of traditional culture and the values they encapsulate. Before the information age, respect for truth came in the boundaries set by definable categories. Music was a symbol of this truth, passed from generation to generation in the forms of Christian chant and hymn. Now either part of a closed monastic community, or demagnetized and thrown into the global market, Christian music and the truth it carries must now compete with tantric chants of Tibetan monks, gangsta rap from the priests of hip-hop culture, and the commercialized stars of contemporary music. This eliding confluence of musical ideas will not disappear in the future.

In our pluralistic world characterized by the chaos of change, church congregations seek to maintain stability and certainty. There are two dangers. On one hand, congregations that protect their music boundaries run the risk of raising walls against the very people they seek to reach. On the other hand, some Christians appear to identify with the culture of the street rather than offering a faith for the street.

In this chapter we present basic ideas for the chapters that follow. First, through several examples, we will see how music is a sound of spiritual harvests. Born in the beat of the street, this music of the cultural heart is outside the walls of the church building. Second, we will discover the world of music through seven basic cultural concepts. We will then define several terms and principles related to this text: the kingdom of God, kingdom music, and kingdom music functions.

The Sound of the Harvest . . .

Harrison was a vivacious Rabai man with a winning smile and willing spirit. Like so many African people, he often spoke in proverbs. Reducing my long questions and abstract explanations into concrete phrases, he would leave me in wonder at his clarity of thought. One day, Harrison's most profound thought sparked my interest in the origins of Christian song.

I was on my way home from Tanzania. Kenya was in the middle of its worst drought in decades and the roads were hot, dusty, and void of the usual Savannah scenery. Dry shrubs and sand whipped around the road in "dust devils." Most wild animals sheltered themselves under trees and bushes that looked more like desert fossils than flora. Turning the bend near Namanga, I noticed several bright red objects glistening from Amboseli as they rolled back and forth in the breeze. They were too large and heavy to be balloons. I pulled off to the side of the road and walked toward what were the remains of a pastoral Maasai's "cash on a hoof." His cattle had died of thirst on the way to the local meat processing plant, where he was planning to sell them for family sustenance. Out of desperation he took the only thing now of value, their hides. Stripped of their covering, the exposed flesh bloated under the searing African sun and soon exploded, bathing the dry landscape in death. Only the wild animals would appreciate this blessing.

When I arrived home, I asked Harrison how the drought had affected his family. "It is hard, Bwana," he lowered his head. "Many people are leaving the village to look for food. Maize was not harvested this year, and we must find money to buy food." My thoughts jumped to his village, where during last year's harvest there had been great celebration of singing and dancing.

27

"Are people making music this year, Harrison?" I inquired. He responded without thought. "*Bwana, bila mavuno hakuna kuimba* [without a harvest there is no singing]."

I did not want to believe that proverb. Later, entering refugee camps near Mozambique and the feeding stations helping the starving thousands in Ethiopia, I heard no music. There was no singing. This was a sad and desperate statement about human life. People without hope could not find the energy, time, or desire to sing. As Abraham Maslow suggested, our first needs are survival needs. Music may not be one of them.

Several days later, I was discussing this proverb with a colleague involved in church planting. Was there a spiritual parallel? "Sounds accurate to me," he observed. "Dead churches have lifeless music. They have nothing to sing about because they are spiritually asleep." For decades these local churches sang nineteenth-century hymns in a dry and ritual mimicry. If music was universal, these translated hymns were not the "universal song." Western spiritual realities were not those of non-Western people. Spiritual creativity lies both within and beyond the boundaries of human culture as I was to discover from a woman named Esther.

I only met her face to face, once. Her appearance revealed nothing of her contribution to global Christianity, yet she was a legend. According to local people, she was the first to sing Christian songs in a style unique to their vernacular language. Esther Joshua was about to answer the question: Where does Christian music come from?

The sun was heavy and sharp, cutting through her tin-roofed coastal house. To stay cool we sat on small stools and leaned against the plastered walls that still held the midnight ocean breezes. Esther hacked and coughed from her emphysema as she sent one of the children peering in the doorway to fetch us a warm soda. A young goat kid scurried and hopped from table, to chair, to floor, and back again. Undaunted by her arthritis, Esther joyously suffered through our conversation.

The local pastor said she had been very blessed, not only because of her musical gift, but also because on each hand she had six fingers and on each foot she had six toes. Revered for her contribution to local Christian life, Esther's personal testimony was now a part of the historical and ecclesial myth. Born in the 1930s to a traditional African village family, she had little use for the religion of the missionaries who built a stone church by the road. Their whole way of life was contrary to hers. These *wazungu* (foreign people who travel in circles) seemed determined to change her way of life. Each Sunday she passed the stone church building built by these partners of colonists who took land, taxed local people, and restricted their travel. Watching from the road, nothing attracted her except for local amusement. Worshipers' hands seemed bound by a book she couldn't read. Singing was stiff without the dancing of celebration and meaningless because it was in a language she didn't speak. "What joy could be found in that place?" she commented to her friends.

Almost as early as she could walk, Esther helped her mother gather firewood and carry water from the nearby river. She loved music, and danced into the night to the drums of celebration, mourning, and healing. At an early age she married a young village man, who recognized her beauty, not only in her dancing, but also for her contributions to the community through hard and faithful work.

As the years passed, her body began to show signs of age. Years of breathing cooking smoke and dust from dry fields caused a lung disease. Like times in the past, she visited her local *mganga* (traditional healer) for medicine. She danced to free the Upeho spirit until the morning hours, but still she found no relief. Her prized chickens were sold to pay the local *mganga*'s services. Drained of spiritual and physical strength, she sank into depression.

One day an African man rode up on a bicycle and introduced himself as John. He was an evangelist from a new group of Christians that was meeting underneath a tree on the edge of the village. "Jesus has the power to heal," he told her. "Pray for me!" she requested. In a miraculous way she was healed. Late that night, in a divine dream, she began to sing a new song about her visitation by Jesus, Son of God, and the healing within her. On Sunday, partly out of curiosity and mostly out of joy, she wanted to share. When John gave those attending the opportunity to tell their personal experiences, she stood and offered her song. Without a thought, she clapped her hands and danced as she rejoiced in song. Others joined in. Esther, the poorest by many standards, sang of hope—a hope she had found in a Savior, a hope for an eternal life beyond her present circumstances.

This story does not end here, however. For if it did, we would not know of Esther's song. Young and gifted singers, acting as musical pollinators, spread Esther's song from village to village, like seeds of a dandelion floating in the breeze. Before long, a body of song was orally codified into the Mijikenda Christian tradition. The Hebrew psalmist, with whom Esther appears to have more in common than with the folks of the stone church, stated the origin for her song:

Sing to the LORD a new song, for he has done marvelous things . . .
The LORD has made his salvation known . . .
Shout for joy . . .
Burst into jubilant song . . .
Let the sea resound . . .
Let the rivers clap their hands . . . let the mountains sing together
    for joy.

(Ps. 98:1–9)

Born in the garden of the heart, harvested in the spirit of the soul, and manifested in the beat of the street, music is the expressive voice of the Christian faith (Corbitt, 1994). From every corner of the present kingdom of God, Christian music grows from spiritual harvests.

As a plant is born, bears fruit, and dies, music also exhibits a life cycle. Bound to the context of its cultural garden, which is ever-changing and dynamic, music finds not an immediate death but a fading relevance to the people who call it their own. In the case of Esther, her children would move to the city, become bilingual, and express their spiritual harvests in the musical styles of their experience. New music is born with a cross-pollinated and grafted heritage from tradition and eventually finds its way into the marketplace of the city street and the world of cyberspace.

. . . And the Beat of the Street

"Where does music come from?" I asked. Mr. Ortiz focused on my face with a quizzical look. Sitting somewhat rigidly in the Baptist church pew of Limon, Costa Rica, he had devoted his life to serving as a trumpet player in the Salvation Army Band. Whether he really believed his answer or wanted to respond to my white face, he gave a response with a resounding "FRANCE!" He was serious. The French colonialists may be proud, but I'm not sure about his African ancestors.

Just one block from the Blackstar Line Hotel, where Jamaican Africanist Marcus Garvey sought to unify the black diaspora against the history of slavery, Mr. Ortiz must have been aware of his African cultural roots. But the syncopated and lively beats of calypso with its roots in Africa could not be his. He was a Christian and Christian music came from Europe.

Somewhere along the way Mr. Ortiz learned that only European hymns were suitable for church. He was unaware, no doubt, that the great Protestant Reformer John Calvin, who so influenced his Baptist theology, would have condemned his trumpet playing in church. Or that, William Booth, the founder of the Salvation Army, might well have used the calypso to reach the people of the streets his bands so effectively marshaled in England.

Caught between the world of tradition and the world of innovation, Mr. Ortiz was somewhat frustrated when the young people wanted to bring the calypso beat into the church. Equally uncomfortable for him was the fact that none of his children or grandchildren seemed to show the slightest interest in learning to play the trumpet. "They just want to play with their new computers." Outside the bounded walls of his sacred music categories, young persons stood in the cultural street with Esther. Like the young people of Limon, the young people of New Jersey had already found an answer for themselves, as I was to discover.

This was a journey to find Christian music in the United States, in the state of New Jersey. Unlike the bumpy roads of East Africa I was stuck in a traffic jam on the Philadelphia Schuylkill Expressway. Drivers were angry and hostile, eager to get home and frustrated with their inability to control the traffic situation. Two-and-a-half hours later I found the location of the "Up All Night" concert by the Contemporary Christian Music (CCM) group Big Tent Revival. It was a nondenominational church set outside the endless tangle of highways between Philadelphia and New Jersey.

The sprawling church complex would soon be transformed into the stage of a Christian "rock" concert with hundreds of screaming young people dancing about the chancel to the music of their Christian "idols." The foyer of the church resembled a shopping mall. Brand T-shirts, performer pictures, cassettes, and CDs covered the walls and tables. Inside the auditorium electronic speakers, amplifiers, and theater lighting overflowed from the pulpit area. At that point, the usual complaints of CCM critics, "It's all commercial, they are in it for the money," were validated.

The concert itself assaulted my senses and my sensibility. A young electrician supervising the concert suggested I wear earplugs and gave me a pair. Young people rushed to the front and began dancing under the assault of sound. The first performers on stage, "Reality Check," could have been any rock group in the country. Dyed hair, hip-hop clothes, and earrings shouted pop culture as loudly as their ear-shattering guitars. I looked around the auditorium. Parents sat in amazement, some in open-mouthed shock, yet all appeared relieved that their children were not in a "secular" context doing the same things, and more. "Where is Christ in all this?" I asked myself.

If, as Marshall McLuhan first suggested, the medium is the message, the message I was getting had nothing to do with Christianity! Later he wrote a book *The Medium Is the Massage,* suggesting that the medium is only part of the message (McLuhan, 1967). I had to dig deeper.

The answer was found backstage. In interviews with groups, The Waiting and Big Tent Revival (which I will draw from later in the book), I learned of a deep spirituality that sought to "build bridges by holding one hand in the culture and the other in the church"— to be in the world and not of the world. Using the latest technology of laptop computers and the Internet, the musicians were answering fan mail related to spiritual issues in their virtual Christian community that included the entire country and beyond. Before the concerts, each group spent time in prayer and Bible study, seeking God's guidance as to how their music could draw the audience to Him and not to them. These contemporary musicians were seeking to make the message relevant by communicating in a language and cultural milieu of a young generation influenced by the media of contemporary culture.

A World of Music

God's world is big and diverse—over 6 billion people speak 6,700 languages. Each language represents at least one culture, and each culture sings and defines music according to its own standards. How can we make sense of Christian music? The answer lies in understanding basic principles about the nature of music itself.

First, all music is a gift of God given freely to all people. Like a vast and fruitful garden, music bears its sounds in every space where humans seek to express themselves. A common grace of divine creation, all people sing, play, dance, and chant their joys of freedom as well as their sorrows and longings. Reflecting their cultures, they express hope, aspiration, and praise. As diverse as God's fearfully and wonderfully made creation (Ps. 139:14), music is always cross-cultural. Its meanings are bound to the people and cultures who make it. *The meaning of music resides in people, not in sounds.* In a general sense, our evaluation of music has more to do with the people who make it, perform it, and respond to it and the context in which it is performed than the music itself.

Second, music is an expressive behavior of human cultures. Culture is the way people organize themselves and go about life. It includes language, roles, rules of interaction, and relationships. Our worldview includes our behaviors, attitudes, beliefs, and values. Music is one way in which members of a culture express their affective or feeling nature. We sing about our life—a life that is lived within our culture. Like the tip of a giant iceberg, music is one of the cultural elements we can see and hear and thus identify.

Third, singing is universal, music is not. As far as we know all cultures sing, but music is not a universal language. Because music is always bound to culture, it adheres to the rules of that culture. It thus becomes a cross-cultural problem when one music is played in another context or culture.

All of us have concepts about music. Our brains are remarkable in that they can take the millions of perceptual schema of our external world and organize them into categories. We can *differentiate* between sounds of birds and those of humans. It is our culture, however, that helps us differentiate between "music" and "nonmusic"

33

(Blacking, 1973, p. 27). In Western cultures, any organized sound may be considered music. People talk of the song of the bird, and even have singing dog contests. Other cultures, however, would consider music as only melody from human beings—a singing bird is ridiculous.

For Esther, the sonic event of the stone church was not music because it did not involve dance. In fact, one Bantu word for music, *ngoma,* is the same word used for the drum, but in the larger context it was the word for a sonic event that included drumming, dancing, and singing. To "sing" a new song without dance would not be singing at all.

Whatever cultural word we use to describe the sonic events of culture, it involves more than sound. We have many *categories* for music within our culture, which we refer to as style. Because music is verbal (having a text) and nonverbal (without words) it has other characteristics or qualities associated with it. Movement, facial expressions, clothes, instruments, and voice characteristics are all cultural markers for what we define as music. To the deaf, music does not include sound, but rhythmic movement and sight.

In Islam, the highest form of music or sonic event is the incantation of the Koran, which is not really considered "music." The term *sawt,* which means sound or voice, is differentiated from *misqa (musiqa),* a term representing other forms of music (Malm, 1995, p. 79). Because *sawt* is linked to the incantation of the Koran, it is sacred.

Fourth, music is bound to a context. Music has no meaning in and of itself apart from the context in which it is used and the culture that makes it. Music is a magnet that draws meaning from people. "The more music is used in a context the more the music means that context" (Best, 1993, p. 54).

Since the early church of the first century, Christians have struggled with the associational baggage of music from ungodly or worldly contexts. Instruments were not allowed as part of Christian worship because they were often associated with the pagan rituals of temple prostitutes and Greek dramas. It was nearly eight centuries before the first instruments were reintroduced into the worship of the Catholic tradition despite a strong Old Testament tradition of temple worship (Hustad, 1993, p. 179). However, when we view the attitudes of early missionaries toward traditional music of other cultures, they struggled with the same evaluation of music outside the sanctuary of Christian worship as we do today. Consider this example from Chinese Christians.

For many years, the Chinese hymn tune Puto, named for an island off the coast of the Chinese Zhejiang Province, was sung by Christians in southern China. Most congregations did not know its origins and "found it quite congenial to their faith" (Chen, 1996, p. 7). But when the hymnal editors discovered its Buddhist origins, they dropped it from the hymnal. Buddhists, contrarily, have quickly assimilated Christian tunes "wrapped up in traditional instrumental accompaniment plus modern electronic sound mixers" (Chen, 1996, p. 8).

Fifth, music is a lifestyle. I can identify and empathize with the people of the stone church, more so than I can with Esther's rural background. And yet Esther and I had much in common. We each were reared within a protective and closed society. My musical worldview was determined by my environment. As the son of a conservative Southern Baptist preacher before the advent of television, I was reared within the four walls of a church building. Esther was reared within the confines of a geographical region relatively free of Western influence.

I am always fascinated and encouraged that young people have the intuitive ability to evaluate their own music, and at the same time express a complex understanding about their culture while those of us outside, looking in, struggle to comprehend. I was talking with a group of young people in the Netherlands during a coffee break of a training session on cross-cultural issues. They kept referring to a music called "house music." So I asked, "What is house music?" Without a thought one young man instructed me, "It's not music, it is a lifestyle." As I understood his explanation, house music is part of a lifestyle of escape. The music is composed on a synthesizer by a single person, using a driving and rapid beat. Young people play the music on "Walkmans" to drive out the sounds of the environment in the external world and within their heads. Often used in connection with drugs at house parties, it is a lifestyle of escape from the realities of everyday life. But so was the heart music of Esther, a lifestyle. She sang to fetch water, harvest corn, and grind meal as part of her agrarian life.

Sixth, music is dynamic like the cultures that make it. The only constant in life is change. Cultures are not monolithic, nor do they remain the same. Music reflects the changes in technology, language, economics, politics, and religion. While it is unclear how this change affects music within different societies, people struggle for a continuity of life in the midst of the change. As we saw in the case of Mr. Ortiz, some of us hold on to the music of the past because it provides stability. Others, as in the case of the Christian rock bands, at least in their youth, take hold of the present and push music to its limits within the boundaries of the church.

Seventh, technology has changed the way we experience music. Marshall McLuhan believed that our perception of the world has been most affected by changes in technology. Western people once relied heavily on the written word; today they are becoming less linear and are taking in everything around them (McLuhan and Powers, 1989). Once literate approaches were the only method of sharing information. Today, we rely on the sensory experience of sight and sound through the medium of modern technology. These contemporary storytellers return us to the preliterate age in a "secondary orality." Many young people would rather learn something from a video than read a book about the same subject!

Music for the Kingdom

Is there such a thing as Christian music? Yes and no. No, in that Christians do not own a special dispensation of musical sounds unique to Christians. So we cannot say that there is a universal Christian music. We often use the term "sacred" to define music of Christians and the term "secular" to define the music of nonbelievers. These terms, however, do not accurately describe the situation because some music has a way of being "sacred" to a particular group of believers, and at the same time, "secular" to others. Consider the debate over rock music in the church. More frequently we may hear the terms "church" and "nonchurch" music, which designates the place where the music is performed. Even when we use "Christian" and "worldly" we have problems because many Christians sing folk songs that are not of the church. Our labels for music often define geographical territory. In addition to these, in this volume I use the term "sanctuary" for the music used in the church context and the term "street" for music outside the church context, although none of these terms adequately describes a mixture of style. I prefer to focus on function of the music and meaning in the text.

We can say that the music of Christians is unique to those who sing, play, and dance their faith. Music is a servant of all God's people and in every culture. It is a gift of common grace. The same song can be sung by Christian and non-Christian alike. However, when used for ministry it takes on a servant role to the kingdom of God. The term "kingdom" has three implications that often confuse our understanding of music.

The Kingdom of God

Our first view of a kingdom is political and social. The people of Esther's stone church were part of an empire—an earthly kingdom. Between the fifteenth and nineteenth centuries, European countries, like the powerful world civilizations before them, established immense geographical and economic kingdoms. Subjugating the masses and maintaining order through direct and indirect rule, they organized standing armies and protected the sovereignty of their acquired colonies. These kingdoms acquired great wealth and power for their monarchs and lords. It is this image of a kingdom that often represents our thoughts of an earthly kingdom.

No less powerful are the social structures humans create to survive and live in the world. While kingdoms, societies, and social structures are essential for life on earth, they do not accurately describe the kingdom of God.

A second view of the kingdom is spiritual. For Christians the kingdom of God should mean "the undisputed sovereignty of God in creation, established and expressed in a complete order of peace, justice and righteousness on a new earth within a new heaven" (Fraser, 1995, p. 1). This kingdom is being fulfilled in the present while looking for consummation in the future. Often pictured as a celestial city of gold in Revelation, with images of a beautiful city-state, the kingdom is "both future and present, personal and social, spiritual and material, gradual and climactic, and involves both divine and human action" (Fraser, 1995, p. 3). It is perfectly complete in the future and potentially whole in the present. Yet this kingdom also stretches from the present to the past in a redemptive history since the beginning of time. Part of this past has been the earthly religious structures that stand between earthly and spiritual power. As Kraybill states, "The kingdom is present in the lives and relationships of people, but the programs and patterns of the church are humanly responses to the kingdom" (Kraybill, 1978, p. 190).

A third view of kingdom is that of religious institutions. The organized church stands somewhat in the middle of these images. It has spiritual designs and uses earthly structures. The institutions, organizations, and ecclesial structures of the kingdom of God have often collaborated with or emulated these earthly empires to establish church kingdoms of equal wealth and influence. It is natural that a vision of God's reign on earth would return in the glory of David in the days of Israel's people of God. It was this same hope that the people of the Gospels held even until the triumphal entry of Jesus in Jerusalem. "Hosanna! Blessed is he who comes in the name of the Lord! Blessed is the coming kingdom of our father David! Hosanna in the highest!" (Mark 11:9–10). Our present age also looks to the future for this perfect kingdom. However, until that time, "the seduction of the church occurs when its institutional forms are shaped by the prevailing cultural values rather than the kingdom perspectives" (Kraybill, 1978, p. 191). How does music relate to these ideas of kingdom: social, spiritual, and church?

Kingdom Music

Music is a part of each of these kingdoms. A society without an expressive nature becomes cold and uncreative. Music is often used to maintain the identity and cultural boundaries of earthly societies. Court musicians often graced the halls of kings to validate their power. Likewise, there is a fine line between music for the kingdom of God and music that maintains the power of earthly kingdom structures. While music must be relevant and functional to the context of earthly societies and structures, it should never be determined by culture. Since music is a human creation, though a gift of God, it must be constantly evaluated for its ultimate servant purpose. Just what is that ultimate purpose?

Kingdom music is, first of all, song. As I will define it throughout the book, song is the expressive, lyric, and symbolic language of people who live in communities of like people. This song grows from the holistic life of the community that we call culture. For Christians, the primary consideration is text and the meaning it expresses and communicates within and without the person and community. This does not mean that instrumental music is not Christian. Rather, it means that instruments are by and large subservient to the voice that sings the text.

Second, music is a transporting art and activity for Christians. In its divine function it often pulls us out of our present reality and focuses emotions and thoughts toward a new understanding and communion with the Creator. There are three facets to this music.

1. Kingdom Music Has a Message.

Any discussion of music in the context of Christianity must begin with God. It does not really begin with music. For without understanding this history of God's active role in the creation, fall, and ultimate redemption of the world, the music of Christians is no different than any other music. The music of Christians is commentary, reflection, and proclamation of the message of God's redemption of a fallen world. It was through the incarnation of Jesus Christ, who came in a cultural context, who died and rose from the dead to become Lord of all who would receive him and his message, that serves as the *song* for those who call him Lord.

The Bible is a not a treatise on music. It is a divine and authoritative guide for living in God's creation. Music is part of human culture and therefore to be created and used by human beings for kingdom purposes.

2. Kingdom Music Has a Purpose.

Music is a tool, an expressive voice to be used within the kingdom of God. There are three overarching purposes for which the Bible emphatically commands all human musical behavior. First, music is to bring glory to God. Both the Old and New Testament writings speak of music used in praise of and to the Creator. From the celebration of the Israelites upon crossing the Red Sea to the unison praise in the celestial city, music serves as an expression of praise.

Second, our human musical actions are to reconcile person to person and person to God. Music is a spiritual ministry of reconciliation.

> So from now on we regard no one from a worldly point of view. Though we once regarded Christ in this way, we do so no longer. Therefore, if anyone is in Christ, he is a new creation; the old has gone, the new has come! All this is from God, who reconciled us to himself through Christ and gave us a ministry of reconciliation; that God was reconciling the world to himself in Christ, not counting men's sins against them. And he has committed to us the ministry of reconciliation. We are therefore Christ's ambassadors, as though God were making his appeal through us. (2 Cor. 5:16–20)

This ministry of reconciliation is accomplished when people and societies are reconciled with the kingdom.

Third, the call to extend the kingdom goes beyond the city gates of power.

> And so Jesus also suffered outside the city gate to make the people holy through his own blood. Let us, then, go to him outside the camp bearing the disgrace he bore. For we do not have an enduring city, but we are looking for a city that is to come. Through Jesus, therefore, let us continually offer to God a sacrifice of praise—the fruit of lips that confess his name. (Heb. 13:12–15)

Christians are called out of the comfort and self-protection of bounded structures to incarnate or live among others as salt and light in the beat of the street. "You are the salt of the earth . . . You are the light of the world. A city on a hill cannot be hidden" (Matt. 5:13–14). Music remains confined to the gardens of the sanctuary and the celestial city of the future when the "worldly" use it successfully in the battle for the street. The very place where Christians are called to be faithful. Music, and the arts in general, must be freed from our narrow categories into a broader, functional worldview. A kingdom worldview involves both a global vision and a historical understanding.

3. Kingdom Music Has a History.

If you look at Figure 1.1, you can see that the spread of the Christian faith has corresponded with the great influences of earthly empires and kingdoms. The solemn beauty of Greek hymns and chants spread with Greek culture. The Roman chant and development of spectacular sanctuary organs and orchestras spread with the Roman and European empires. The tumultuous age of liberty spurned a growth of new hymnody in the Reformation. On the wings of colonialism came the modern missionary movement and the beginnings of hymnody in the emerging church. Today, in the information age, a global community sings in hundreds of languages and musical styles. Is there a role and function for music that serves a spiritual kingdom?

From the beginnings of the church, Christians have struggled with several issues: Should songs be only Scripture? Can instruments be used? Is worship music the sole responsibility of an ordained (or designated) class, or does it belong to the congregation? Can music outside the church context be used for the kingdom? Throughout the text we will discuss these issues in greater depth, and I encourage you to refer back to Figure 1.1 for historical perspective.

Holistic Ministry

The kingdom of God is not limited to the sanctuary, but extends to city streets and beyond; it is past, present, and future; it includes every part of life. In this section, we discover how a holistic ministry functions within the kingdom, both earthly and spiritual. Music anthropologist Alan P. Merriam (1964) makes an important distinction for this discussion. When we discuss music in ministry, most people think of its uses, not its functions. The distinction is clear. "'Use' refers to the situation in which music is employed in human action; "function" concerns the reasons for its employment and particularly the broader purpose it serves" (Merriam, 1964, p. 210). For example, music is used before the sermon in a choir anthem, or as congregational song, a wedding song, or an offertory interlude.

41

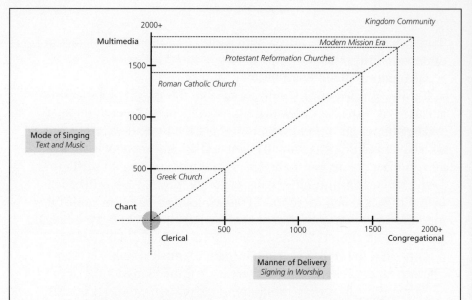

New Testament Church—A.D. *33–200* **Mode.** Chant. Instruments probably forbidden. **Manner.** Clerical and community. **Issues.** How to include the cultures of new converts and maintain purity.

Greek—Patristic Orthodox—Church—A.D. 200–500 **Mode.** Chant. Instruments forbidden. **Manner.** Liturgy develops with primarily clerical performance of music. Congregation becomes "active" listeners. **Issues.** Maintaining a musical identity apart from the non-Christian world.

Roman Catholic Church—A.D. 600–1400 **Mode.** Codification of the Latin chant. Introduction of organ and other instruments. The development of polyphony. **Manner.** Highly controlled clerical performance of the liturgy. Development of the Schola Cantorum and choirs. **Issues.** Centralization of papal authority and liturgy. Debate over use of instruments and nonchanted music and the overuse of secular materials with liturgical music.

Protestant Reformation Churches—A.D. 1500–1750 **Mode.** The hymn and choral music become more prominent. Psalm singing increases. Instrumental music and accompaniment grows. **Manner.** Congregational participation in singing eclipses clergy control. **Issues.** A continual debate over the role of instruments in congregational singing. Humanly composed hymns versus strictly Psalms and Scripture. Influences from outside the church.

Modern Mission Era—A.D. 1750–1950 **Mode.** Primarily the evangelistic (translated) hymn. Choirs. Roman (Latin chant) The piano and organ, Western orchestral instruments are the only instruments allowed in worship—with some exception. **Manner.** Each tradition is carried forward to the mission field: congregational in Protestant missions, clerical in Catholic traditions. Chant continues in the Orthodox church. **Issues.** Associational elements of traditional styles and instruments of music.

Kingdom Community—The Emerging Church—1950– **Mode.** All styles of music practiced from chant to multimedia. Incorporation of every available instrument both in-culture and cross-culture. Music enhanced through electronics including amplification, the overhead, computers, synthesizers, MTV, and television. **Manner.** While orthodox traditions continue, music of the emerging church is congregational. However, with the advent of electronics and commercialization, a new class of performing "priestly" musicians threatens the participative nature of worship. **Issues.** Spectator worship. Commercialization. Secularization. Unity in diversity.

Figure 1.1 Global Music Perspective

[1]Based on Myers 1996, pp. 8–9.

These uses tell us the what, when, where, and how of music. However, they don't tell us the "why" of its existence—for what purpose music exists in the local kingdom community.

Merriam suggests that there are a number of greater functions of music within society: emotional expression, aesthetic enjoyment, entertainment, symbolic expression, physical response, conformity to social norms, validation of social institutions, stability and continuity of culture, and integration of society. These functions are found in every social society, church- and nonchurch-related. For example, just as music helps young members of a tribal group integrate into the community in rites of passage songs, so also the music of worship helps integrate new members into the rite of the community worship experience. These functions, however, are not what the church would consider ministry or service to the local church, although music does function in these ways as well.

Donald P. Hustad suggests that music is not an entity unto itself, but serves higher purposes or functions of the church. First, music functions in Christian worship (Greek *leitourgia*) as a way to express God's presence and an effective method of communication in worship. Second, music in proclamation *(kerygma)* narrates salvation history and calls people to faith. Third, in Christian education *(didache)* music imparts information about God and service to him through gifts. Fourth, in pastoral care *(diakonia)* music is a healer of the human spirit and activity as a result of human relationships. Finally, in fellowship *(koinania)* music builds community by strengthening bonds of love (Hustad, 1993).

Both of these concepts of functional music apply to the church. As part of the present kingdom, like in earthly societies, music performs, serves, and supports the kingdom in a number of ministry roles in communities of faith. Often, however, we view the ministry of music in the kingdom community only from a worship perspective.

Music has multiple roles to perform. When we focus only on music in the role of priest or proclaimer, music remains underutilized and produces an unhealthy community. Music is priest when it transports and directs worshiping people toward a relationship with the living God. Music is proclaimer when it communicates the good news of the kingdom to the people of the present world. It is a prophet when it stands on the boundary of faith and belief and calls

the fallen world and "straying" church toward the justice and righteousness of the perfect and future city. Music is poet when it brings
healing and reconciliation to the physically ill, psychologically disturbed, emotionally wounded, and community of brokenness.
Music is preacher when it provides understanding of the kingdom
to those who call themselves its subjects. And music is professor
when it welcomes and educates the newborn into the community
of faith through time, history, and ecclesial structures.

These functions of music are not simple, but complex; holistic,
and not so easily dichotomized between sacred and secular definitions. One song can function in several roles at the same time,
depending on the context and participants. For example, the hymn
"Amazing Grace" was sung at a funeral where thousands gathered
in Arkansas to honor and remember the victims of an ambush when
two boys opened rifle fire on schoolchildren. In the ministry function, the hymn served in a priestly role to direct the spiritual focus
toward God. For most, it functioned as healer, soothing hurting souls.
Yet, on a societal level, it served to validate the structure and role of
the church within American culture.

Conclusion

In this chapter we have looked at how music is defined, used, and
functions within culture. Instead of giving specific rules for evaluating music, I have proposed basic concepts to guide the musician
and minister in gaining a kingdom worldview for music. Music, like
food, clothing, or other cultural artifacts, is to be evaluated based
on its cultural value. Music (which has many definitions) is a creative expression that brings life and meaning to the people who call
themselves Christian.

I have come to appreciate and learn from different people and the
music they make. In six continents, Christians sing of the same Lord,
but their sound has many voices. These voices are gifts of ministry that
fulfill important functions in the kingdom. As my friend commented,
they are the sound of the harvest. However, from the safety of our own
cultural sanctuaries, the beats of their streets can be threatening. These

cultural others have their own songs to sing. Yet the kingdom uses their music in much the same way—for their part of the kingdom.

Esther Joshua, as far as I know, was not literate. Like many women of her time and place, she never learned to read or write, never attended formal school. Though she had not read the Bible, her music was biblical. Her song of hope was a song of the heart. Like David of the Old Testament, in *action* she danced before the Lord in joy. Her song was one of God: "he will take great delight in you, he will quiet you with his love, he will rejoice over you with singing" (Zeph. 3:17b). And with the psalmist she sang to the Lord a new song, for he had done marvelous things; his right hand and his holy arm had worked salvation for her. She could shout for joy, burst into jubilant song, and make music (paraphrase of Ps. 98:1, 4–5). Her response was one like Joel's: "I will pour out my Spirit on all people. Your sons and daughters will prophesy, your old men will dream dreams, your young men will see visions" (Joel 2:28).

Her singing was motivated by her integrity and honest intent of the heart, "For out of the overflow of the heart the mouth speaks" (Matt. 12:34b). Esther wanted nothing more than to share her good news and rejoice in the company of other believers. With Paul she could agree "that the only thing that counts is faith expressing itself through love" (Gal. 5:6b). Her singing was with the "spirit and the mind also."

What about the results of her singing? Esther's style of singing became a testimony to many others like her—people who would not have heard this message of salvation without it. Within two decades, hundreds of songs like hers were pollinated about the countryside and a musical style was born and codified into Christian practice, thereby giving identity to a local group of people.

Had we taken Esther's music at "face value" we might have concluded, as did many early missionaries, that it is not worthy of Christian praise, that it has no value and possibly is even evil. Were you to hear the music, you would definitely not understand it, and out of context, it would be meaningless to you. But by entering into this story and understanding the context, you can see its value.

But can we say any less for the people of the stone church or the Christian rock bands in New Jersey? In reality, we do not know until we know the people involved and how music is functioning for their kingdom communities. We do know that music was a sign of their harvests, a SONG of their salvation. The question that next comes to us is this: If these people are worshiping the same Lord, why is there so much conflict in the church, and how can we ever sing eternal praise together? We now turn to our next chapter, where we consider the difficulties of unified worship.

Questions for Discussion

1. Can you think of a time when a special song came to you as a result of a liberating experience? Is there a special song you sing in times of trouble or joy?
2. As a result of changing society, what conflicts divide your own church community?
3. How would you define music?
4. Using a song you have heard or sung recently, describe how it is associated with the context in which you heard it.
5. Describe a particular musical style and explain how it is part of a lifestyle.
6. How has technology affected the way you play, perform, or listen to music?
7. What words do you often use to describe the music of Christians? How might they reflect an association to a geographical context?
8. Have you ever considered your church's music ministry as a "holistic" ministry? In what ways?

Exercises

1. Select a member of your congregation, or another person, who enjoys singing. Interview her or him regarding how music has ministered to her or him in a special way. In a class discussion, compare your different testimonies about music.

2. Using the description of a holistic kingdom which includes all of life, but different rules for living, what terms would you use to define music used by Christians? Or debate this concept: all music is potentially evil.

3. Using the map of the historical church, trace your own church's history. Include major events and the music that came with this history.

4. List the six major functions for a holistic ministry: priest (worship), prophet (justice), proclaimer, healer (healing), preacher (theology), teacher (education). Under each heading list ways in which your congregation is already involved in these ministries?

Music as Priest

Then the king of Assyria gave this order: "Have one of the priests you took captive from Samaria go back to live there and teach the people what the god of the land requires." So one of the priests who had been exiled from Samaria came to live in Bethel and taught them how to worship the LORD. Nevertheless, each national group made its own gods in the several towns where they settled, and set them up in the shrines the people of Samaria had made at the high places. . . . They worshiped the LORD, but they also served their own gods in accordance with the customs of the nations from which they had been brought.

(2 Kings 17:27–33)

I am in them and you in me. May they be brought to complete unity to let the world know that you sent me and have loved them even as you have loved me.

(John 17:23)

After this I looked and there before me was a great multitude that no one could count, from every nation, tribe, people and language, standing before the throne and in front of the Lamb. They were wearing white robes and were holding palm branches in their hands. And they cried out in a loud voice: "Salvation belongs to our God, who sits on the throne, and to the Lamb."

(Rev. 7:9)

Discussing worship is both holy ground and dangerous ground. It is holy ground because worship style, as opposed to worship itself, is what people often hold sacred about God and their relationship to him. It is dangerous ground, first, because entire denominations have been created in order to experience relevant worship, sometimes based on theological differences, but more often on history and culture. It is also dangerous ground because worship involves a cultural perspective. Culture is a hidden dimension of life (not bound by overt rules of behavior) that we generally take for granted. As such, the influence it has on our beliefs, values, and attitudes carries into our worship experience. How we worship is seldom taught, but is transferred through experience (worship culture). With rare exceptions, music is central to our worship culture. As such, our preference and selection of music have much to do with our cultural preferences and aesthetic standards. Our expression of worship is intimately bound to the cultural symbols we use to communicate with each other and with God.

The primary purpose of music in the kingdom is to worship God. However, the function of music is one of expressive unifier. Music serves as priest when it unifies the community in communication with God. This metaphor implies that music is representative and mediator of the community's musical voice of worship. There is, however, a difficulty in worship that threatens the contemporary church in an urbanized world. Ubiquitous music creates confusion.

The urban world is a cultural bazaar. A wide variety of ideas and values, drawn from different civilizations, competes for the attention of potential consumers (Mazrui, 1986, p. 97). Lost in a maze of culture, ethnicity, sociological class, and denominational traditions, contemporary Christians, like lost tribes, are looking for a place to feel at home. As Doran and Troeger ask, "How will we lead the church to worship God in a way that draws the best of what each tribe has to offer without reinforcing the fragmentation and the struggle for domination that characterize our culture?" (Doran and Troeger, 1992, p. 16).

In a study of eight documents on Roman Catholic worship since Vatican II (1962–65), Jan Michael Joncas (1997, pp. 113–15) describes five trends that apply to every tribe of the kingdom:

1. There is confusion on "what constitutes proper liturgical music."
2. "The treasury of sacred music consisting of Gregorian chant, Ars Nova and Renaissance polyphony, Baroque, Classical, and Romantic Masses, Requiems, and motets has almost completely disappeared from Roman Rite Worship." (And for many evangelicals this includes the traditional hymn and choir anthems.)
3. The impact of sound technology and mass media has changed worshipers from participants to consumers. The result is conflict when individual tastes do not conform to community concerns.
4. More than in any other time in history, we live in a pluralistic music environment, where we find music from every faith tradition.
5. The role of the musician is also changing. Is he or she to be a professional in ministry or to serve the church as an avocation?

In addition to these concerns, we find a blending of worship traditions, where music from one tradition is converging on another (Liesch, 1996, p. 81). If you have changed geographical locations and tried to find a new church home, you know the confusion. In what I call *worship vertigo,* you may experience ecclesiastic culture shock to find Baptist worship that appears more like Pentecostal worship, Presbyterian more like Baptist, and Catholic more like Congregationalist. Church clergy, musicians, and congregations are struggling to make worship relevant, but in the process there is a loss of identity and continuity.

In response to this confusion, many people are thronging to the charismatic and seeker-friendly worship churches; others feel manipulated and detached from the Christian faith. Journalist Yonat Shimron recently reported that in the traditional Bible Belt of the Southern United States, where evangelical churches dominate, many people are converting to Orthodox Christianity. New Orthodox churches are "being built at a rate of 50 a year." The Orthodox Church in the United States, with 5.5 million members, already has more members than the Anglican and Presbyterian churches combined (Shimron, 1997, p. B5).

These people are searching for the roots of the faith that has been uncorrupted by contemporary culture. Others find a safe place in familiar cultural and ethnic patterns. Still others, a new breed of cyber communities of the Internet, find their worship in virtual communities outside temporal space and time. Is it possible for citizens of the kingdom be unified? Should they be?

In this chapter we will look at how music functions in worship to create unity. First, we will define worship using a model of cultural and ritual communication. Second, we will discover how music creates unity—and sometimes disunity—among different cultures. We will consider basic cultural, ecclesiastic, and historical traditions that contribute to the problem. Third, we will consider basic principles for planning effective worship, including the role of the musician. Finally, we will look at a case study of kingdom worship.

The Sound of the Harvest . . .

Chiang Mai, Thailand. It's 6:00 P.M. and worshipers are beginning to gather for evening worship. Flower gardens and lawns provide a serene and welcome setting at the Seven Fountains Seminary. The wood-frame building is void of chairs; only mats provide a place to sit. At the front of the room, a communion table holds baskets of wafers and a single silver cup of wine. The table is on a raised platform. In the center of the platform is a candle holder in the shape of a lotus flower. On the wall is a picture of Jesus, whose hands are in the Thai *wai* greeting. Worshipers gather on the mats and then take a reflective and silent cross-legged position—in complete silence. The pastors enter and sit behind the table. One of the participants takes a small acoustic guitar and gently strums a few chords of introduction as worshipers quietly chant a unison chorus in the Thai language. It is a beautiful service, a perfect balance of silent reflection, form, and community song. One leaves with peace of heart, refreshed in spirit.

... And the Beat of the Street

Santa Loisa, Puerto Rico. 6:00 P.M. on Tuesday. Just blocks from the Atlantic Ocean, this is a bustling town of the open air. On the beach, warm ocean breezes caress sunbathers, and fishermen repair their nets amidst daily stories and anecdotes. Just blocks away, on the streets, pedestrians jostle with buses and taxis. The latest hit tunes of reggae and rap blast from the lowriders (cars) of young men. On nearly every corner is a church, and on Sundays hymns, songs, and spiritual songs compete with bantering conversation and street hawkers' cries. It is at dusk, however, that the sound of street gives way to the voice of the sanctuary.

The heavy thump and beat of drums and the scream of electric guitars pour into the neighborhood street. Inside the cement building soloists sing praises into a microphone. Worshipers dance about the aisles shouting, waving their arms, singing, and speaking in tongues. Maracas and tambourines are passed between members as one grows tired or fails to pick up the beat. The music continues for over thirty minutes as ushers greet newcomers with a welcome smile and a yell in the ear, "Buenos Dias!" It is a beautiful service— alive, noisy, exuberant, and friendly.

The Service of Worship

The English word "worship" comes from the Anglo-Saxon *weorth-scipe,* meaning to attribute worth to an object. In its highest meaning, "To worship God is to ascribe to Him supreme worth, for He alone is worthy" (Martin, 1975, p. 10). But how do we ascribe worth to God? In the Old Testament *hishahawah* means a "bowing down," to prostrate in complete submission. In the Greek translation, *proskunein* carries the same intent of "submissive lowliness and deep respect" (Martin, 1975, p. 11). A second term is *abodah,* translated service, which implies that a believer's life should be one of complete service, as a servant to God (Martin, 1975, p. 11).

Our worship of God has to do with both attitude and action, faith and belief. How we express our attitudes and actions of worship is

53

determined by our individual history and culture. It is through language and symbols we are able to express these attitudes. Through belief we verbalize our worship, but in faith we express it in action. Music is one of these expressive languages.

The purpose of music is to be an expression of service, praise, and sacrifice. This is the focus of music, why it is present in worship. However, its function, or how it works within the kingdom community, is to unify separate voices into a single voice of purpose—praise. The basic musical language of worship is found among the members of the community "who share a common habitat and who live some kind of corporate life based on common institutions, common local traditions, and common beliefs and values" (Nketia, 1974, pp. 21–22). Music provides an opportunity to create, participate in music as a form of community experience, and express group sentiment.

In this chapter we will define the worship service as a *dialogue with God in an apex celebration event within the life of Christian communities.* In this definition, worship neither specifically begins nor ends. Rather, it is the community focal point on God and communion with God. It also calls for continual response outside the worship event. It is this focus of continual spiritual energy from the community that builds and solidifies the community for lifelong worship, faith, and service. Worship is living in constant communion with God and becoming like God in the humility of service and prayer. This apex worship event is experienced differently by various communities. Symbols change and are synthesized into the community, depending on the culture(s) of the participants. Yet each community reconfirms God in salvation history, and retells the salvation story within its context.

The apex worship event is one of communal dialogue with God and with each other. This dialogue uses language and metaphors encased in music that have meaning to us and express our emotions. This dialogue takes place in four distinct *content* aspects of the worship, which may contain subfunctions: praise, prayer, proclamation, and response (healing).

Praise. Praise and prayer are direct ways the community can communicate with God. While there are spoken prayers, the majority of communication takes place through singing. (A popular Christian proverb says, "Singing is praying twice.") In hymns, psalms, and spiritual songs the voice of the church is, first of all, praise. That is, the focus of music is directed toward God.

Prayer. Praise turns to prayer when the focus of the congregation turns from praise to God to the self-realization of sin and separation from God. Prayer also involves a focus on the needs of the community and offering of self for his service.

Preaching. God speaks to the community in Scripture, personal revelations in the form of testimonies (and prophecy), and the sermon. This proclamation extends outside the sanctuary into the street through the prophecy of justice and proclamation of evangelism (which we will discuss in subsequent chapters).

Response. Response is also important. Worship is not complete without a holistic response from the individual and the community. Individuals recommit to spiritual integrity through confession of personal sin. A kingdom community must also confess and renew its role as a lighthouse to society, in which its witness extends beyond the walls of the worship event.

The members of the community live in constant yearning to attain unity, unity with God and unity with each other. The apex service offers an event when the community can come together and hope to find unity. Each person comes with fears, doubts, and needs. The community comes face to face with God, and in his presence seeks affirmation and healing. As the community builds physical unity with one another through praise, it comes to a point of realizing the sins and powers that prohibit unity. There is an expectancy of renewed revelation from God—that he will speak. This happens through Scripture and sermon. But there is a further need for healing—intellectually, physically, emotionally, and spiritually. It is not until these healings take place that there is resolution within the body of believers. The event is not totally complete; it is a process. The apex event does provide a measure of resolution that allows the individual to grow and mature in personal faith and community responsibility. From this event, the individual responds in continued life service.

Negotiating Unity

To set the stage for our discussion on music in worship and how it functions to unify, I will tell a brief metaphorical story. I ask you to participate by becoming a citizen in the kingdom of Babki. Your name is Not Knowing. The kingdom of Babki is ruled by a king named Baba. Baba has many sons and daughters, and to each of these children he has given a province of the kingdom. Each child has built a house in the middle of the province. Although there are highways connecting the provinces, very few people have the opportunity to travel to other provinces.

You were born in the province of Bibko, and when you were twelve years old, Bibi, the first son of Baba, invited you to his house. You set out early one day on the highway and arrived at about noon. When you arrived Bibi called you by your name, Not Knowing, and welcomed you into the house. You did not know what to expect so Bibi gave you a tour. Inside the house were a number of rooms. In the first room, you met a group of people who fell to the ground when Bibi entered and kept very silent. You noticed sweet music playing in the background, and saw an object on a table. Under the object was a written word, Bibi Ba. You progressed to the next room, the next, and finally arrived at a room with a very large table set with all kinds of food. You couldn't help but hear the same music throughout the house, and could occasionally catch a phrase or two that sounded like Bibi Bobo, Bibi Bobo. You also noticed that in each room was a Bibi Ba. When asked to sit at the long table you noticed that all waited for Bibi to be seated. And in front of him was a Bibi Ba. After a wonderful meal Bibi escorted you out the back door. He said, "Good-bye, my friend. You are welcome the next time you pass this way. No longer are you Not Knowing, but from this day you will be called, Now Knowing."

During the next several weeks, you notice people from Bibi's house. They greet you, "Hello, Now Knowing." Occasionally, you even hear them whistling the Bibi Bobo as they pass on the road. When you return to the house of Bibi, you are greeted as Now Knowing. When you enter the first room you fall to the ground when Bibi enters, like you have seen the others do. You even begin to sing phrases of Bibi Bobo. As you pass through the house, it becomes more familiar and you notice more words to the Bibi Bobo song. You see other objects and more gestures that the Now Knowing make to each other. Eventually, you feel at home. And each time you leave, you feel as if you are Now Knowing More.

What I have just described for you is a very basic cultural model of ritual communication. For most people, this is how worship is learned. It becomes a cultural worship home. Over time, it becomes comfortable, acceptable, and unconscious. In other words, you do not have to think about the process, the symbols, or the songs. They also become attached to the context (Bibi's house) and the people you meet there. So much so, that to hear the Bibi Bobo song in another house can create confusion, or comfort. While you may be Now Knowing in Bibi's house, when you go to his sister's house in the province of Tatka, you become Not Knowing again, and must learn new songs and symbols.

For example, the Christians of Chiang Mai and Loiza, Puerto Rico share a basic and common faith and belief in the kingdom of God. But their habitat (provinces), traditions, and community experience are quite different. Imagine if members from these two churches were to gather in one place. The commonality of community would be diffuse. Creating unity with residences from different provinces and nations can be confusing, and uncomfortable. Participants entering another worship culture may experience worship vertigo.

Vertigo

To the casual observer, the missionary practitioner, and the church historian, these cross-cultural worship events can be devastating to the balance that tradition has afforded churches in the past century. In some cases, missionaries and national leaders respond by complaining of secularism, materialism, sinfulness, and excess in the church. They encourage a return to traditional theological education and hegemonic postures in an attempt to find balance. This state is not unlike the culture shock caused by the cross-cultural experience. I prefer to call it ecclesial vertigo, where generations have lost their sense of balance, order, and equilibrium among dynamic Christian communities. These emerging Christian communities from around the world are discovering religious freedom through biblical self-discovery, guidance of the Holy Spirit, and spiritual renewal amid political, social, economic, and cultural upheaval. This apparent confusion is a "a process of working out multiple syntheses of available options" (Chernoff, 1985, p. 155).

While some church members and leaders may be worried and confused by their loss of tradition, I believe these expressive Christians are not. As reportedly seen on a Ghanaian bus, "Observers are worried, believers are enjoying" (Chernoff, 1985, p. 156).

This is particularly important to church denominations that have established traditions (particularly in music and worship). In many countries Christian churches maintain a majority; in others they are a minority. As such, they are especially vulnerable to exposing doctrines and practices that have been under the church's control but are now placed in the religious "marketplace." The Christian "buyer" not only loves the Bible, but reads it and interprets its message in light of his or her own dynamic culture (Barrett, 1971, p. 143; Shorter, 1978, pp. 74–75).

Dynamic Convergence

An explanation for this vertigo experience can be illustrated by a principle I will call *dynamic convergence.* Dynamic convergence is the point of contact between divergent cultures (including church cultures). Once experiencing vertigo, the cultures must enter into what Jak Njoku (1990) has called *differential negotiation,* where all people learn from each other and negotiate change.

I can illustrate dynamic convergence and the resulting vertigo by a personal example. For a number of years I was the choir master of an African church. The pastor of this church was also a missionary from the United States. In this church were Western missionaries, Western ex-patriates (nonmissionary), Abaluyia, Kikuyu, Luo and other Kenyans, West Africans, Southern Africans, Japanese, Filipino, South Americans, and other nationalities. Finding unity and community in this group was an almost impossible task. Church members were not only Baptists, but came from a variety of denominations, including Anglican and Pentecostal. And yet they met weekly for public worship. Sometimes, in a worship event, unity was expressed, but many times it was not. The reason was that the church could not come to terms with the vertigo caused by the dynamic convergence of its diverse community. There was considerable disagreement on worship styles.

One Sunday, an African student and accomplished *litunguu* (African stringed lyre) player was to play and sing in the worship service. After being introduced to the congregation, he attached his leg bells and placed the seven-string lyre on his knee. He explained the meaning of the song he would sing since it would be in a language most people did not understand. He began to play and sing. As he sang, the lively rhythm soon began to bring smiles to the faces of the congregation. Suddenly, one woman jumped up from her seat and began to wave her arms and dance, giving the *kigelegele* voice trill of approval and excitement. For a moment the service was suspended in spiritual vertigo. Some people wanted to participate, but sat looking around at others who visibly expressed disapproval. Some were shocked. At the close of the song there was a wave of applause throughout the congregation and also relief that things had not gotten out of hand.

This experience offers an opportunity to discuss the continual problem of community in a divergent kingdom. The majority of the world's Christians are no longer from the West (Schreiter, 1990, p. 3). This shift in community is offering new symbolic expressions for worship events in the life of the kingdom of God. Christians in worship in the late twentieth century draw on many different traditions and church cultus or worship practices (Leaver, 1987, p. 1) at a *musical bazaar.* These different symbols of worship expression come from Catholic, Anglican, American Evangelical, Pentecostal, Independent Church, and African traditions, as well as Western popular music and culture.

These expressions have come within the grasp of every Christian. A number of forces have aided significantly in this negotiation, including independence, a world communication order, urbanization, Christian spiritual maturation, and a growing world theological scholarship. But we must also count the view of community and cultural identity that strives for consensus. The need for community consensus allows for convergence and the subsequent process of negotiation. While many are loyal to their denomination, informally the community of Christ knows no such barrier.

In essence, the process is one of developing a contemporary ritual. Ritual is defined as *the sharing of meaning through the practice of collective symbols* (Land, 1989, p. 413). These collective symbols include singing (in accepted forms and language), dancing, raising of hands, and other expressions. Music is our focus. This dynamic convergence and the resulting worship practice (cultus or rite) is the process of coming to consensus with a new worship experience that can express community. This community must be expressed on different levels that have a church community parallel. Each of these communities converges at some point with the larger community (see Figure 2.1). In this process, negotiating means both sharing and giving up certain worship expressions. We will look at this process from four different perspectives: social worship organization, cultural concepts about worship, worship format, and worship expression.

Social Level

The first level of negotiation takes place within the social organization of the community. This convergence happens on five basic levels:

1. The individual worship service is the private worship (devotional), where each Christian interacts and communicates with God personally and privately.
2. Family/clan worship is the small service by monolinguistic families and clans, best exemplified by the house church and rural family church.
3. Community/tribal worship is the service most experience, taking place in the community church and suburban church with homogeneous peoples.

4. Nation/multilingual worship is the large urban church with members of different ethnic and sociological backgrounds.
5. Kingdom worship is the international gathering of many diverse communities. This can most often be seen in large crusades and international conferences.

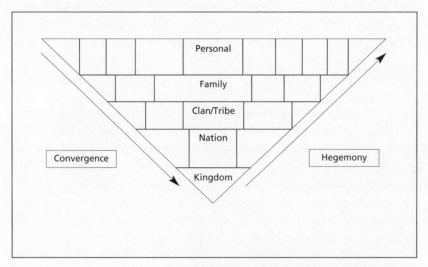

Figure 2.1. Converging Traditions

Each of these types of Christian community allows for certain freedoms and individual expressions. Each level demands giving up or negotiating individuality for the community of Christ, particularly in response to the wider community. The symbols in family worship are easiest to negotiate. However, as the community grows, symbols of ritual such as worship languages, form, and music expression that bind the community and allows the community to communicate with itself and God must be found (negotiated). Music expressed in family worship may not express national worship. The development of symbol in the larger context is a historical and sociopolitical process.

This is one reason that choruses, praise songs, *coritos* (Spanish), short songs (Asian), or *pambios* (Swahili) are so popular. It is not just their lively nature; they become a common musical language because of their simplicity. They take less time to teach, and they are common to many of the world's cultures, even in translated versions.

A second consideration, as we saw in the introduction, is that there are political reasons that people do not want to negotiate aspects of their worship identity. Ethnic groups that have been marginalized and held psychologically captive by dominant groups need their worship style, especially if they have been forced to conform.

Cultural Concepts of Worship

Each participant comes to a worship service with a personal experience in Christ and a specific cultural and sociopolitical context. Each person has an image or idea of the community and certain basic life and spiritual needs. I can explain this with a return to the Nairobi congregation.

After the service I just described, I was outside the worship hall visiting with choir members. My daughter Laura, then six years old, ran across the church lawn and jumped into my arms. We hugged each other, laughing and joking, and then just as quickly as she came, she jumped down and ran off to find her friends.

Mary, the ecstatic dancer of the worship service I just described, watched all of this from the doorway of the church. "Nathan, I want to ask you a question. I really don't understand you white missionaries. You kiss your children and hug them publicly, you even hug your wives in public, which is a show of emotion we sometimes find unacceptable. Why is it you can't hug God?"

Later, we were able to discuss this concept of *hugging God.* What was taking place was the point of convergence between our two cultures (our multiple cultures), north-south, clan-nation, and nation-kingdom. This unexpected event brought the congregation to the point where they had to negotiate the assimilation of this expression into the community in worship. What Mary was saying in this question was, "Won't you hug God with me? Join me in expressing praise to God in the emotional way that I practice at home. Can we express praise in the same way, together?" She was stating the sentiment of African theologian John S. Mbiti: "This community of faith is externally expressed, where Christians are more at home in dancing their faith, in celebrating their faith, in shouting their faith (through jubilation), singing their faith, being possessed by the Holy Spirit of their faith and demonstrating the frontiers of their faith" (Mbiti, 1986, p. 127).

Hugging God is just one such cultural concept of worship. In what Melva Wilson Costen calls a "binding thread ... woven over the years from slavery to the present age," to many African Americans, worship is *empowerment*. These patterns of worship "provide a tapestry of styles that empower and liberate African Americans to act responsibly in a world that seeks to limit power to a few" (Costen, 1993, p. 119).

Theologian Justo González describes Hispanic Christian worship as a *fiesta*. "It is a celebration of the mighty deeds of God. It is a get-together of the family of God" (González, 1996, p. 20). In this worship as fiesta, like our Puerto Rican example, worship may seem chaotic, but it is planned, just not rehearsed. It is more like "planning a party more than rehearsing a performance." Worship is participatory, emotional, festive, interactive, sensual, and moving. There is a strong sense of family (González, 1996, pp. 20–23).

In the contemporary context of the technological, primarily Western world, worship is *technique*. For these churches, worshiping correctly, in proper order, time, and style, consumes the church's energy. Driven by technology, the church must discover ways to bring the worship experience to the busy lives of urban people. This concern becomes especially critical when worship is televised or broadcast on radio. Worship workshops may become worship services themselves, where participants are trained in the latest theory and method of worship.

A good path expresses a concept of worship among the Kiowa Native American people. Native Americans are deeply spiritual people and their traditional religion was and is bound in ceremonies, which are often very demanding. Native American people have a tradition of travel on well-worn paths that laid the foundation for much of the highway system in the United States. Walking a good path implies a life free of anger, strife, and prejudice. Spirituality is holistic in that Native Americans experience good in humility, calling on God for every aspect of their daily lives. Many traditional Christian songs speak of personal experience on this good path. These people identify with the psalms because the metaphors of paths and journeys reflect their voice (Daney and Thompson, 1998).

In this conceptual level of negotiating unity, there are two approaches. By far the most prominent has been for the less powerful to acquiesce to the more dominant group. As nations and ethnic groups become stronger in their praise, prayer, preaching, and response, their voice becomes clearer and on more equal terms with the majority worship culture. These concepts do not mean a relativist gospel, but provide clearer pictures of God and broaden the metaphors and language by which all people in the kingdom can worship. While I may not have the cultural experience of hugging God, or overcoming slavery, or participating in great rituals, there are times when the concepts of hugging God, empowerment, and a spiritual walk can express my praise and service. These concepts and metaphors enliven the worship format, or ritual.

Worship Forms

The content of worship must be placed in some type of form. Forms vary according to different theologies, worship traditions, and cultures. Liesch conveniently categorizes these into three traditions: liturgical, thematic, and flowing praise (see Figure 2.2). The form is the ritual or cultus of the worship. Some evangelicals chafe at the word "ritual," primarily as a reaction to the pre-Reformation rituals in the Orthodox liturgical traditions. However, in the anthropological context a ritual is the organization of symbols and movements into time and space. Without rituals (and smaller ritualizations), we could not find a pathway into a familiar shelter (Driver, 1993, p. 16). Rituals help us move into a space and a time that we hold sacred. As we saw in the ritual story of Babki, the form (or ritual) that assists the worshiper helps transform him or her from one status to another. Form is the structure by which we organize our worship. Even the most "free" worship traditions have a structure, or form, or ritual—from the more complex liturgical tradition to the free-flowing praise worship.

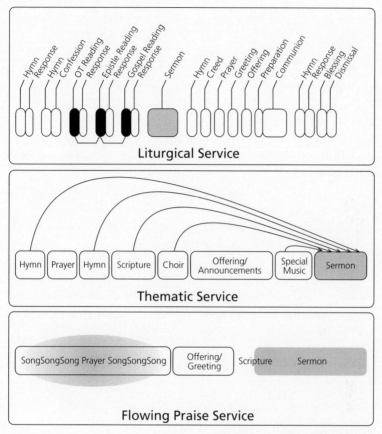

Figure 2.2. Worship Forms
(Liesch, 1996, p. 81; used with permission)

Worship forms (rituals) help us collectively express and experience the worship experience. In the larger kingdom communities, negotiating meaning involves learning the worship format from many options and styles. This is often a process of simplification and reduction of symbols from many different groups to find common ground. "Ecumenical" worship requires that divisive doctrinal issues give way to collective faith issues. Many Christians are often unaware of the ecumenical nature of hymns, songs, and spiritual songs, which grow from and are sung in every denomination. At a deeper level, we use cultural symbols to express ourselves and communicate within this form.

Communicating through Worship Signals

In the worship context, we bring our own cultural and worship communication. Learning to share visible signal systems of the new culture incorporates newcomers into the worship culture. In the multicultural worship, worshipers must negotiate their communication signals.

- Spoken language or verbal signals. Mama Esther can sing "All My Chickens Had Gone to the Witch Doctor" in Malindi, Kenya, and chances are she can express unity with the local congregation (Corbitt, 1988, p. 24). But this song only creates curiosity outside her community; at best it helps in understanding of diversity (and this is necessary). Likewise, the Western Christian can sing "God of Earth and Outer Space" and be regarded with the same curiosity in the rural equatorial church.
- Sound or audio communication, including music. Music is a language in sound; therefore, each culture has its own musical language.
- Written language. Communicative and worship language varies from culture to culture.
- Objects and artifacts. In the contemporary setting the drum, electric guitar, piano, and a host of instruments have been freed from sinful and pagan associations. Many pastors believe that a coat and tie are important for propriety in the pulpit (even in the dust and heat of equatorial summer). Some pastors wear robes and collars. The cross is definitely a unifying symbol in every Christian culture. Some churches have flowers on a table. Others highlight the Bible at the front of the church.
- Body language or kinesics. We express our praise in a variety of fashions—lifting hands, jumping, dancing, shouting, silence.

The Bible provides a variety of postures for worship: *silence* (Hab. 2:20), *walking humbly* (Mic. 6:6–10), *going barefoot* (Josh. 5:15), *bowing* (Exod. 20:5), *lifting hands* (Exod. 17:15), *shouting and falling down* (Lev. 9:24), *bowing down* (Matt. 2:11), *kneeling* (2 Chron. 7:3), *standing up* (Neh. 9:5).

- Space. Another important differential is the use of space in worship. We enclose space according to our culture. The way we manage the use of space and the resulting acoustics influences our mode of worship in music, posture, and other elements. For example, great cathedrals can create a cold and distant atmosphere, but they provide tremendous acoustics for melismatic and nonrhythmic (in some cases) chants and choirs. But in the open village center, long, slow phrases do not carry as well as syncopated monosyllabic rhythmic drumming and singing.

- Art and pictures. Many churches are void of any art, as if to say that art is idolatrous in worship. Yet many churches communicate through their art and icons. Consider the pictures over a baptistry, pictures of Jesus in the church, or the icons found in Orthodox churches.

- Light and color, or optical communication. Creating a mood for worship, some churches have vibrant and festive colors, while others prefer darker tones. Each of these creates a culturally determined mood.

- Time. The temporal organization of worship reflects a culture's concern for time as either a commodity (as in the West) as opposed to an event, where time is not a concern.

- Touch and smell. Olfactory communication is expressed in worship through the burning of incense, perfumes worshipers may wear, even the smell of a building. The communal wine and bread have a taste. Our smell and taste impressions are active long after we leave the service, and remind us of the worship event.

- Numbers. For Christians the number 3 is sacred representing a triune God. (Smith, 1992, pp. 144–65).

As you can see, when a nonmember joins a certain community in worship, it takes some time to acculturate (learn) a new worship event. In the broader worship experiences of kingdom communities, planning takes into consideration many of these elements. Worship committees ask questions like, Will we have dancers? Will we burn incense? Will guitars be appropriate? These external signals of cultural communication, when combined within the worship event, reveal deeper issues of beliefs and values regarding how someone should worship.

Cultural Values in Worship

Beneath our structures, concepts, and signal systems there are cultural values and preferences. Not polarized ideas, these worship values are more like dimensions. Their importance depends on culture, tradition, and even personal preference, and vary with age and experience (see Figure 2.3). These dimensions intersect at different levels.

Dimension A: Artistic/Functional. Differences in ideas about music center on two ideas: what is good music, and what the purpose of music is. The answer to the first depends on the second. When cultures view music as an "artistic" expression, then music is evaluated based on its artistic excellence. When music is a functional part of worship, it is not necessarily based on a standard of excellence in itself, but by how well it fulfills its function. For example, in the worship of the Puerto Rican Pentecostal church, the music was considered good because it created an atmosphere of unity for participants.

In contrast, in many high church traditions, perfection is strived for by a soloist or choir, which are highly valued for their artistic expression. This value results in a *spectator-oriented* as opposed to *participatory orientation* of functional worship music. This can be seen by the architectural design of buildings, which places the congregation as spectators in long, square sanctuaries as opposed to the semicircular design of many participatory sanctuaries. While this will be discussed in greater detail in chapter 8, this does not mean that congregations who favor functional music do not pursue some excellence, or that artistic music does not function as ministry. Just as functional music can have its own standards of aesthetics, artistic music when placed under God's service can lead in a priestly function.

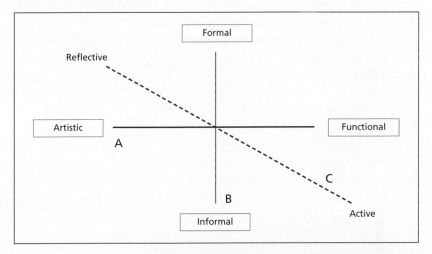

Figure 2.3. Dimensions of Worship Values

Dimension B: Formal/Informal. As we noted above, all worship services have form or structure. Formal structures have well-defined boundaries within the worship context. Orthodox traditions are very formal, with exact movements of priests and celebrants. Informal structure allows for a much wider latitude of behavior within the worship event. Consider Pentecostal worship, where participants stand and move about the sanctuary when led by joy and the Spirit.

Some people have the freedom of "antistructure" and are not bothered by a lack of exactitude and predictable order. This is directly related to the crisis orientation value of different cultures (Lingenfelter and Mayers, 1986, pp. 69ff.). The crisis-oriented person plans for almost every eventuality with a multitude of contingency plans. Change becomes predictable. In worship, I have heard a number of pastors, when planning worship, say, "We want to have planned spontaneity." There is a definite Western concept of the *expectation of predictability.* The unpredictable convergence produces vertigo. In African societies, there is what we can call the *expectancy of the unexpected,* or a noncrisis orientation to life. This noncrisis orientation allows the African to be flexible and adjust at

69

an astounding pace to changes that have affected the continent, religious or otherwise.

Yet there are times in our lives when we move between each of these dimensions. For example, for many years I have worshiped in the "expectancy of the unexpected" congregations. Recently, however, as a result of a fast-paced and sometimes chaotic life, I also desire structure.

Dimension C: Reflective/Active. In the reflective extreme, worshipers meditate quietly and reflect in silence. You saw this in the Thai worship example. In the active extreme, the worshipers participate often in boisterous praise. Many people are not basically emotional in relation to the worship event. They do not actively and outwardly express their emotions. Reflective worshipers often seek an inner response to their faith. They can also have an *intellectual* approach to worship. In fact, it has been stated that in Western culture people have moved toward thinking about religion and not experiencing religion (Goodman, 1988, p. 35). This is evidenced in the very few opportunities the congregation has to express emotion in the worship service. Our hymns, with many stanzas, are often symbolic expressions, unifying our intellects, but only occasionally our emotions.

Let's now apply this to personal, cultural, and ecclesial tradition. A negative reaction by one Christian community to an expressive element of another Christian community is often due to the concern that sharing in the practice will result in being drawn into a closer identity to an outside group. For example, some Baptists will not lift their hands for fear of being "Pentecostal." Other groups will not wear robes to avoid being considered Catholic.

While there are other cultural dimensions we will mention throughout the text, these three illustrate problems in negotiating unity in worship through music. There is one final area that we will mention briefly, and discuss in more detail in our chapter on music as prophecy, that is the context of worship.

Both the immediate and general context of the worship event directly affect the communicative language, structure, concepts, and values of worshipers. Every worship participant brings to the event the context of the broader culture. These become concerns for the entire community. We cannot avoid the fact that our worship in its many differences is determined by the sociopolitical context of the worshiping community. The Old Testament is full of worship symbols, hymns, and prayers that draw on the liberation from Egypt and wandering in the desert to the conquest of a new land. In South Africa during the 1980s, one did not enter a church without the political suppression affecting the realm of the spiritual. One can see this as well in the Western church from the language used in hymns during the World War periods. One of the challenges of the next century is to discover language that will speak to the needs of the world's communities in response to Christ. Our worship events and Christian service of worship cannot ignore the needs of those around us.

Designing Worship

As we have seen, culture expresses itself in the worship event. People cannot and will not accept the expressive means or lifestyle of another culture with which they have little or no affinity. Authentic worship demands that the cultural language used be understood by those who constitute the culture (Whelan, 1983, p. 180).

Worship languages and cultures are in constant transition. "Liturgy is bound to fossilize when it loses touch with human life. As soon as it becomes extrinsic to contemporary experience, it sickens. Its sure destiny then is the grave. As a fossil, it has the power to arouse curiosity, but it cannot inspire living faith. And it becomes absurd when it pretends to give meaning it does not and cannot give" (Magesa, 1975, p. 208).

We live in a day and age where the soccer or football game is the religious rite of the city (Goodman, 1988, p. 162) and where the rock concert is the religious rite of the youth culture led by the musician-priests of our day (Spencer, 1989, p. 5). Ritual does not guarantee worship of God; in fact, it can become a pathway to the wrong end. In Christian rock concerts, it is sometimes difficult to decide what and where worship is especially for those of us from another generation. There are four criteria for worship music that must be central whenever the community of Christians gathers for the specific purpose of worshiping the Triune God:

1. The music should be Christ-centered.
2. The music should be God-directed.
3. The music should be Spirit-empowered.
4. The music should be expressive of and edifying to the church (as community).

Celebration provides the community with a time of rest, a time of gathering together of a social grouping to retain and continue the bonds of society; it helps maintain the bond of the society and the departed and it keeps the bonds of society with the divine. In the Christian worship experience, music has a role to play in providing unity (Magesa, 1975, pp. 207–8).

1. Unity through texts that express community thought in light of biblical revelation.
2. Unity through music forms that express corporate emotion.
3. Unity through songs of local history of personal faith. These include gospel songs, songs of personal testimony, and new songs for the local community.
4. Unity through songs of biblical salvation history. This includes singing Scripture songs, setting psalms to music, learning about hymns from other lands, including the West, and learning about their historical significance.
5. Unity through songs of broader kingdom faith. This includes listening to and singing contemporary songs of larger communities. It also means encouraging the learning of new songs for and from the larger community worship event. Much sharing takes place today via the encouragement of the Christian volunteer movement.

Christian Worship at Its Best

Planning kingdom worship, based on our discussion, involves four basic principles:

1. Respecting the voice of other kingdom communities. Hugging God together involves some exciting concepts for the worshiper. It

is this concept of worship that African cultures have to offer the kingdom of God in biblical worship. It brings to mind a physical, emotional, and spiritual response to a loving, personal God who desires to be with his children. It is a celebration of community. One is reminded of Miriam's response to God's acts in Exodus 15 or the response of angels in Revelation 5. It is spontaneous. It is personal. Martin describes aspects of worship as the centrality of Christ, an awareness of the Holy Spirit, and a concern for others and the upbuilding of the community (Martin, 1982, pp. 195–97). Hugging God is but one way of expanding our worship vocabulary and experience. The fullness of God's glory, and the mystery of worship unfold and blossom as we enrich our worship, past the limitations of our present experience, and into the experience of fellow believers around the world.

2. Hard work. Experimenting with new concepts of music, however, will not bring quality into worship nor will music bring community. As Cornel West states, "Inclusion indeed yields new perspectives, critical orientation, and questions. It makes possible new dialogues, frameworks, and outworks. Yet only discipline, energy, and talent can produce quality" (West, 1993, p. 42).

The word "community" also implies a family of believers who care for each other and extend the event of worship in continued love and concern for each other outside the event. If people do not want others, cannot understand them, or are unprepared to share power or resources or to listen to other groups, they will always remain on the fringe.

3. Developing new mental worship maps. As we learn how music functions in worship, we are better able to share in the experience of others. Our concepts, beliefs, and values are our mental maps or frameworks for indexing what we experience. It is a spiritually liberating experience to share in the reflective/active, formal/informal, and artistic/functional worship of other Christian cultures.

4. Creating third worship cultures. Negotiating unity can take several approaches. Some seek unity through diversity and try to understand each culture on its own terms. In this musical apartheid, each group goes its separate way in worship while respecting the right of others to express themselves as they feel led. This has been promoted in the extreme by some with a call for

73

the exclusion of Western hymns in local churches to allow for the development of local hymnody. While this may be worthy, it certainly is not practical. Dynamic convergence is ever present, particularly through the radio, audio, and television media and modern transportation.

A second approach to unity in diversity accommodates all cultures through eclectic worship. This has value in that people of the kingdom learn to respect the diversity of world Christians.

A third approach is to use common songs found in all cultures. Hymnody is ecumenical in that many congregations share the same hymns and songs, though they may appear in different denominational hymnals (Hawn, 1996, p. 26). In international worship, leaders often select hymns and choruses that serve as a common bond to all participants from around the globe.

A fourth approach, implied in the universal Christian song of Revelation, is to create a third culture music, where people of different Christian practices and cultures create new songs. This has proven effective in a monastic community in Taizé, France. This community began in 1940, when Brother Roger came to the village to offer refuge to political refugees of World War II. Today thousands of people from every nation visit Taizé weekly to experience the community's worship. They are encouraged to experience the "wellspring" in their hearts. This living "parable of communion" has composed chantlike songs that provide a new Christian music that appeals transculturally to its many visitors.

Each of these approaches has its place. A truly universal song is certainly an ideal, but as the early church was given flaming tongues to express their praise, so will worship express the harvest of many cultures in the beats of a thousand streets.

Music in Kingdom Worship

As I travel throughout the world and share in different worship services, I am sometimes burdened by the lack of Christian community song. I see many churches searching for music that will help the community of Christians gathered to express unified praise and worship as a community. The selection of songs is often dictated by the taste of a pastor or worship leader, well-meaning, but without the assistance needed from gifted, trained, and ministry-conscious musicians. Here are some practical positive steps the pastor and church can take to develop kingdom community culture songs.

1. Recognize the need for a vital worship event.
2. Recognize music as a gift to the body of Christ to be developed and used.
3. Select a worship committee or hold focus group discussions on the needs of the congregation, including musical and family cultures.
4. Teach about worship, and its biblical, historical, and cultural practice, starting from the home cell group to sermons and demonstration of different worship formats, encouraging participation and creativity.
5. Encourage new songs by and from the congregation, including hymnwriting contests, song festivals, and visiting scholars and musicians.
6. Start from the cell group (home unit) Bible classes and other small groups, sharing new songs and encouraging songs from the group, using these in the meeting of the larger community.
7. Encourage musicians. Help them find a home in the church. Use their talents, provide them with instruments, and give them extra training at local music schools.
8. Identify and disciple musicians, incorporating them into the church.
9. Use a choir or music group as a worship leader.
10. Involve the congregation in songs, choirs, and other musical expressions.
11. Encourage and expect diversity, but strive for unity with symbolic music expression evolving from the church.
12. Rely on the Holy Spirit to guide the church in a meaningful worship experience. Plan for worship, but expect the unexpected (even if you have to plan a response).

One Church, Many Tents: Worship and Ministry in Singapore

William Wan is used to diversity. Growing up in Singapore, he was converted to Christianity while at a boys' boarding school. He and his cohorts began a small fellowship in 1963. It began to grow and with the advice of a missionary grew to become the thriving Bartley Christian Church in Singapore. Singapore has 221 square miles with a population of diverse peoples of 2.7 million. It is a newly industrialized country that trades throughout Asia and the world. Its cosmopolitan nature has influenced the type of church that thrives.

Fifteen years ago, Dr. Wan moved to the United States where he has pastored a multiethnic Methodist church in Washington, D.C. During those years he led the church to incorporate the changing community into a church with 30 percent Anglos, 60 percent Asian, and 10 percent African American members from the surrounding community. During that time the church made a move from a traditional Methodist congregation meeting in a building with stained glass windows and pipe organ to a multidimensional church meeting in a local theater, using praise music with a worship team and electronic instruments. This architectural transition is reflective of contemporary trends that have greatly influenced worship forms. In the traditional church one expects to find stained glass, a pipe organ, a minister of music and choir director, and traditional hymns. However, in the theater, the worship is more celebrative and involves praise and prayer and a worship team with guitars and drums. Interestingly, this also shows a change in American culture, from one of formality to informality, hierarchy to community participation.

In Washington, Wan encouraged a variety of styles to meet the needs of the members. He wrote hymns for special occasions that encouraged a community amidst diversity. One is "God of People, God of Culture" set to the tune of "God of Grace, God of Glory." The traditional tune was well known; the new text reflected a change in social organization combining the common ground of all with a changing and growing theological understanding of the kingdom of God.

In 1996, Wan returned as senior pastor of the church he helped found in Singapore. The motto of the church is "One Church, Many Tents." This vision statement guides the ministry of the church in a cosmopolitan and international city-state.

One Church, Many Tents has influenced the nature of worship. Three times a year twelve tent (satellite) congregations meet in a theater for prayer and praise. Each week there are eight worship services in English. Adapted to the international business context, one meets on Saturday to accommodate the businesspeople who must work with businesspeople from Japan, Indonesia, and other countries and enjoy playing golf on Sunday. There are also three Chinese services and one Filipino service. The church is divided into eleven zones, then into areas, and then into contact groups. Wan states that this concept has helped the church have the financial resources for ministry, yet create small enough groups to build community.

The church owns two small buildings that hold three hundred people. These are used for weekly services. They have avoided the acquisition of property, as an unnecessary part of "church" and have focused on people. The twelve professional ministers have been educated in many parts of the world, including Australia, the United States, England, and New Zealand.

Fifteen years ago, the church made a conscious effort to move toward a "celebrative" worship format, something less structured. At the same time neighboring churches were influenced by Pentecostal choruses—yet, they avoid labels of charismatic/noncharismatic, even though they clap hands and hold healing services.

In the healing services, they have a time of prayer and praise and then anoint members in need with oil. These services are held once a month. They seek to heal the illnesses of spirit, emotion, mind, and body. At times they will go to members' homes and remove idols, common to some Asian cultures, exorcise spirits, and cast out demons. Music is used, but has a subordinate and servant role. They seek to minister to the whole person though music and worship.

While threatening to the traditional worship patterns of the church in much of the world, this example illustrates the innovative response of a Christian community to their changing context. Worship forms of the past may be irrelevant to the people of the future.

Making worship meaningful requires thoughtful change based on biblical principles.

Conclusion

Jesus said that the greatest commandment was to love the Lord God with our whole heart and our neighbor as ourselves (Luke 10:27). The condition of our heart—having no other gods, being broken before God, and celebrating his power in creative redemption—has been the spiritual condition for worship. How we have chosen to express that heart condition has provided us with the diversity of life worship and more than occasionally created conflicts. Our task is to find the common denominators of our belief and try in our expressive worship, through the power of the Holy Sprit, to transcend our cultural differences while recognizing our uniqueness. It is possible. We want to glorify and bring honor to God. Transcultural worship can degenerate into a circus of events, with the glorification of the music, participants, and speakers. We can pray and plan that at the name of Christ every knee will bow and every tongue confess him Lord and Master of our lives.

Traditional community provides an extended family that cares for its members year in and year out with special events to celebrate life and focus the community inward, outward, backward, and upward. The love of God through Jesus Christ has brought us into the family of God. It is an extended family focused on God through Jesus Christ and energized through the Spirit with a responsibility to love one another and bring others into that family. God does not intend cell groups to become prisons or churches to become tribal homelands.

As in the spontaneity of a young child who wants to express her love for her father and be reassured of his love for her, can we "hug God" together? It takes commitment, hard work, and the continual understanding of the family of God as community.

The psalmist wrote many years ago that we should sing a new song unto the Lord. *The basic question in churches today may not be one of which old songs to sing but where the new songs for us to sing are.* A growing and vital community of God must always express faith. New songs have been a sign of the harvest in every major revival and renewal movement in Christian history. People are hungry for community, celebration, and communication with God.

> Sing to the LORD a new song, for he has done wonderful things. . . . Shout for joy to the LORD, all the earth; burst into jubilant song with music.
>
> (Ps. 98:1, 4)

Questions for Discussion

1. There are many denominational differences in worship we have not discussed here. Does your church have a definition of worship?
2. Read Exodus 38 and 39 and Numbers 8:5–23. Describe the ritual process. What communication signals can you find?
3. Is there a time when you have experienced worship vertigo when attending another church? Can you determine why?
4. Have you ever thought of your worship experience as a spiritual rite of passage? Do you agree or disagree with this concept? Why or why not?
5. Is your family worship different than your community worship?
6. What would you say is the underlying cultural concept of your worship? Is it related to any of those mentioned in this chapter?
7. Draw a diagram of your church's worship service. Compare these with those of other students.
8. Using these comparisons, what communication signals might you have to negotiate in order to feel at home? Are these biblical?
9. Using Figure 2.3, where would you place your church worship on the graph?

10. In the case study presented of Dr. Wan, what adjustments is your church community making in light of changing technology and sociological trends?

Exercises

1. Divide the class into several groups. Go out into several different community worship services and map the worship service using the categories mentioned in this chapter. As a class project, compare your findings. Include both theological and doctrinal issues. What worship cultural changes might you have to make to bring these congregations together for a community service? If you do not have this opportunity, use the two case studies from Thailand and Puerto Rico.
2. If you have a theologically mixed group of students, plan a joint worship service. Prior to planning, however, write a definition of worship.
3. There are theological reasons worship services are designed the way they are. Write a research report on the theological background of your church. If you are nondenominational, you may wish to interview your church pastor for information.

3

Music as Prophet

Oh, my anguish, my anguish! I writhe in pain. Oh, the agony of my heart! My heart pounds within me,
I cannot keep silent. For I have heard the sound of the trumpet;
I have heard the battle cry. Disaster follows disaster; the whole land lies in ruins.
In an instant my tents are destroyed, my shelter in a moment.
How long must I see the battle standard and hear the sound of the trumpet?

(Jer. 4:19–21)

After that you will go to Gibeah of God, where there is a Philistine out-post. As you approach the town, you will meet a procession of prophets coming down from the high place with lyres, tambourines, flutes and harps being played before them, and they will be proph-esying. The Spirit of the LORD will come upon you in power, and you will prophesy with them; and you will be changed into a different per-son. Once these signs are fulfilled, do whatever your hand finds to do, for God is with you.

(1 Sam. 10:5–8)

If music functions in worship to unify people in a voice of praise, music as it functions in prophecy often divides. While its ultimate goal is to bring people into a righteous and just kingdom under the grace of God, it often speaks more to the ills of society than to its benefits. One response is to proclaim the gospel without attending to the social needs of community. As urban pastor John M. Perkins explains, "God was beginning to show me that the gospel had to be more than just 'evangelism.' The gospel rightly understood is holistic—it responds to man as a whole person; it doesn't single out just spiritual or physical needs and speak only to those" (Perkins, 1982, pp. 22–23). As the gospel is holistic, so is music. While music is a vehicle for worship and evangelism, it also calls for justice.

Musical prophets stand on the edge between the sanctuary and the street and provide a vision of God's future reign. Music is prophecy when it leads people to truth and justice. Music is not a fortune-telling device, but a sonic tool that foretells future consequences based on present realities. At times, this musical truth lies outside the boundaries of a just and righteous kingdom. Yet at other times, it is the voice of the kingdom to an unjust world.

In this chapter we'll look at the musicians who make us uncomfortable, yet, when heard, cannot be ignored. First, we will look at how music functions as an indirect warning, banner of war, and leaven in the bread. Second, we will discuss the characteristics of musical prophets in the kingdom, whose empowered sense of justice is like Jeremiah's "fire in the bones." Third, we will suggest principles for interpreting the messages of prophetic music, which often sounds more like "noise in the city" than the music of praise. Finally, we will look at ways musicians and congregations can utilize music in justice. In these ways, we will learn an objective approach to evaluating music's prophetic voice.

The Sound of the Harvest . . .

Jahad laid on his reed mat at dawn, when the full moon surrenders to the rising sun. The earthen walls no longer held the heat of the desert sun and the chill of the morning pinched his feet stretching from under his small blanket. Jahad anxiously clutched the ram's horn *yobel* next to his reed sleeping mat.

For seven years he had anticipated this morning. His father, who lay quietly across the room, had waited forty-nine years. "Father, it is time! Can I play it now?" He could contain his excitement no longer. Muffled sounds of distant yobels masked the raucous tones that slowly moved in a wave across the valley. "No, son. First we must remember Yahweh who gave us this day."

This was the beginning of the Year of Jubilee. A historical foundation of God's law would free Jahad and his family from indentured service. Their land, taken years ago when drought had forced them into their present circumstance, would be returned. As Jahad's father canted the law, the growing sound of trumpeting yobels signaled a day of justice.

> Count off seven sabbaths of years—seven times seven years—so that the seven sabbaths of years amount to a period of forty-nine years. Then have the trumpet sounded everywhere on the tenth day of the seventh month; on the Day of Atonement sound the trumpet throughout your land. Consecrate the fiftieth year and proclaim liberty throughout the land to all its inhabitants. It shall be a jubilee for you; each one of you is to return to his family property and each to his own clan. The fiftieth year shall be a jubilee for you; do not sow and do not reap what grows of itself or harvest the untended vines. For it is a jubilee and is to be holy for you; eat only what is taken directly from the fields. In this Year of Jubilee everyone is to return to his own property." (Lev. 25:8–13)

Jahad's father then took his own *yobel.* "Now we can blow the trumpets of Jubilee, my son. Today we are free."

... And the Beat of the Street

It was billed as the "Sound and the Fury," and later dubbed the "Bite of the Century." Evander Holyfield was to meet former heavyweight boxing champion Mike Tyson in Las Vegas, Nevada. Thousands of bloodthirsty fans worked themselves into a frenzy, as they peered at the roped battlefield. Soon the davidian "underdog" would confront the Goliath of heavyweights.

Inside their dressing rooms, each fighter began to build courage. Electronic choirs on audiotapes went before them in battle as each one made his way to the canvas. First Holyfield, accompanied by a multicultural entourage, seemed to pray down the aisle to the words of gospel musician Fred Hammond, "When the Spirit of the Lord comes upon me, I will dance like David danced," blaring from the public address system.

In reverent silence, if only for a moment, sportscasters and the crowd bowed to the opening Christian contender's music. This reverence was interrupted by crashing, driving, and booming music throbbing from the opponent's hall. Mike Tyson bullied his way down the aisle, accompanied by the percussive voice of gangsta rapper, The Notorious B.I.G.'s, "Let's get it on."

Like all battles, when the music stops, the fighting starts. Within minutes, the disciplined and ruled feinting and jabs gave way to a street "brawl" as fighters shoved and clinched around the ring. Then the unimaginable happened. While in a hold Tyson turned his head and grabbed Holyfield's ear with his teeth, yanking and twisting his head. Before order was restored, blood poured from Holyfield's ear, now missing a sizable chunk of sinew and flesh. Tyson was disqualified (later suspended from boxing for a year) and Holyfield stood victorious without throwing a knockout punch.

Prophecy

In this chapter we will use the words "prophecy" and "prophesy" interchangeably, both derived from the Greek word *propheteuo*, which means foretelling future events, but it also includes the acts of prompting, teaching, refuting, reproving, admonishing, even comforting. The primary purpose of prophecy is to make apparent the truth and ultimate will of God in each generation, person, and society. So in this chapter, prophecy is to speak of future consequences based on present actions; to prophesy is to preach.

Through the Old Testament prophets, God called his people to be a righteous nation that focused on the social responsibilities of justice and righteousness. There was both a prophetic call to righteous and just living based on the law, and a prophetic foretelling of a Messiah who would fulfill the law in a demonstration of God's plan. In the New Testament gospel, Jesus fulfilled both the law and this prophetic concern in a ministry to the poor and marginalized of both society and religious institutions. In the letters to the early churches by the apostle Paul, prophecy in 1 Corinthians 14:3–4 is defined as a gift of the Spirit given to believers in order to build the church through edification, exhortation, and comfort. The gift of prophecy calls both the world and the church to the ultimate will of God in redemption.

Many contemporary Christians see the gift of prophecy as the realm of the preacher in the pulpit on Sundays. Prophets can also enter the streets of society, as in the Old Testament, and call all people to proclaim justice and righteousness. It is possible that God can also use those outside the established church, from urban wastelands and remote areas of the world, to remind the redeemed people of God of their social responsibilities to God's kingdom.

Many Christians find this subject of social responsibility uncomfortable for two related reasons. First, Christians of the suburban West live in relative physical safety and economic distance from the world of poverty, war, violence, and disease. Second, part of this discomfort derives from opposing practices of faith. These different faith practices influence how music is used.

According to black theologian Michael Eric Dyson, there are two faiths—one priestly, the other prophetic. A priestly faith cultivates a spiritual life, nurtures church growth, and develops a pastoral theology (Dyson, 1996, p. 47). Related to what theologian Nicholas Wolterstorff (1983) calls an avertive religion, the goal is to turn away and separate oneself from the present reality. In avertive approaches to religion there is often a distinction between the sacred and secular worlds (Wolterstorff, 1983). Music often finds a comfortable and refined home in this aspect of faith. Musicians express the highest forms of their "sacred" art in the image of Old Testament temple worship. Music in this context is often used for building up the church. The uncomfortable aspect comes when music is not used for God's praise, but as a tool of communication for justice outside the sanctuary.

A prophetic faith, as Dyson defines it, draws its vision from the biblical concepts of the Year of Jubilee and the kingdom of God, focuses on "social justice, the institutional nature of sin, and the redistribution of wealth" (Dyson, 1996, p. 47). This formative religion seeks the *re*formation of the social world and finds life out of the sanctuary and in the streets of the city (Wolterstorff, 1983).

It is here where the sound of the harvest marches into the street and directly confronts the world. Music becomes a voice of the poor and a tool of the prophet. Artistic refinement gives way to the language of the street. Sanctuary comforts become ponderous burdens for this spiritual war.

What does it mean to be in the world and not of the world? Rural and isolated communities may not understand the historical and cultural context for this biblical mandate. The culture of the New Testament may have been much closer to present-day multicultural and global urbanization, where people of different cultures and faiths live in close proximity to one another. There are three basic ways communities interact with the world: they can encapsulate themselves, separating themselves completely from the world; they can assimilate every cultural aspect of the world to the point of losing their identity; or they may acculturate by appropriating those behaviors of the world that bring glory to God. The final chapter of Hebrews encourages the people of faith to live outside the city walls. This did not mean a move to the country; rather, it means that we are to understand the attraction of power and convenience that the walls of the city hold.

Music as Prophecy in the Kingdom

The opening stories set the stage for one of the most exciting, dangerous, and controversial functions of music—prophecy. In the first story, a fictional account based on the Leviticus passage, a single trumpet call expressed the symbolic hope for justice and righteousness wherever people are persecuted, bound, and enslaved by life's circumstances. Yet, wherever evil unbalances the scales of justice and sin corrupts human relationships, conflict often results in fighting. In the second story, based on a heavyweight boxing match, music instills courage and flies as a musical banner before opposing forces.

Jon Michael Spencer, in *Protest and Praise,* provides a useful distinction for prophetic music, drawing from the Civil Rights Movement of the 1960s. First, prophetic music inspires and encourages the marginalized, poor, and oppressed, who sing in and of their struggle for justice within their own historical context. In this case we find music where "Singing not only occupied the tongue to control violent outbursts of profanity, but it also diffused some of the hostility of the oppressors" (Spencer, 1990, p. 94). This is the music of demonstrators who directly confront their opposition.

Second, gifted musical prophets write and perform topical songs bringing attention to specific deeds of unrighteousness and injustice within the world (Spencer, 1990, p. 83). In this case, however, we find a more reflective and poetic commentary on the evils of injustice and unrighteousness that calls people to take action. This is the music of popular singers and socially minded hymn writers and composers who bring a holistic vision to the kingdom. Music's power to both communicate and inspire has four distinct uses within these two categories of singing and commenting: mediation, call to arms, banner of war, and leaven in bread.

Mediation

Few people enjoy conflict and most avoid it by looking for ways to diffuse and redirect the anger and hostility that leads to open conflict or physical violence. Music as a mediator is an indirect form of communication. First, the language of music is often metaphorical and, therefore, meaning is not immediately understood by the listener. Second, melody couches and softens harsh words. Anger, anxiety, and fear are redirected into the emotional energy of singing. Finally, when sung in the right context, music can lead to surprising results, demonstrated in the following example, where the emotions of conflict diffused into humor.

The tensions were high in a North African remote outpost. Drought had stolen every bit of grain and left people eating roots and berries. Tom led a small group of American volunteers to help distribute food in this outpost, and had carefully planned for equal distribution of donated grain. It was not easy. Thousands of people, many near death, joined a snaking line near the makeshift center. Their next week's meals beckoned them from a locked building behind Tom's table. They were hungry, tired, and anxious.

Tom didn't speak the local language, so he was forced to use a translator. Everything he said was received through the filter of a local chief. Tom carefully explained the need for orderly distribution; he really wanted to avoid a food riot. People began to form a line and things appeared to go well until an old grandmother worked her way from several hundred yards away and placed herself squarely in front of the line.

Now, a young man can be handled with some force, but who would touch a grandmother? Tom explained the rule and the need for order. There were many young children in the front of the line; some had been waiting for food for a week. The old woman would not hear it. She began to argue and, before Tom could control his own emotions, the argument escalated into a shouting match. The old grandmother was becoming more and more belligerent and pulling the crowd in with her.

Unbeknownst to Tom, the country's security forces, who were quietly observing from the side, decided to take action. From behind the mask of a napping ragtag military, they sprang forward, arms loaded, cocked, and ready to fire—and all pointed at Tom. This was a life-and-death situation!

While saying his last prayers before meeting his Maker, Tom was given inspiration. From deep in his memory and with all the voice he could muster, he prophesied using an old Elvis Presley song, "You ain't nothin' but a hound dog, just a cryin' all the time."

No one could translate this message, and if they did, the old woman may have been even more offended. But the shock was so great to hear this angry American sing that everyone—nervous soldiers, anxious crowd, and belligerent old grandmother—began to laugh. They began to reestablish order and food was served.

In this example, Tom was very frustrated—he couldn't speak the language and the situation was out of control. He was powerless. Music mediated the conflict on two levels. First, whether he meant it or not, he called the cantankerous old grandmother a "hound dog" (a very offensive term). It was a metaphor for someone difficult to deal with; it allowed him to voice his frustration. Had she understood the meaning, things might have been worse—even fatal! On another level, however, music was a surprising and disarming display of humor. Who could not laugh at a crazy American singing in the face of danger?

Music softens our messages in a way we could not or would not dare attempt with words. Because it is indirect, the hearer has a way out—a way to save face and maintain the relationship—rather than having to respond directly and risk open conflict. Many Westerners who value problem solving over the maintenance of relationships often miss the subtleties of music mediation. Reared in a "what you see is what you get" culture, they prefer to fight for the truth of the moment with harsh words, thus risking a loss of redemptive resolution. While it takes patience and perceptual alertness to decode the messages of mediating music, it is a valuable skill for understanding. When conflict is unattended, however, music's greater power inspires people to action.

Call to Arms

Music inspires and instills courage. The expression of the artist/musician transports the hearer beyond his or her present reality. When the oppressed sing "Thy Kingdom come," they see more than a heavenly home. Music frees the human spirit to soar above the reality of the present situation. This vision of hope calls for a response.

Jahaziel, the descendant of a great tabernacle musician Asaph, knew the power of music to excite and instill courage. He counseled Jehoshaphat, who was about to do battle with the formidable Moabites. He said, "Do not be afraid or discouraged because of this vast army. For the battle is not yours, but God's." So after counsel, Jehoshaphat "appointed men to sing to the LORD and to praise him for splendor of his holiness as they went out at the head of the army, saying, 'Give thanks to the LORD, for his love endures forever'" (2 Chron. 20ff.).

As we will see in the chapter on music and healing, music has action potential. As a source of courage, people charge to music, march to music, and cheer with music. It intensifies emotions, unifies beliefs, and accompanies actions. This same potential for positive action becomes a banner of loyalty and war.

Banner of War

Music is like a banner that flies in the face of the enemy. As we saw in the example from the Tyson-Holyfield fight, music both inspired the fighters and declared their loyalties. It is the rallying point for soldiers and citizens. The stories of many national anthems illustrate this point.

Japanese forces occupied Korea between 1910 and 1945. Like all occupations by foreign powers, Japan eliminated freedom of expression and dissidents left the country. Among these political refugees were musicians, artists, and other intellectuals. During this time, a composer began to write a poem expressing the beauty of the country. The poem was more than a description of the physical beauty of the mountains and rivers; it was a banner call to solidarity and identity against a foreign oppressor. That poem soon became the national anthem. National anthems have had such power that one British member of Parliament called for banning their singing at international soccer matches to avoid the violence that often accompanies the competition.

Whether on the battlefield of justice or in the streets of violence, music is the voice of war where good and evil come face to face like two heavyweight boxers. At first reading of this second story, one may want to side with Holyfield because of his Christian music. Both fighters waved their music before them like the colors of a cavalry troop. As we will see, however, these banners have several levels, lest we prejudge the gangsta rap of Mike Tyson. We will discover that the music of the street may also have a message for the kingdom.

The world, by now, is not immune to the lyrics of many rap groups preaching violence. A group in Mexico calls themselves "Control Machete," selecting their name to bring attention to both the control and potential for violence in the urban environment. They "speak of violence because violence exists, because we see it, because we live it" (Kline, 1997).

This musical voice of war is a way of gaining a hearing when the oppressed and disadvantaged feel that others are not listening. In the United States, during the Civil Rights Movement of the 1960s, many black prisoners were forbidden to speak during their confinement. Singing became a way of "talking back" in self-assertion. Singing is "an irreplaceable survival tool for the oppressed" (Spencer, 1990, p. 92).

As Jon Michael Spencer reports of Dr. Martin Luther King's love for the song "We Are Soldiers in the Army," "'We did not hesitate to call our movement an army,' said King, 'But it was a special army . . . that would sing but not slay. . . . Singing not only occupied the tongue to control violent outbursts of profanity, but it also diffused some of the hostility of the oppressors. . . . Singing was both a defensive weapon of mitigation as well as an offensive banner of courageous self-assertion'" (Spencer, 1990, pp. 94–95).

If music is a way of talking back, it can also be a way of *shouting down*. While attending an independent church service in Zimbabwe, I witnessed an unusual use of music of prophecy. The group is called the Apostles of John, named after an African prophet who declared himself the Jesus of black people in the 1930s. During the open-air worship services, which adhere to literal interpretation of Scripture, a number of "prophets" speak before the congregation. The prophets' lives are under the constant scrutiny of the congregation. On this occasion, an old prophet stood before the congregation and began to prophesy (preach). From the back of the congregation a number of elders grew uneasy, talking among themselves about where they had seen him the previous night. Almost without warning they stood and, with the rest of the worshipers in tow, began to sing so loudly his words were no longer heard. Recognizing the futility of continuing, he withdrew from his position and joined the congregation. He would have to repent and build trust with them before the congregation would listen again.

Sometimes music itself is a weapon. Gideon was a great warrior, but in the face of insurmountable odds he needed a strategy that would thoroughly overwhelm his enemies. Below his small force of three hundred men, the Midianites and Amelikites settled in the valley, "thick as locusts. Their camels could no more be counted than the sand on the seashore." To each soldier he gave a trumpet and a torch covered by a clay pot. In the early morning hours he struck the enemy with surprise, like a "round loaf of barley bread tumbling into the Midianite camp." Blowing trumpets and crashing pots they shouted, "A sword for the LORD and for Gideon." Frightened by the sound, the Midianites turned on themselves in fighting before they realized their situation and fled (Judg. 7). Just as sound can surprise, music can be a weapon of mental fatigue.

In 1997, a Peruvian group of leftist rebels called *Tupac Amaru* took control of the Japanese ambassador's residence and held diplomats hostage in a stand-off that lasted several months. In the tensions that followed, it did not appear that weapons would be the immediate solution. Yet neither side could remain silent. Using a public address system, the police blared military songs toward the guerrillas. The guerrillas retorted by singing revolutionary anthems. Like two cheerleading squads at a football match, though with consequences greater than a lost game, they competed in musical battle. When neither side would acquiesce, the singing stopped. The Peruvian military opened fire and all dissidents were killed, finally freeing the seventy-two hostages.

Music's language is political—dividing separate loyalties. It is more than a song but also an indirect political expression. On a recent trip to Korea, Heewon Chang, a Korean educational anthropologist now living in the United States, was surprised to attend her home church and find a quartet of young people singing a Korean folk tune, set in four parts with Christian words. South Korea is one of the world's most Christianized nations; Western hymnody and classical music have served the church until only recently. Because these hymns are still the staple of worship, the young people believe that they are the voice of a Western culture. This was more than a simple expression of identity. It was both a statement of the rejection of foreign ideas and a reflection of the struggle to make the gospel Korea's own.

Part of music's appeal is not only its beauty but its deeper value as a boundary marker, a creation of an "us-and-them." Imagine a soldier, upon hearing the advancing band of an opposing army saying, "Their music is prettier than ours. I think I'll switch sides." Or consider your own response if by government or church decree you were forbidden to sing the music of your childhood. In each of the above examples, music has been a prophetic voice across a chasm of conflict outside of a social or religious group. As we discussed in the introduction, identity clarification is a necessary stage on the road to the kingdom city. Prophetic music also calls a community to follow a standard of justice. When a society, or a kingdom community, does not live by rules of justice, the prophet sings out.

Leaven in Bread

In a just society, there is no need for a prophet. But where injustice and sin prevail, music is sung both as defiance and prophecy, calling the society to a higher standard. A first, and almost universal, response by the establishment to this protest is censorship. But beneath the surface, this music calls for justice. For example, the Chinese rock star Cui Jian is known as a rebel in his country. One of his songs, "Nothing to My Name," was a rally anthem for the student-led demonstrations for democracy in Beijing. Following the massive killing of demonstrators by the army on June 4, 1989, Cui was banned from public performance. The government later instituted a campaign against "unorthodox music and drama . . . at profit-making performances" (Kline, 1997). Many Americans would applaud the rebel because he was inviting youth to stand up for democracy. Indeed he is a "prophet" singing for justice. And yet Americans are not so open to criticism of their own injustices.

The 1960s and 1970s were tumultuous years for the United States. Youth not only called into question the war in Southeast Asia, but many citizens called for an accounting of the unjust treatment of African Americans who had suffered without full freedom or participation in society stemming from slavery several hundred years before. Many participative and topical songs of this period brought courage to demonstrators and pointed directly to social injustice of which Christians had participated. However, they were not the first to do so and their roots can be found in the great hymn writers of the nineteenth century.

Following the American Civil War, which was fought over slavery, Reconstruction brought a new societal evil. In 1871 Henry Ward Beecher declared, "We are in more danger from overgrown organized money than we ever were from slavery; the battle of the future is to be one of gold" (Bailey, 1950, p. 558). What James Truslow Adams called "the Age of the Dinosaurs" and Matthew Josephson called the epoch of "Robber Barons" became a time of tremendous economic growth in the hands of a few exploiting men who industrialized the North, grabbed western lands under expansive railroads, and discovered vast reserves of oil. Under political and sometimes religious corruption, the nation's populace suffered. Large cities bulged with poor folk looking for work. Immigrants from the South, as well as overseas, worked for meager wages and survived in squalid slums. The church had to respond with a prophetic gospel.

As religious writer Albert Edward Bailey pointed out, evangelical hymns of the nineteenth century had a "mystic approach," a "zeal for individual conversion," and an "ideal of God's kingdom as an . . . eternal city in heaven." High Anglican hymns "looked back with nostalgia to the historic church, its theology, its liturgy." The hymns of a new social gospel wanted "the slums abolished, poverty and sickness banished, the will to grab transformed into the will to serve, and all our faith and energy devoted to bringing into being a brotherhood on earth" (Bailey, 1950, p. 560).

An excellent example is the Methodist preacher and writer Frank Mason North (1850–1935). Born in New York City, where he spent his life in ministry, he served parishioners from many nations who lived in poverty. Inspired by Jesus' parable of the "Wedding Banquet" he based his hymn on this verse: "So the servants went out into the streets and gathered all the people they could find, both good and bad, and the wedding hall was filled with the guests" (Matt. 22:9).

Where Cross the Crowded Ways of Life
Where cross the crowded ways of life,
Where sound the cries of race and clan,
Above the noise of selfish strife,
We hear thy voice, O Son of man.

In haunts of wretchedness and need,
And shadowed thresholds dark with fears,
From paths where hide the lures of greed,
We catch the vision of thy tears.

From tender childhood's helplessness,
From woman's grief, man's burden'd toil,
From famished souls, from sorrow's stress,
Thy heart hath never known recoil.

The cup of water giv'n for thee
Still holds the freshness of thy grace;
Yet long these multitudes to see
The sweet compassion of thy face.

Master, from the mountain side,
Make haste to heal these hearts of pain;
Among these restless throngs abide,
Tread the city's streets again.

Till sons of men shall learn they love,
And follow where thy feet have trod;
Till glorious from thy heav'n above,
Shall come the city of God.

At the cusp of the twenty-first century, the world faces social problems demanding contemporary prophetic words calling the church to faithfulness and responsible justice. Of eternal importance is the prophetic call of the world's people to the grace of God. Songs of prophecy bring inspiration and courage to the marginalized, serve as battle standards for the courageous, and preach social responsibility to a fallen world. Without the musical prophet, however, there would be no such music.

The Musical Prophet

Ever since Saul saw a vision with the musicians and prophets of the mountain, music and prophecy have been partners. The prophet's role is to call the kingdom to righteous relationships with other kingdom citizens. The prophet is often mistrusted because of the potential for revelation of truth and the exposure of evil intentions and acts.

At times a thorn in the flesh, a prod toward action, or a slap in the face, the prophet will not be denied a voice. Musicians inspire the imaginations of the oppressed toward a better world than the one they presently experience (Castuera, 1992). Even in the rational world of urban and suburban elite, their vision of reality helps shape a social existence that provides an alternative to social forces (Wolterstorff, 1983, p. 138). What causes the prophet to sing is a vision for a just kingdom.

Fire in the Bones

Musical prophets are gifted in three ways. In these ways, they ignite a deeply felt flame that calls others to action. First, they possess a strong sense of reality of the social world around them. Their social and spiritual vision affords them a perception outside the analytical and rational world. They see and hear where others who have eyes and ears fail to use them.

Second, like the prophet Micah, they are empowered with a sense of justice, a "discernment for what is right engendered by the infilling of the Holy Spirit" (Candeliaria, 1992, p. 43). Armed with this vision, they are often fearless in their criticism of sin in social, political, and religious institutions and their leaders.

These gifts result in a calling so strong that they courageously stand on street corners and roam in the markets of humanity because they cannot keep quiet. Like Jeremiah, they have a burning passion to sing: "But if I say, 'I will not mention him or speak any more in his name,' his word is in my heart like a fire, a fire shut up in my bones. I am weary of holding it in, indeed, I cannot" (Jer. 20:9).

Many of these prophets are offensive and confrontational. In speaking of the hip-hop/rap group, Public Enemy, Michael Eric Dyson defines the nature of the music prophets in their "insistent, uncompromising demands, their cantankerous assertions of truth, their whole-boiled quest for justice fits the portfolio of all prophets possessed of a vision that just won't go away. Their discomfort rises from the irritating gift of sight laid on them, a burden that only increases when the times are inhospitable to their message. Like the Old Testament prophet Jeremiah, if they don't tell their story, it's like a fire shut up in their bones. But when they do speak, agree with them or not, the flame burns us all" (Dyson, 1996, p. 171).

To many Christians, the vulgar, abusive, and violent lyrics of contemporary music of the street has no place in the church. But one cannot deny the reality that many of these "prophets" follow—a tradition of calling a people of God to righteousness and justice. Their language is no more violent or offensive than that of the Old Testament prophets who called Israel to repentance: "Therefore I cut you in pieces with my prophets, I killed you with the words of my mouth; my judgments flashed like lightning upon you. For I desire mercy, not sacrifice, and acknowledgment of God rather than burnt offerings" (Hos. 6:5–6). An especially poignant prophecy comes from Amos:

Woe to you who long for the day of the LORD . . .
Away with the noise of your songs!
I will not listen to the music of your harps.
But let justice roll on like a river, righteousness like a never-failing
    stream. . . .
Woe to you who are complacent in Zion, and to you who feel
    secure. . . .
You lie on beds inlaid with ivory and lounge on your couches.
You dine on choice lambs and fattened calves.
You strum away on your harps like David and improvise on musical
    instruments.
You drink wine by the bowlful and use the finest lotions, but you do
    not grieve over the ruin of Joseph.
Therefore you will be the first to go into exile; your feasting and
    lounging will end.

(Amos 5 and 6)

Like an Old Testament prophet, nineteenth-century Congregationalist minister Washington Gladden had strong words for the people of political power and well-hearted colleagues who thwarted efforts for labor reform, of which he was a proponent. Written first as a devotional poem, the following verse was too confrontational to be included in the now famous hymn, "O Master Let Me Walk with Thee" (Bailey, 1950, p. 563).

O master let me walk with thee
Before the taunting Pharisees;

Help me to bear the sting of spite,
The hate of men who hide thy light,
The sore distrust of souls sincere
Who cannot read thy judgments clear,
The dullness of the multitude
Who dimly guess that thou art good.

Washington Gladden (1879)

Finally, musical prophets, as we saw with Frank Mason North, often live with a problem that gives them an authentic voice. There is a link between prophetic texts and the exploitation that dominates their world (Dyson, 1996, p. 178). As we saw with Control Machete, many popular groups understand the problems of society because that is their personal experience. It is no surprise that Isaiah would use the song of a prostitute, proving at least, that he was a man acquainted with the music of the street: "Take up a harp, walk through the city, O prostitute forgotten; play the harp well, sing many a song, so that you will be remembered" (Isa. 23:16). Prostitutes, gangsters, rabble rousers—not the kind of people we normally think of as prophets. Yet, even within the walls of Christendom, prophets and the movements they spurn have generally come from the periphery of the established church, outside the gates of institutional Christianity. Even within the kingdom, though not always accepted, new theologies develop around justice.

Harvey Cox, in his *Religion in the Secular City,* draws a parallel between the new liberation theologies of the world's cities and the Protestant Reformation. These movements "crop up" from the "periphery of cultural and intellectual life" (Cox, 1984, p. 263). Cox outlines several characteristics of these movements that give insight into the conditions precipitating social prophets. First, the prophetic movements of Asia, Latin America, Africa, and the ghettos of the city rarely begin in the capital. They are movements outside the gates of power and privilege. Second, these theological movements accompany political and social upheavals. As such, they also attract false prophets who would use the time for their own purposes. Third, new movements recover and proclaim lost or neglected aspects of a holistic truth of God. As Martin Luther called for a saving faith, contemporary prophets call for social faith that focuses on the poor and marginalized—a truth found throughout Scripture. Fourth, though these "libertarian" theologies do not have the central personalities of the Reformation, their populist impact is felt strongly in Catholic and Reformed traditions. The sound of the harvest is no more clearly heard in the beat of the street than the people of these movements.

So what do we do with these prophets who will not go away? Do they offer guidance for the kingdom community? Below we consider two possible options. In the first, we will take a more *reactive* strategy and look at how to use discernment in thinking about prophetic music. In the second strategy, we will discover how to be *proactive* in becoming part of the solution to injustice within our own musical worlds.

Discerning the Truth of Prophecies

The urban world can be a crowded, smoggy, busy, and unfriendly place. We are perplexed by what it means and seek to know what all the music and noise mean. We can identify with the Israelite Joab, who centuries ago was the first to ask, "What is the meaning of all the noise in the city?" Adonijah, David's son, had just crowned himself king and offered a great feast when it was interrupted by the celebration music of David's first choice, Solomon (1 Kings 1:28ff.). Sometimes the music is just noise, but sometimes it brings us back to reality.

Discerning the meaning of what we often consider noisy street music is no easy task. Initially, people are often confused or angered by the intrusion on their lives. At other times, like Adonijah, people cannot hear the message because they are involved in activities outside the will of God. Infected by the disease of spiritual blindness, they cannot see truth (John 9:41). The music calls them to the reality and truth of their situation.

Musical prophets, however, are not exclusive to Christianity but are found in many cultures. Most cultures can differentiate between true and false prophets. There is also a mistrust of prophets, particularly those who lose credibility and authenticity because of their wealth and power. However, not all words of a prophet edify and point to truth. There are several principles for the kingdom we can use to evaluate prophets and their utterances.

First, prophecy is a gift to the church. Paul in 1 Corinthians 12 explains the nature of prophecy as a spiritual gift to ultimately edify the kingdom community: "Follow the way of love and eagerly desire spiritual gifts, especially the gift of prophecy. . . . But everyone who prophesies speaks to men for their strengthening, encouragement and comfort" (1 Cor. 14:1, 3). People in comfort might expect that strengthening means encouragement of their present lifestyle. However, prophecy can often have a biting edge that brings sin to light.

Second, Christians should pray for the "eyes and ears" of Jesus in seeking the counsel of the Lord (1 Kings 22:5) in both personal and social life. More than spiritual foresight, prophecy calls for "hands and feet" to bring the kingdom into being. Christians need some honest self-discovery of their response to a holistic gospel. It is said that the black spirituals had an understanding of this holistic gospel. "No theological interpretation of the black spirituals can be valid that ignores the cultural environment that created them" (Cone, 1991, p. 20). Culture is one of many factors that goes into making music of the street.

Third, when confronted by the songs of the street, Christians would do well to follow the advice given to the Israelites who faced prophets attracting citizens to follow other gods: "If you hear it said about one of the towns the LORD your God is giving you to live in that wicked men have arisen among you and have led the people of their town astray, saying, 'Let us go and worship other gods' (gods you have not known), then you must inquire, probe and investigate it thoroughly" (Deut. 13:12–14). Sometimes it is difficult to hear what people are saying because they are talking too loud, but testing the spirits is a necessary part of discernment (1 Thess. 5:19). This noise becomes a distraction and thus we dismiss the meaning because we have not taken the time to really listen. We will look at how to analyze the text of music in Chapter 6.

Fourth, there should be no mistake that the primary goal of musical prophecy is the redemption of a fallen world. Music of the street that preaches violence for its own sake, or self-gratification and glorification, is a false prophetic message. As Dyson suggests of urban rappers, it is easy to criticize rap music. The language is offensive, the in-your-face manner of performers, unabandoned and confronting music makes it the antithesis of "good" music for many. In many Christian circles, the music is demonized. It is easier to objectify the performer as Satan, when, as Dyson says, "The much more difficult task is to find out what conditions cause their anger and hostility. A more ennobling pursuit is to establish open lines of communication with gangsta rappers, to ask them why they speak and act as they do" (Dyson, 1996, pp. xiii–xiv). While we may not approve of Mike Tyson, his music gives an indication of a society that must deal with its own social structures. It is only with dialogue that we can more clearly see what appears in part (1 Cor. 13:9) in the songs of the street.

The test of truth is in the fruits of the prophet. Fruits are the product of a season of labor, the manifestation in a harvest. As Jesus said, "Whoever is not with me is against me" (Luke 11:23). Fruits are the test of a prophet. False prophets will "die of their own words" (2 Peter 1:20–2:2).

Finally, once false and evil prophecies are discovered, the church should confront them with the full weight of God's truth in the street. In the sanctuary, however, a proactive ministry of justice shines bright.

A Prophetic Music Ministry

In the previous section, we looked at principles for interpreting the words of prophets. Now, we want to look at living a life of justice within the sanctuary and on the street. Not only is the prophet called to preach; but many congregations who may feel uncomfortable moving in the street often forget that within the congregational setting they preach justice by their actions toward outsiders.

Ministry of Faithfulness

Our times call for a prophet. For nearly twenty years the repressive Ethiopian government closed down churches, scattered believers, and imprisoned their leaders. Persecution was not limited to the church, however, as opposition leaders were detained and beaten, while others mysteriously disappeared. Forced under-ground, the faithful group met in secrecy. Using passwords and cau-tious observation, small groups met in houses, keeping the faith alive. It was a clear and courageous voice that maintained their hopes.

Born to Christian parents with a love for music and God's word, Tesfaye Gabbisso began composing songs at an early age. Drawn from a meditative life in Scripture and prayer, his songs preached hope to the faithful people of Ethiopia during the communist rule in the 1970s and 1980s. He sang publicly at Pentecostal youth rallies. His recorded songs were shared throughout the country (Balisky, 1997).

A ministry of social justice takes spiritual sight and courage to the street. The consequences of speaking out takes courage, as the apos-tle Paul found out on many occasions. In Acts 16, we find an unusu-ally good story that involves singing. One day Paul was walking the streets on his way to pray. There was a young slave girl who had a gift of prophecy. Her owners made a good deal of money from her fortune telling. Every time Paul passed on his way to church, the young slave girl would shout in the streets, "These men are servants of the Most High God, who are telling you the way to be saved."

After several days of this, Paul grew increasingly irritated. He turned to her and commanded the spirit that was speaking through her, "In the name of Jesus Christ, I command you to come out of her." At once, the spirit left her. As you can imagine, her owners were furious about their loss of income. They instigated a riot among the local people simply by telling the truth, "These men are Jews, and are throwing our city into an uproar by advocating customs unlaw-ful for us Romans to accept or practice."

Paul and Silas were stripped, beaten, and thrown in jail, where they prayed and sang. The jailor was startled in the night when, as the result of an earthquake, the jail doors were flung wide open. Had the prisoners escaped he would have lost his life, so he drew his sword to commit suicide. Paul called out from his cell: "Don't harm yourself! We are all here!" The jailor called for the lights, rushed in, and fell trembling before Paul and Silas. He then brought them out and asked, "Sirs, what must I do to be saved?"

In his book, *Christ outside the Gate*, Orlando Costas explores mis-sion beyond Christendom. Referring to Hebrews 13:12, Costas presents us with several convincing arguments for a prophetic ministry of justice.

First, there is a new place of salvation. Before Jesus, salvation was found in the temple. "With Jesus there came a fundamental shift in the location of salvation: the center was moved to the periphery. Jesus died in the wilderness among the outcast and disenfranchised. The unclean and defiled territory became holy ground as he took upon himself the function of the temple" (Costas, 1992, p. 189). Second, there was also a shift in focus of salvation. "Salvation means, in other words, freedom to confess Christ in the service of outsiders." Finally, no longer does one see salvation as an "individual benefit" or "privileged possession." A radical transformation calls one to share in Christ's suffering by serving the poor, the powerless, and the oppressed (Costas, 1992, p. 194). It is on the street, outside the walls of the sanctuary, where the faithful meet those in need of God. Musicians are called to faithfully minister outside the choir loft and pulpit microphone among the marginalized.

Ministry of Incarnation

A ministry of incarnation is a ministry of involvement. While our closest relationship to the Creator comes in the gardens of our hearts, it is to the city streets that we direct our feet. Any approach to a justice ministry must take place with people in the context of their daily lives. Responses to need must come from the inside. This is more than singing songs in the language of others, and attempting to contextualize the message. It has to do with broader life issues of where and how people live, with their physical as well as spiritual needs.

In speaking of the translation of Scripture into contemporary translations, specifically related to rap, Dyson warns,

> Indiscriminant, anachronistic slang can't do the job that real love and respect will to win their appreciation and gain their ears and eyes. The real challenge is to translate the gospel into action—to sever it from bourgeois respectability and moralistic condemnation and use it as a weapon of the suffering and oppressed to make justice a reality. What black youth need are jobs and spiritual renewal, moral passion and enough money to act with decency and self-respect. Then,

103

they can afford to be themselves in a world that respects the variety of black life. (Dyson, 1996, p. 138)

It is now popular for many churches to take singing tours and concerts around the world "on mission." While these provide good Christian entertainment for the hearer and add a new perspective for the singer in building relationships with others, longer term relationships are required. "If you don't live in the urban community and allow it to become part of you, you might see what needs fixing but you won't understand the reasons these problems have developed. This lack of understanding will make your approach irrelevant" (Perkins, 1993, p. 31). A ministry of incarnation means living with people in the context of their pain, suffering, and need.

Ministry of Reconciliation

Christians are called to reconcile the world to God, "who reconciled us to himself through Christ and gave us the ministry of reconciliation: that God was reconciling the world to himself in Christ, not counting men's sins against them" (2 Cor. 5:18–19). In the United States, there is a divided church based on race. Perkins, in describing the theological solutions, finds a limit to basic theological orientations. European theology is liberation for Europeans who came to America and eventually subjugated non-whites through colonialization and slavery. "'Black Theology' is an expression of response to white oppression . . . while liberation theology has often stopped short of a strong message of spiritual liberation." An authentic church, part of what Perkins calls a reconciliation theology, absorbs pain, proclaims hope in a despairing world, points to God's authority, brings people together, spends lavishly on the needy, reflects God's character, and protects the vulnerable (Perkins, 1982, p. 41). Can music be a part of this reconciliation? An interesting example comes from Sarajevo, Bosnia.

President Bill Clinton called it a "harmony of disparate voices" where one could distinguish the tuba from the violin but not the Muslim from the Croat or the Serb (CNN Headline News, December 22, 1997). During the 1990s, one of the worst wars in Europe involved Muslim, Croat, and Serbian factions in the wake of the

Soviet break-up. No city was more devastated by ethnic division than Sarajevo. Indiscriminate acts of war broke the city apart, turning it into rubble. Those who could leave escaped while other residents sank into a collective depression of survival. A city with a long music tradition, musicians refused to join the killing and determined to make their music a symbol of peace. Throughout the conflict, Muslim, Croatian, and Serbian instrumentalists maintained a rehearsal schedule in a unified demonstration of hope and justice.

Ministry of Confrontation

When the gospel takes the street seriously, prophecy has a ministry of confrontation. Contemporary Christian musicians, who commonly are criticized for their commercialism, have courageously confronted the secularized faith of the mainstream culture. They seek to build bridges by holding one hand in the church and the other in the world. Their ministry not only confronts a secular society in need of a Savior but disturbs the comfort of the sanctuary into a ministry of service.

Ministry of Inclusion

Perhaps the greatest prophetic role of music comes in inclusion. In Matthew 22, Jesus tells the story of a wedding banquet. In this story, a king prepares a great banquet in honor of his son. When those he invited do not come, he decides, "The wedding banquet is ready, but those I invited did not deserve to come. Go to the street corners and invite to the banquet anyone who will come." So the servants go out into the streets and gather all the people they can find, both good and bad, and the wedding hall is filled with guests.

Musicians of the sanctuary fail to have a ministry in the street. Musicians can exclude the street in a number of ways: they restrict membership in choirs to the talented; they create an unfriendly environment based on wealth; they develop complicated rituals; or they exclude the voices of world Christians.

1. *Exclusion based on gifts and abilities.* One of the conflicts based upon aesthetics and concepts of music has to do with who should

105

sing in a choir. In an "artful" attempt, the church seeks to produce the highest standard of music. In order to reach this goal, the choir master does two things. He or she may set performance standards for musicians, or he or she may hire professional singers to supplement volunteer voices. When the church follows a "priestly and avertive" perspective, under the model of Old Testament temple worship, only the "gifted" are given the opportunity for "special" music. This is, in my opinion, an easy approach to music ministry. The harder, and more redemptive, approach is to work to include all who desire to participate. "We must struggle to make the church the place where the only credential to gain a hearing is a cry of agony, and not power or savior-faire, or position, or items with which to bargain" (Baert, 1992, p. 70).

This inclusion does not rest with the "less-gifted" musicians, but the challenged as well. Often the deaf are excluded from worship participation. This takes place when no provisions are made for them in worship. In many cases they are treated as an outcast group by providing for their worship outside the context of the worshiping community. Yet deaf *singing* brings a beauty of movement to the worship context as songs are interpreted with the hands and arms.

2. *Exclusion based on wealth.* Expensive instruments and sanctuaries can create an unfriendly, intimidating space for the poor and marginalized. "God wants to convert our elaborate, expensive and exclusive temples, where there is no more room for people who might be different from us, into stables, where all humanity can come and worship him freely in open, loving oneness, without distinction" (Rosado, 1992, p. 79).

3. *Complex worship rituals.* As we addressed in the chapter on worship, rituals are an effective way of giving identity, form, and structure to a community. However, when forms and worship rituals become cold and formalized, or too complex, outsiders do not feel welcome. One of the real appeals of the "seeker-friendly" worship styles of the Vineyard churches is their contextualizing the worship to the contemporary context. They have created a friendly space in which many people can find their place.

4. *Excluding the voices of world Christians.* In talking with a church musician about his inclusion of world hymns in congregational singing, he responded, "We don't sing those songs, we're not politi-

cal." Unfortunately, many Western Christians believe that they do not have a political orientation. They may fear that hymns sung from the Third World will allow liberation theology to creep into their church. As we have seen, the majority of the world's Christians are now outside the Western world. When we fail to hear their voice and sing their songs, we prepare a banquet and fail to invite part of the family.

It is when the gospel makes "somebody" out of the "nobodies" of society, when it restores the self-worth of the marginalized, when it enables the oppressed to have a reason for hope, when it empowers the poor to struggle and suffer for liberation and peace, that it is truly good news of a new order of life—the saving power of God (Rom. 1:16) (Costas, 1992, p. 17).

Ministry of Contemplation

A final concern for justice has to do with contemplation. Wolterstorff rightly calls attention to the role of worship in justice. Many people "neglect inwardness" at their own peril in the development of spirituality. There is a "rhythmic alteration of work and worship, labor and liturgy," a contribution of a Christian's way of "being-in-the-world."

Until recently, most books on social justice did not include worship as an important element. We are both laborers and worshipers. There is a rhythm in remembering worship as an interchange between actions of proclamation and the actions of worship (Wolterstorff, 1983, p. 157). A prophetic ministry on the street, without the contemplation of the sanctuary, leaves the prophet with an angry and distant voice.

Returning to the story of Tesfaye the Ethiopian prophet, his life sums up this ministry of justice. It was not just his singing that proved so prophetic, for there is more to Tesfaye's story. As a youth leader in the Pentecostal church, he continued to sing during the communist years. When word of his leadership reached the officials, he was arrested and thrown into prison. Like Paul and Silas he sang his songs, giving courage and hope to bring salvation to those around him. But unlike Paul and Silas whose prison doors flew open wide,

107

Tesfaye was placed in solitary confinement. Yet, he continued to pray, meditate, and sing. It was this faithfulness, as a prophet who came from a test with Satan in the desert, that gave his music authenticity (Balisky, 1997).

Summary

In this chapter, we have considered the role of music as prophet. A prophet calls the people of God's kingdom to righteousness and justice, and invites the world to a knowledge of the kingdom's grace. Musical prophets have an intuitive gift of the Spirit, which marks the dividing line of truth between good and evil. At times, God uses prophets within the congregation to call the faithful to right and just action. But at other times, God may choose to use those outside the kingdom looking in to cajole a soft and privileged class.

Music is an excellent tool of the prophet. First, as indirect communication, music softens, even veils, the message. Those who have their hearts and ears tuned to the holistic nature of the kingdom respond out of faithfulness. One is not forced into obedience, but must seek the kingdom. Second, music inspires and has the affective (emotional) character to sacramentally transport our human experience into a more perfect vision of God's eternal city. Third, music inspires people to action. Unified in song, people are encouraged and empowered to act.

To many people, like Joab, we ask, "What is the meaning of all this noise in the city?" The prophetic messages of song can offend because they are carried in the language of the street. The prophetic song can also speak to the evil of one generation or culture and lose power in the next. To interpret the truth of a message, hearers must first seek the counsel of God. Because of the symbolic and metaphorical nature of prophetic song, seekers of truth must look at the message, the messenger, and the sociological context from which they come.

Finally, musicians who seek a ministry of prophecy have a sixfold calling. First, musicians are called to faithfulness. This faithfulness to a holistic gospel seeks justice and righteousness for the poor and marginalized of the world. Second, this ministry of faithfulness is in a reformative faith on the street. In the model of Christ, a reformative faith is one of incarnation. Third, a prophetic ministry seeks the reconciliation of the world to God's grace. Fourth, music as prophecy is confrontational and identifies evil wherever evil presents itself. Fifth, once confronted, a prophetic ministry is an inclusive faith where the marginalized find a home in the kingdom. Finally, musical prophets cannot hear the voice of God without contemplation. A prophetic ministry on the street, without the contemplation of the sanctuary, leaves the prophet an angry and distant voice.

Questions for Discussion

1. Based on this chapter, can you think of prophetic music in your culture? Church?
2. Do you believe Christian musicians should use music for such purposes as political dissent?
3. Can a priestly faith and a prophetic faith be found in the same church? If so, how could their music complement both aspects?
4. Are there ways in which your church excludes others based on gifts and abilities, wealth, worship rituals, or world hymns? What would have to change to have a just worship service?
5. What are some ways that musicians can be involved in bringing justice and righteousness to the world?

Exercises

1. As a group, select a contemporary song from a popular singer that speaks about justice. Analyze the song to discover the meaning. Also, look to see what metaphors he or she is using.

Are they indirectly communicating a message outsiders may misunderstand?

2. Debate this statement: Because popular musicians are often paid by record companies, their message has no credibility.

3. Interview a number of musicians in your community, or go online on the Internet. Ask them about their concerns for justice issues such as the environment, violence in society, poverty, or other issues.

4. Write an essay comparing a contemporary musical prophet to the Old Testament prophet Jeremiah.

5. Listen to several recordings of popular Christian musicians. Analyze their songs for issues related to prophetic issues of justice and righteousness.

Music as Proclaimer

You who ride on white donkeys, sitting on your saddle blankets, and you who walk along the road, consider the voices of the singers at the watering places. They recite the righteous acts of the LORD, the righteous acts of his warriors in Israel.

(Judg. 5:10–11)

Sing to the LORD, praise his name; proclaim his salvation day after day.

(Ps. 96:2)

Music functions as proclamation when it declares and communicates a simple message of salvation. This proclamation function is determined by the text of the music and its desired message. Music is a medium of communication. In the chapter on worship, we learned how music is part of cultural communication. In this chapter, we look at how music can also serve as persuasive communication.

First, we will define proclamation. Second, we will consider the ways in which music proclaims and communicates. Third, we will consider the needs of the audiences who hear the message regarding music selection and context when planning proclamation events. Finally, we will consider the necessary attributes of gospel proclaimers.

The Sound of the Harvest . . .

When looking at Solomon, one could only catch a glimpse of his past. Behind his smile were the dark crevices of an addict and thief. Born in an impoverished equatorial town, Solomon, like many of his friends, responded to poverty and a hopeless future by escape through drugs and alcohol. Soon, he and his friends had chosen a profession of fraudulent means to support their daily fix. Each day was a challenge as they panhandled from city travelers. They pilfered for their daily necessities among the rural farmers who came to sell their produce. At the end of the day, they gathered at the "Happy Times Bar" to trade stories and drink their earnings far into the night.

Their real day of celebration came on Saturday. Tradesmen, farmers, and craftsmen plied their wares in the town market accompanied by the hawking of sundry politicians and preachers in the town gardens. This was a fruitful day for the "Happy Times" gang. The evening entertainment was always provided by Solomon, who especially enjoyed mimicking the preacher and his choir. Though he loved the music of the singers, he could not resist the chuckles of his nighttime audience as he recanted the message of the day. "Jesus saves, Jesus saves!" he boomed in a loud voice and then strode about the room wildly pointing in accusation, spitting warnings in the faces of his cackling audience.

One Saturday Solomon did not make it to Happy Times. The sun had been unusually harsh that day and to quench his thirst he began drinking well before noon. While staggering about the market he lost his footing and fell from the path near the goat market, landing in a trash pit. This was not any trash pit, for near the goat market was the butcher. While little of a goat was ever thrown away, remains were tossed into this pit. Under the hot sun the stench and filth warded off curious eyes. Asleep in the comfort of his squalor, he didn't awake until the next morning. Animal blood was now caked in his hair and on his face. Had he not already been sick from his binge, he would have been repulsed by his circumstance. Only recognition of the disparity of one's life brings a vision of salvation.

In a small voice, Solomon began to sing the words of the choir, "Jesus saves, Jesus saves." He wasn't sure of the meaning, but the call was appealing. A smile of joy and peaceful presence beckoned Solomon to a new life. He wanted this. Climbing from the pit he made his way to the home of the choir—the Sunday worship service. Today would be a new day. His life was about to change.

Soon after, Solomon was a man with a mission. Every morning he awoke to the ancient words of the psalmist: "He lifted me out of the slimy pit, out of the mud and mire; he set my feet on a rock and gave me a firm place to stand. He put a new song in my mouth, a hymn of praise to our God" (Ps. 40:2–3).

Armed with a new life and a message of salvation, Solomon marched into the "Happy Times" bar with a higher purpose. He slid onto the polished bench and rested his elbow on the table. Other customers ambled in and out of the doorway, which opened to the dusty street filled with donkey carts, stray goats, and weary travelers. A haggard barmaid, who doubled as a prostitute in the evenings, shuffled forward and asked Solomon for his order. "I'll have an orange soda," he quietly requested. No one seemed to notice him. Each small group of dazed and slurred storytellers chronicled memorable events. Peering at the rim of the soda bottle, Solomon began to sing,

Mukuru tanju kori muoge? Wogotwe ni Shaitani, Jesu nia ugwita.

The local, traditional melody pierced the ears of at least those who sat at his table. After finishing his soda, Solomon quietly stood up and walked into the street. A man who had been sitting at the table followed him down the street. The man knew the meaning of the story and wanted Solomon to talk with him about it. He also knew Solomon.

As Solomon tells it, for the first years of his life he had been bound by Satan. He was now freed by the power of Christ. Jesus called him out of an old life into a changed, new one. Each week he returned to the bar to proclaim a new life to his old friends. As the one who followed him into the street, there were questions about the prophetic—yet proverbial—text he proclaimed in the bar. (The text in English says, "Are you bound? It is Satan. Jesus is calling you.")

113

. . . And the Beat of the Street

All Fred Caban wanted to do was play rock music. He loved the guitar and after graduating from high school he joined a local touring band. This was in the turbulent 1960s in the United States—the "antidecade." Young people began to question every institutional authority including, and especially, God and country. A popular magazine voiced the defiance by declaring "God is dead." Disillusioned by the war in Vietnam, racism, and segregation, young people protested loudly and defiantly. "Sex, drugs, and rock 'n' roll" became the motto of a youthful counterculture. As DiSabatino describes it, "Rock music became the primary vehicle of communication for the youth subculture. Song lyrics were transformed into sacred elements of worship to the altars of self-indulgent adolescence where rock musicians served as high priests and priestesses" (DiSabatino, 1997).

Like many of his young generation, Caban, amidst the stormy and defiant activity, was seeking truth. One night while traveling with his band he entered a small coffeehouse, where Christian young people gathered to live the message of Christ. Fascinated by their commitment, he accepted a copy of the Gospel of John. He read, prayed, and waited for answers. In the still of the night, "I started to pray and had an experience where Jesus came to me and touched me on the shoulder and I actually saw him and he basically called me to follow him" (DiSabatino, 1997).

After being baptized in the Pacific Ocean by members of the coffeehouse, Caban decided to proclaim this gospel message in the language he knew and one that would speak to his generation. He formed a Christian rock band and named it "Agape." They sang songs of Jesus to a rock beat and preached the gospel as "musical missionaries to a counterculture." Other musicians like Caban gave birth to the "Jesus Music" of a Christian movement that would eventually lead to the development of present-day contemporary Christian music.

Music as Proclamation

Though these stories happened on different continents, and in diverse cultures and languages, they illustrate one point: music is used to proclaim the gospel of Jesus Christ. I have also recounted these stories for another reason. When most people think of the terms "evangelism" and "mission," they think of a preacher in a revival service or crusade, someone handing out tracts on a street corner, or a television evangelist in a flashy suit backed by a choir and small band. Music can be used in these events, but that does not mean that music is proclamation. Music as proclamation communicates the essence of Christianity. It is a natural extension of one's experience within his or her culture as we saw when Solomon sang a local melody or Fred Caban used rock music. This communication becomes more difficult when crossing cultures. If either of these persons had entered the other's culture, there would have been confusion, not communication.

Other than worship, the most frequent role of music in the life of the church is proclamation, or public declaration, of the Good News of Jesus Christ. Since the mid-twentieth century, three words have been used to describe this proclamation function: witness, mission, and evangelism. While they are often used interchangeably, each has a distinct meaning.

First, to *witness* is to share one's personal experience with Christ. Certainly Solomon gave witness to his new life by returning to the Happy Times Bar and singing a song about his life experience. Many personal songs of testimony share a "witness" or "testify" to a change in lives as a result of a new relationship with a living God through Jesus Christ. Such musical witness is born of experience and placed within the immediate context, language, and culture of the one sharing the experience.

Second, *mission* is an important word in the life of the church. Theologian John Stott states that "[mission] . . . is a comprehensive word, embracing everything which God sends his people into the world to do. It, therefore, includes evangelism and social responsibility, since both are authentic expressions of the love to serve man in his need" (Stott, 1975, p. 35).

Since 1950 music has become a vital tool of the church's mission. Seminaries and colleges offer courses in church music to train ministers of music. The field of "Christian" ethnomusicology grows, and cross-cultural servants teach music as part of the mission of the

115

church in many parts of the world. But not all music used in the proclamation mission of the church is evangelism.

The word "evangelism" comes from the Greek *evangelizomai*, which means to bring the good news *(euangelion)*. In 1978, a special task force of the Lausanne Conference on World Evangelization set out to define clearly the nature of evangelism:

> To evangelize is to spread the good news that Jesus Christ died for our sins and was raised from the dead according to the Scriptures, and that as the reigning Lord he now offers the forgiveness of sins and the liberating gifts of the Spirit to all who repent and believe. Our Christian presence in the world is indispensable to evangelism, and it is that kind of dialogue whose purpose is to listen sensitively in order to understand. But evangelism itself is the proclamation of the historical, biblical Christ as Savior and Lord, with a view to persuading people to come to him personally and so be reconciled to God. In issuing the gospel invitation we have no liberty to conceal the cost of discipleship. Jesus still calls all who would follow him to deny themselves, take up their cross, and identify themselves with his new community. The results of evangelism include obedience to Christ, incorporation into his Church and responsible service in the world. (*The Willowbank Report*, 1978, p. 318)

There is a lot in this statement. Communicating this definition of the gospel is not easy if at first one were to take this statement and share it with a nonbeliever, as the report explained. Consider the problems we might find. Could someone who didn't speak English understand? Could this be set in a song that people could enjoy? How would you explain concepts like the "universality of sin" or the "transforming power of the Holy Spirit"? It is difficult enough with words; it is even more difficult when placed in the form of music. For this reason, music proclamation's message must be simple and understandable to a variety of audiences with different needs. It is not focused on informational statements about the gospel, but on the person and message of Jesus Christ.

Looking at the word "proclaim" in a biblical concordance, one finds a number of references in the Old and New Testaments where followers of Jesus are told to proclaim good news.

Public proclamation was encouraged by Jesus in Matthew 10:27, when he told his disciples to speak in the daylight and proclaim from the rooftops.

Response is the goal of proclamation. In the New Testament cultural context, proclamation was more than speaking or preaching, but involved dialogue and a call for response. We see this in Paul's proclamation on Mars Hill in Acts 17:16–28, where he received both negative and positive response to his proclamation. His method also included proclamation that was outside the walls of religious worship.

Outside the church and in the *marketplace,* Paul entered into a dialogue with nonbelievers on their terms. He contextualized the message within their worldview and belief system.

Costly consequences are possible for our call and commitment to proclamation. Jesus admonished those who would follow him that proclamation was more essential than one's commitment to many cultural norms and earthly responsibilities (Luke 9:61–62).

Liberating and saving proclamation meets people where they have heart-felt and real needs. Jesus, quoting from Isaiah, explained why he came—to preach good news to the poor, proclaim freedom to prisoners, sight for the blind, and release for the oppressed (Luke 4:18–19). This was a holistic gospel.

A *whole and complete gospel* meets more than the eternal spiritual needs of people, but speaks to their present life circumstances.

Being informed through experience, the writer of 1 John 1:3 says that he has seen and touched the message. The message is part of his own life experience.

The message of the gospel is the person of Jesus Christ. Christians are not called to proclaim information, but a person. "We proclaim him, admonishing and teaching everyone with all wisdom, so that we may present everyone perfect in Christ" (Col. 1:28).

Music as Communication

How does music communicate meaning? First, meaning, or what we understand, is in people and not in objects. Music serves as a channel in which a message is carried from a sender to a receiver. With the advent of radio and television in the 1950s, a transmission model of communication became popular. It presented the idea that a *message* was placed in a form *(medium)* using *signal systems,* such as words, sounds, and symbols. This message was *transmitted* through the medium to a *receiver.* There could be *noise,* which distorted the message. *Feedback* was necessary to see if the message had been received. Later, human communication researchers began to extend this model to include a loop of communication where the process of transmission and feedback was repeated until understanding was created in a transaction of communication. Today we also understand the impact of the *context* on communication. Culture, how we organize ourselves in social groups and go about life, creates a *filter* through which we screen the messages we send and receive. Both senders and receivers have immediate *reference groups* of family and friends who influence what is sent and how a message is received. Music can be analyzed using this communication model to appreciate the intricacies of music in communication and music *as* communication.

Ethnomusicologist Roberta King, building on these communication principles, views music as transactional music communication. Meaning is communicated in music through linguistic, music, movement, performer, and instrument channels, whereby the sender and receiver transact in a process—much like a dialogue. Music is a pathway to communication (King, 1989).

The Song as a Path

Music has real power to motivate. It calls for and creates an emotional response in humans. When combined with words, it can have a powerful effect on the hearer. When you listen to a new song, you go through a process of listening conditioned by your personality and your culture. At first your emotions are jolted by the sounds you hear. Then you make a choice. If you like the music, you then explore the meaning of the text. If the words make sense and have meaning to you, you then begin to internalize the music. Some African cul-

118

tures call this "eating the words." Before you take any action, you evaluate the words against your own worldview, of which your belief system is a part. You may then make a conscious effort to change your behavior. Alternatively, if the music does not appeal to you and your musical preferences, you change the station on the radio or ignore the song by thinking about something else. This is one reason marketers and advertisers try to write catchy (appealing) songs for selling their products. They want to "grab" your attention and hold on to your emotions so they can get you to think about their product, persuading you to change your consumer behavior in favor of their product. And it works! Can you think of a time when you have stopped what you are doing to listen to a song because you liked the sound and were drawn into the event?

Because of its power to motivate, music has tremendous appeal. For this reason, music is often used as an attractive part of proclamation events. Crusades, evangelistic rallies, and revivals often feature a soloist or music group who will appeal to the musical tastes of an audience. At the same time, music can also manipulate. The power of music to affect emotions can create an atmosphere in which people respond solely out of emotion without cognitive understanding. Like people who may be motivated by advertising to change brands because the tune is catchy, people may also be motivated to change religions because they like the music—and they never understand the meaning of their decision.

Can a sound really save or liberate someone? No. But the sound can be a sign that points toward salvation. Here is an example of sound and music used in saving someone. If you were walking along the lakeshore and watched as someone walked near the edge of a pier, would you sing loudly in a beautiful, operatic voice, "Don't walk much farther, you're about to fall off the pier"? You might get the person's attention, but I doubt if the words would be understood in time. You would have better results if you took an airhorn and blasted a sound to get his or her attention. Then you would shout, instead of singing, because your chances of being understood are better.

These two examples illustrate how sound and organized sounds we call music communicate a message in proclamation. First, sound is a signal. It is a physical phenomenon that has the ability to carry external stimuli to the body. You, through cultural learning, assign meaning to that sound. It is a nonverbal signal like smell, touch, taste, or sight. When this signal points to something outside itself, it is called a sign. In the examples above, the signal of the airhorn was a sign of danger. A beautiful operatic tone usually is a sign of music, but in this case, it could have signaled craziness.

Second, sound and music are symbols. A symbol is any sign, word, or object, to which we, through our culture, assign meaning. This meaning is usually an abstract concept. For example, the word "airhorn" is a symbol we identify with danger. Music can be symbolic and represent a host of other meanings to a receiver. To some people rock 'n' roll music is a symbol of sex, drugs, and alcohol. When they hear and see the music, they prejudicially think of the contextual acts that go along with the music. This is a generalization, of course, because not all rock 'n' roll musicians do drugs; some are even followers of Jesus. The generalization, however, creates a stereotype. You can see why it has been difficult for many to accept this music in congregational worship when there are so many associations tied to the music.

Third, meaning is contextual. Since we also assign the meaning as a noisemaker to the airhorn at a ball game, the sound can signal two different meanings, depending on the context. You can see how using even one sound could be a confusing way to relay your message.

When we apply these ideas to music and proclamation, we can draw several conclusions. *Music is a signal system.* It is an organization of sounds that, when produced, act as a stimulus to receivers.

Music is a sign that something is taking place. In many societies, beating drums are used as a signal to call people, because they know that it is a sign that something is about to happen. The brass and curved bell have become a sign of the church, especially in the days when church bells called out the morning hour of worship.

Music is part of a culture's symbolic language. The collective signals and signs of a musical performance in culture, (e.g., movement, sound, sights, colors, etc.) can take on a larger symbolic meaning than just the music that is being played. *The further it is taken out of its intended cultural context, the more music loses its intended communicative power.*

Music can be used in the direct communication of ideas. This is true in some African societies, where drumming is used as a tool for direct communication. But since music often has other cultural symbolic meanings, words take precedence over musical sound in communicating direct ideas. The way in which music and text is heard and affects people is determined in part by culture. In many cultures, music remains a communication medium, like the example of Solomon's "proclamation." Solomon was actually speaking to his friends through music. Music softened the direct words, which might have been considered harsh. We might imagine that Western music does not communicate; nevertheless, it does. Westerners do not value music as a form of communication. It is often viewed as mere entertainment and the communication takes place on a more subconscious level.

Music for proclamation, without text, must have a strong association with a specific text recognizable to the audience. As we have already noted, music is a powerful form of communication. But is it possible to expect too much from music? To conclude this discussion, here are some things that we do know about music as communication.

1. The meaning of music and musician varies from culture to culture. In some cultures, an instrumentalist who cannot improvise is not a "musician." Other cultures do not consider a person a musician unless he or she can read music.
2. Music is a vehicle of communication, and as such, it has no meaning apart from that assigned by the culture in which it is sent or received. The meaning of music is assigned by society. Music is universal, heard everywhere, but value is assigned to music by specific cultures.
3. Music is not inherently bad or good. The value, or aesthetic quality, we place on music is determined by our worldview. It is a human communication system, like language.
4. We cannot expect music to act as a person, because the meaning we assign to music is determined by people. Yet music and the musician create meaning.
5. Music appeals first to the emotions, then to the mind. For this reason, the proclaimer is concerned with both music and text;

121

studies reveal that a weakness in either may reduce the reception of both.

6. Even if our message is understood, the hearer may choose not to accept our message. Therefore, our goal of understanding may be reached, even though we may not like or agree with the outcome.

7. The Holy Spirit may choose to use that which we consider inappropriate for God's purposes. This does not mean we do not plan or work to match music, text, and audience. It simply means that the world is a big place and God is a big God. God works in ways we sometimes don't understand.

Music, at best, is an aid in proclaiming the gospel message. Through emotional and reflective qualities, it has the capacity of being used by the Spirit to convict of sin. By prophetic and apostolic text, it can direct the listener (and singer) to a living Christ. Music, without text, can create a mood if the proper associations are attached to the melody, rhythm, and instrumentation. But as proclamation, music requires a specific text that communicates and proclaims the message of Christ. Recently, instrumental music (without words) was used in a radio program targeted to a remote ethnic group. A listener responded, "Why doesn't your music have any teaching? Please provide words to the sounds so that we may receive good teaching."

Liberating Words

Words have power. Herbert Klem's important work, *Oral Communication of the Scripture,* stresses the difference between Western and African concepts of words. Westerners interpret words as phonological symbols; they have no power in themselves to control or change an event. However, in Africa and other societies, words uttered in the right circumstances can bring about a change in events (Klem, 1982, p. 113). It is not difficult for many non-Western people to accept and believe that Jesus could pronounce a storm into submission or call forth a person from the dead. Yet, Westerners also use words to bring about change and so words are the foundational element in proclamation. Unless words are placed into the language and worldview of the hearer, they have no meaning, or are misunderstood.

Missiologists use the term "contextualization" to explain the process of placing the message into the frame of reference of the receiver. Hymn translators have often had difficulty in finding a *dynamic equivalent,* or equal meaning, in the new culture. For example, in some cultures where animal sacrifice was practiced as well as cannibalism, new converts were often confused when they read the passages where Jesus said, "This is my body broken for you, take and eat." It took a lot of explanation before people could understand that this was a metaphor, not a literal practice.

To illustrate the process of contextualization, try this experiment. You may be familiar with this line from a hymn, "Now wash me and I shall be whiter than snow." In the first translations of this hymn, for congregations around the equator, the translators would either use the word "snow" or find an equivalent in the new language. What word would you use to illustrate this concept to people who have never seen snow or do not know what it is? Difficult, isn't it? If you expand this principle of contextualization to the gospel outlined in the previous Willowbank statement, you can see how sometimes there can be much confusion in understanding the gospel.

An additional concern regarding the language we use has to do with the thought processes of people. People of many cultures are concrete relational thinkers, as opposed to many Western cultural people, who are abstract thinkers. The Willowbank statement is an abstract and objective way of discussing the gospel. In abstract and objective discussion of the gospel, we reduce difficult concepts to single words and then use many more words to explain their meaning. However, in concrete relational thinking, we require an experience of life, as related in stories, parables, and jokes, to explain concepts in a personal and subjective way. Personal salvation and relationship with Jesus is best communicated in concrete, personal, and subjective terms. Each culture requires a proclamation of the gospel in the language that creates understanding. Words and their message should be simple and personal.

123

The Audience as Receivers

We have already discussed the central role an audience has in the communication process. They are the primary focus for our message. The more we know about our audience, the better we are able to create understanding. There are at least three considerations when thinking about our audience. First, we need to know where they are in terms of knowledge about the gospel. Second, different people have needs based on their social status. Third, people have preferences for different types of music.

Language of Identity. As I described in the introduction, each of us has a music identity. We have a heart language in which we communicate most often. We have preferences for music styles. We have value associations regarding the music we consider sacred, secular, or profane. Solomon understood the traditional music of his tribe; Fred, the rock music of his counterculture. We communicate naturally with those who are like us. We have to learn new music styles when we communicate with those who are different. Even within our own culture, and to a greater degree, *across* cultures, we are also identified by the music we use to communicate. If Fred Caban had been singing in the market center of the equatorial village, in Solomon's culture, Caban's received message may have been more about what he was wearing and the style of music than about his intended evangelistic text. This is one reason the older generation within his own culture disliked the music. They could not separate the association of sex, drugs, and rock 'n' roll from that type of music. The first consideration in music and communication is to understand the identity of our audience and the perception of our identity.

Information and Receptivity. Jim Engel, several years ago, developed a model for understanding how people move through the process of decision making in becoming Christians (Smith, 1992, p. 326). In his model, drawn from change process studies, he outlined the cognitive process by which people used information about God to make a commitment and incorporate themselves into the community of believers.

124

In the decision-making model we find that there are two axes of direction. First, people need enough cognitive information about Christianity to help them make a decision. At the same time, they must move in a growing positive direction to make a decision. It is the role of the communicator to create understanding about the gospel. It is the role of the Holy Spirit to convict of sin. Our responsibility is to communicate the gospel in a language that others will understand. Once they understand, people may choose not to accept our message and invitation. This, too, is feedback.

Social Status and Life Needs. In his *The Becomers,* Keith Miller proposed that Maslow's hierarchy of needs had implications for communicating the gospel to selective audiences (Miller, 1973, pp. 89–109). Maslow proposed that all people have basic life needs. Until the basic physiological needs of food, clothing, shelter, and safety were met, they would not be concerned for higher life needs of love, self-esteem, or self-actualization. Miller proposed that as people moved upward socially, they responded to different appeals of the gospel. In other words, we respond to different concepts of Christ and salvation based on our place in life. For example, impoverished people have a need for food, clothing, and shelter and readily hear a message of Jesus as Healer and Bread of Life, whereas those who have their basic needs met might be more concerned with the assurance that God is Love. When proclaiming Christ, it is important to understand the sociological position and needs of the audience. It is true, in the evangelical concern, that all people need Christ. A good communicator is careful to understand the needs that Christ can meet in the immediate context.

Music Selection. In many countries closed to the gospel, music may be one of the only verbal ways in which the message of the gospel can be shared. Music veils the words and softens their meaning so that people do not take them as a direct threat. Music has different meanings. Several ethnomusicologists have assisted missionaries in closed countries by placing biblical history into the local language and music of the community. One person hired traditional and professional musicians to help write a series of songs on salvation history that was later broadcast over radio. Some may be offended or question the integrity of using non-Christians to write and sing for the purpose of evangelism. But this was an honest and

125

first attempt to bring people into the awareness of the gospel and create an interest.

Music can serve in three ways to build bridges between non-Christians and Christians. Music is proclamation when it creates a friendly and welcome space for decision. The purpose is to move from the unknown to the known. By understanding where people are in their life process, we can better use music as proclamation. In Figure 4.1, you can see a summary of what types of music are most appropriate for proclamation.

1. Bridging Songs. Bridging songs begin with an understanding of the audience and assist hearers in moving from what they know to what they don't know. For example, a number of Christian broad-casting stations have programs targeted at young people with little or no knowledge of the gospel. As a way to attract their attention and build on what they do know, they may play non-Christian music that has a positive message. It is difficult to know whether the music is specifically Christian, but it is not anti-Christian.

Bridging songs also speak to real-life needs and are outside the perimeters of the local church. Some cross-cultural community developers use music as a teaching aid where "Christian" music might be unacceptable. In many countries, it is illegal for residents to convert to Christianity or for visitors to give Christian verbal witness. One may not directly evangelize. One ethnomusicologist was assisting missionaries in a Muslim country to develop a strategy helping people move from the known to the unknown. There was a good deal of development work being done in the country. Songs related to Scripture and development were prepared on a cassette and played during work. She explains, "There are five facts about Jesus which are a good starting point. Jesus was born of a virgin—so the song begins there (perhaps giving the Sura reference in the Koran) and gives the rest of the Gospel story of his birth. The same principle applies to the Koranic statements—He was sinless; He did miracles; He was called 'the Word of God,' and it will be by Jesus that we will all be judged at the Last Day." She assisted these cross-cultural workers in finding local musicians who were Christian and who could use local story-song style with familiar instruments (Scott, Evans, 1990, July 17).

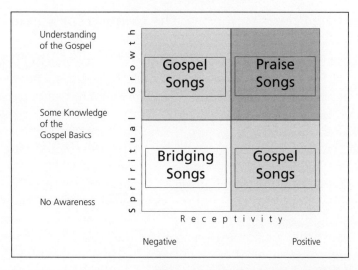

Figure 4.1. Music in Proclamation

2. Gospel Songs. The gospel song is a simple story of salvation. It is subjective and relates personal experience. Used both outside and inside the perimeters of the organized church, it provides the audience with the basic gospel story and calls for a response.

Many local Christians write songs that are highly contextualized. In many countries of Africa, it is common to find train or bus songs that tell of the ticket to heaven. These songs, too, are often outside the boundaries and perimeters of the organized church and create a friendly space within the context of the "world."

3. Praise Songs. Praise songs aid a newly planted church or Christian community to praise and worship. These songs are not abstract, but give a simple and concrete idea of God. Most people will praise God, even though their concept and belief may be otherwise. It is natural for most people to praise a higher being. "God Is So Good" is an example of a proclamation praise or worship song. It has been translated into almost every language. It is easy to sing in terms of both music and text. In the contemporary urban environment, seeker services of "worship evangelism" make good use of these songs in praise and worship because they create a friendly space for outsiders.

127

Creating Friendly Spaces: The Context for Music

Music should be shared where people who need to hear the message can hear it. This may seem like an odd suggestion. Chances are that most people in the Happy Times Bar would not enter the local church building, where Christians don't drink, to listen to the singing. Solomon was merely proclaiming the message where those who needed to hear the message could hear it. He also created a friendly space for receiving and responding to the message.

Henri Nouwen, in *The Wounded Healer,* talks of creating a "friendly space" for people to come to the knowledge of Christ (Nouwen, 1972). Some people involve themselves in confrontational evangelism. And while there may be a place for the gospel to confront the spiritual nature in all of us, people confronting people often leads to the destruction of relationships rather than building them. At the heart of "friendly space" is the concern and respect for people, for their beliefs and their culture.

Following a lecture on this topic, I gave my class the assignment of designing an evangelistic event using music in a local village that was predominantly Muslim. They decided to follow the traditional form of having the choir and preacher stand in the village center. Throughout the meeting people yelled insults, joked, and stood amazed that this little band of Christians would dare enter their space. During the traditional salvation "invitation," I began to see the reason this honest attempt at proclamation was failing so miserably. The class had not created a friendly space. We were in a town where we were not known. We stood in a direct line facing a culture that was highly collectivist and valued circles of community.

We actually had no credibility in this community. We might as well have been strangers who walked into the village and begun throwing rocks at the mosque. In other countries this has led to riots. Had we created a circle, a more acceptable space to the culture, at least the space would have been friendlier. We learned this the following night.

In a mud and tin-roof church just a mile from the village center, local Christians gathered at dusk to spend the night singing, praying, preaching, and sharing their testimony. It was a warm tropical night; hurricane lamps from the trees provided light outside the building. Benches were placed in a circle facing the church entrance. Singers and preachers would enter the semicircle to face the congregation. Behind the people the open area was partly hidden by palm trees and scrub brush, which separated the church from the sandy road leading to the village center. It was dark and remote so the meeting was undisturbed by automobiles.

Throughout the night as people sang, rejoiced, danced, and prayed, we began to feel a part of our own world, far removed from the world of confrontation we had experienced earlier in the day. We became tired and our singing began to slow as the desire to sleep pulled us into a sinking state. And then something unusual happened. An American friend was visiting; he played the guitar and enjoyed children. The preacher asked if he would present a song. Mark was a tall man and we were expecting a booming bass voice. But when he began to sing his high tenor voice startled all of us. It also startled another audience. From the silence of the night, all around the perimeter of the scrub brush and palm trees, arose a thunderous laughter of surprise, not ridicule. We realized that scores of village people had been standing at the edge of our meeting, listening to all that had been said and sung. Needless to say, this cloud of witnesses enthused the congregation to a renewed life of singing. They had become proclaimers and created a friendly space for the community around them.

The concept of incarnation, as evidenced in the theology and life of Christ, shows us that Jesus lived with those outside the parameters of religion. He was even accused of being a drunk and cavorting with prostitutes. There is a fine line here for most of us. It is easy to slip into old habits. Many who arrive at Christianity come out of a life at "rock bottom." We have to divorce ourselves from people, places, and things that remind us of this old life. So there is caution. Yet the fact remains, this fine line of participation can be problematic. In Joseph Aldrich's exceptional book, *Life-Style Evangelism*, he explains that our best work is done through relationships (Aldrich, 1981). Musicians are proclaimers who live in a world outside the concert hall and performance arena, where life meets the musician who has met the Savior.

Proclaimers or Performers?

In the days before television and radio, many villages and towns had a town crier. The town crier was sent by the king to each of the villages in the kingdom to make official announcements. The town crier was a proclaimer; he announced the news of the king. These could be messages about a special royal visit, impending danger, or even celebrations. Throughout the Bible we read of such proclaimers. The most famous proclaimer was the angel who visited Mary, and later Joseph, to give them the news about the birth of Jesus.

The town crier's message, sometimes introduced with the sound of a trumpet and accompanied with regal flags and robes, may have sounded like this: "Hear ye, hear ye, by order of the king, you are to assemble on the fifth day of the fourth month for a visit from the royal family, in celebration of our land's victory over the invaders." The town crier or proclaimer was sent by *one with authority*. He was the voice of one with greater power. As such, he had *credibility* with the village people. They knew his message was from the king. The *message was delivered with a clear and strong voice* so that there was no misunderstanding it. There was a special *relationship* with the townspeople in that they knew him to be the town crier who brought news from afar. Through their *response* to his message, the king would know if the town crier had delivered the message with competence. I imagine that if no one attended the special event, the town crier lost his job, and maybe his head (Kraft, 1991).

Each culture has role expectations for its musicians and artists. They are, sometimes, expected to be eccentric, emotional, and flighty. In some cultures, musicians represent a special class, loved for the music they produce and despised (but tolerated) for their immoral behavior. There are many positive expectations as well.

Musicians are valued for their ability to motivate through music—to move the hearer emotionally. We expect musicians to demonstrate skill on their instrument or with their voice, though that skill is determined by culture. As proclaimers, like the town crier, musicians are more than musicians, but messengers of their king, and as such have high musical standards and ethical standards. Musical proclaimers are expected to motivate, present a clear message, love people, live the life they sing, and present a proclamation of personal experience. These are the biblical expectations of proclamation. There are also unwritten expectations that have been placed on proclamation through tradition and history, which we will consider as a prerequisite to specific musical discussion.

James tells us "Do not merely listen to the word. . . . Do what it says" (James 1:22). In the Lausanne statement above, we read a doctrinal statement of the gospel. It says little about our daily doing of the gospel. C. S. Lewis commented that we are not to be good people but *new* people in response to the gospel (Lewis, 1952, p. 182). This requires change. Doctrinal statements provide us with a mental map, a belief system, for sorting though life's information. Eventually, however, we must experience and act on that belief.

Proclamation is every Christian's responsibility. The musician has special gifts to proclaim in specific ways. However, proclamation is more than singing a song or playing a melody. It involves the whole life of the proclaimer. People evaluate the message not only by the sound of the song but by the life of the singer. This is the reason that relationships are important. Many Western societies rely heavily on information. This has increased in the information explosion of the late twentieth century. Proclaiming the gospel is not just sharing information, although information is important. Proclamation is as much about sharing yourself. This sharing comes through relationships. In John 4, we find that Jesus was not lecturing the Samaritan woman about the doctrinal aspects of the Jewish faith. He developed a relationship with her by meeting on common ground and sharing common needs. He connected with her and entered into dialogue. Music, too, is relational. As we saw in the first chapter, music is often used to build community.

Music proclaimers, who merely sing and then leave, have shared an emotional moment and cognitive information, but a relationship has not been developed for people to evaluate what the gospel means. Audiences often rely on spiritual interpreters, such as friends or other Christians they might know who are the "doers" of the words they are hearing. They learn by example. People with little knowledge of the gospel or Christians can only evaluate what they hear through the best and worst of the Christians they know. They move through a process toward conversion.

The words we sing or the melodies we play cannot be separated from the person who creates them. If on the way to the studio or a concert, a musician cannot stop to help those in need, and thus ignores those around him or her, then the message in a sense is canceled out. If a young college student travels to a distant land to be involved in music proclamation, but does not take the time to learn something of a local culture, the message of the combined media of music and person sends mixed signals. Our sung and played messages have the greatest chance of proclaiming when we relate and partner, and when we as messengers have as much credibility as our message.

An African preacher once told a group of American missionaries, "If you've only come to preach to my soul, go to the graveyard, because that's the only place where the soul and the body are separate." Not only is the musician's whole life to be proclamation but we are to proclaim to whole people, not just spiritual beings. People have real physical needs, emotional needs, and social needs, as well as spiritual needs. When proclamation is targeted for the spiritual person, we make a partial gospel. Jesus' life illustrated that he was concerned for the whole person. The implication for music proclamation is that musicians and their music fulfill real needs of people.

Musicians, who are excellent performers, enjoy sharing their craft through performance and teaching. Yet, a learning attitude can create friendly dialogue with interested individuals. New styles of music, new perspectives, even new friends come from being open to learn about others. Is there, then, an effective method for music proclamation? We now look at several case studies.

Proclamation

Just as prophecy calls *from* the street for justice, proclamation takes *to* the streets a message of hope. While prophets are often single voices, proclaimers are partners with other believers of the kingdom in witness, mission, and evangelism. This ministry speaks both to people intraculturally (within a culture) and cross-culturally (across cultures). There are three ways in which music is part of proclamation in the contemporary context related to our three types of songs: as a bridge, as welcome worship, and as gospel messenger.

First, music supplements other media presentations, such as radio broadcasts and television programs. Listener expectations for quality comparable to that of mainstream music are often so high that truly talented and gifted musicians are needed in this ministry. In virtually every part of the world where the church is present, talented musicians offer their gifts in a service of proclamation. Because many come from nonchurch backgrounds, they often receive a skeptical eye from church people who consider their music worldly. One cannot deny, however, that they are a bridge between belief and nonbelief.

One such group is the contemporary Christian music group, Jars of Clay, based in the United States. In the early years of their music ministry they made a conscious attempt, like many Christian bands, to sing at "secular" nightclubs. This strategy was driven by their desire to be Christians *in* the culture. They discovered that the greatest barrier to their witness was members of the church, who did not trust their motives and felt uncomfortable in this context. In an attempt to have a bridge-building ministry, where they could "hold one hand in the church and the other hand in society," they began giving concerts in neutral places, like theaters. They find this venue practical because nonbelievers do not feel comfortable in a church building, and believers are usually threatened by the drinking and other activities of clubs. It is a safe, protected, and friendly space, where non-Christians and Christians can interact.

Because the texts of their songs do not proclaim the gospel directly, they indirectly proclaim a message that depends on the witness of other believers. As I have witnessed with other contemporary Christian music groups, many people ask questions, based on the song's message. A dialogue is established in the virtual world of the Internet. These musicians are faithful and articulate in sharing their belief after the song has ended. I was even shocked to know that they hold to strict rules of behavior during concert tours, to maintain credibility in their witness (Lowell, 1997).

A second approach has been called "worship evangelism" by author Sally Morgenthaler. As a welcome worship, Morgenthaler clearly states that the purpose of worship is not evangelism but "worship is to glorify God, not to win lost souls" (Morgenthaler, 1995, p. 87). But in this worship, like the singing of Paul and Silas in prison, unbelievers hear the truth about God (through worship songs, prayers, communion, baptism, Scripture, testimonies, drama, etc.); and second—most importantly—they observe the real relationship between worshipers and God. For this to happen, there are four essential elements. First, there is a "nearness—a sense of God's presence" in the service. Second, Christ is the center of the worship with a focus on relevant communication of his message. Third, worship must be a place of vulnerability, where there is space to lament, where sinners are welcome, and where real-life problems are addressed. Finally, evangelism worship is a place of interaction and participation with God and each other (Morgenthaler, 1995, pp. 96–123). Out of worship, however, the faithful are called to enter the world with their message of proclamation.

A number of years ago, a group of nine students from Samford University in the United States traveled to the city of Kitwe in the Copperbelt of Zambia. They were hosted by the Copperbelt Baptist Association. Over two weeks they sang twenty-nine concerts in secondary schools and colleges. A week before they arrived in Zambia, a coup attempt occurred. Outdoor rallies and meetings were canceled by the government. School concerts were the only place the group was allowed to sing outside the local churches. Their audiences averaged 1,250 young people at each concert.

The local church association, working with cross-cultural missionary Ed Miller and school authorities, designed a concert that would also include local school choirs. Christian music is part of most school choir repertoires. In addition to the choir singing of gospel texts, a Zambian adult or youth was selected to share a brief testimony of his or her experience with Christ. At the close of the concert an invitation or verbal call was given to the students (for knowing Christ, prayer, Bible study, or counseling problems). The response was so great that all those calling themselves Christians or wanting to meet the performers were asked to leave the auditorium. Only those wishing to know more about Christ or needing guidance were asked to remain. Ten to 15 percent of the student body remained; many young people made decisions. Counselors met with the students to interpret and explain the gospel message.

According to Miller, this response could be attributed to three factors: the hunger of the students for spiritual things, the excellence of the musical performance, and the genuineness of the people who shared in proclaiming through song. Another missionary observer surmised the response to be great because a simple statement of "invitation to a living Christ who could change lives today" was used rather than the religious jargon so often used by Christian groups.

It is sometimes difficult to know why people respond to music proclamation. It could be a response to the emotion of the text, the entertainment, or the culture the proclaimer represents. Certainly this can be the case when the focus is on the excellence of the music or the performance of the "entertainer." Responding to this concern, Miller cited an earlier example where a similar response was received during concerts by a visiting group. The sincerity and genuineness expressed in the Christian character of the proclaimers made the performance successful. Certainly excellent music—as defined by culture—is important, but the genuineness of the messenger is of primary concern.

Miller stated that he learned a lesson from this experience. "The need and interest in the gospel is outside the church, and the local church is often unaware of this openness." While a number of Bible studies were begun and many were incorporated into the forty local churches, the lack of follow-up by the local church was a significant weakness. Miller further reported the important role prayer had played in the initial and continued proclamation events.

From these three case studies we can draw several conclusions. First, prayer is essential to, during, and following the event. In each case, prayer played a fundamental role. Second, planning, especially in the cross-cultural context of traveling mission groups, is absolutely critical. Even with the best planning, as we saw in the coup attempt of Zambia, things go wrong. This planning should always involve leaders on both sides of the event and in cooperation with local Christians. This relationship between cross-cultural Christians is as important as the one believers should develop with nonbelievers.

Third, because music communicates different messages to different people, a relationship should be established between proclaimers and hearers. Proclaimers and receivers need time to interact, ask questions, seek clarification, and develop relationships. Fourth, a verbal explanation-interpretation of the message should accompany the music proclamation. This is sometimes done through personal testimony, a sermon, or, as in the case of concerts, through the Internet. Fifth, within this welcome space an opportunity should be provided to respond to the proclamation. While some groups give an open "altar call," this may prove embarrassing to some people, or, in the case of many cultures, people may respond out of politeness to the guest, without any personal commitment. Finally, follow-up, including counseling and leading to the incorporation into a local church community, is essential (Smith, 1992, pp. 332–34).

Summary

In this chapter we have considered music as proclamation, which witnesses to the salvation experience, relates in mission to the world, and evangelizes by calling people to a life of faith in Jesus Christ. Music proclaims the gospel when words, music and actions communicate a simple message of salvation. Using a transactional or dialogical model of communication, music is a process shared by performers and hearers, in which meaning is created in text, music, instruments, movement, and even dress, within a communication event. Because of its emotional power, music can motivate as well as manipulate.

For effective communication to take place, the message is placed within the language and context of the hearer. This is done cross-culturally through a process of contextualization when the gospel is inculturated into the receiving culture, often using dynamic equivalents—or relevant metaphors. As receivers of the message, individuals and audiences listen out of personal interest and life needs.

Understanding the audience is crucial in selecting music. Bridging songs help build bridges of trust and information about God, especially where there is little knowledge of him. Gospel songs are simple stories of salvation that invite the hearer into the kingdom. Praise songs create a welcome atmosphere for outsiders to quickly find a friendly space in what are often complicated worship rituals.

It is within these friendly spaces that music proclamation serves best. People are welcomed into a friendly space to hear, dialogue, and respond to the message of salvation. The ability of people to hear within this space is directly related to the authenticity and credibility of the proclaimer. For this reason, proclamation events are best held in cooperation with local Christian communities. This local involvement involves prayer, planning, preparation, and follow-up.

Questions for Discussion

1. Why do you believe that contemporary Christian music has gained such popularity around the world? Has this made proclamation easier or more difficult? For example, are people coming to know the Christ of culture, or the values of Western culture?
2. If you were asked to use music in proclamation, how might you dress, talk, sing, play, or choose instruments for urban young people as opposed to rural farmers?
3. What are some ways in which musicians can give witness in their own community?
4. What dangers do musicians face when trying to give witness outside the confines of their local church?
5. Do you think it is acceptable for a non-Christian to record salvation songs for use in proclaiming the gospel in countries closed to Christian missionaries and witness? Can you give a biblical example to support your opinion?

Exercises

1. Interview friends you know about how music played a role in their decision to follow Christ.
2. Look for articles in missions magazines on how others use music in evangelism.
3. Take one of your favorite hymns. On a piece of paper create two columns. Title the left column, **my culture**, and the right column **other culture**. In the left column write each line of the hymn. This is the hymn that you understand. In the right column, select another culture of which you are aware. For example, if you are in an urban area think of a rural culture. Or perhaps you have traveled to a country outside your own. Now write in the second column a contextualized version of the lines in the first column. Find a dynamic equivalent for the words that might pose problems in understanding.
4. Visit several different churches near you. Draw a diagram of the evangelistic service. What physical characteristics create or prohibit a "friendly space" for those outside the Christian community? At the same time have a class member or friend keep track of the dialogue and order of the service. Are there words, movements, and symbols that do not foster understanding? What would you change to create a friendly space?
5. Design your own proclamation event where you create a friendly space with music and space. Then experiment with the help of your class.
6. Listen to music from different musicians that you hear on the radio, cassette, or compact disc. Write out the words and see how they try to contextualize the gospel in contemporary contexts. Do they proclaim the gospel in the meaning of the Willowbank definition given at the beginning of the chapter? What might you change?
7. Select a group of people with whom you are familiar. Design a music proclamation event specifically for that group of people. Follow the principles at the end of the chapter. How might this event look and sound different in another culture, socioeconomic class, gender, or age-set?

8. Search the Bible for parables and stories that give a proclamation of the gospel (e.g., the lost coin). How might this be
   presented using a multimedia approach of music, drama, and
   dance in your context?

Music as Healer

Now the Spirit of the LORD had departed from Saul, and an evil spirit from the LORD tormented him. Saul's attendants said to him, "See, an evil spirit from God is tormenting you. Let our lord command his servants here to search for someone who can play the harp. He will play when the evil spirit from God comes upon you, and you will feel better." So Saul said to his attendants, "Find someone who plays well and bring him to me."

(1 Sam. 16:14–17)

Jesus went through all the towns and villages, teaching in their synagogues, preaching the good news of the kingdom and healing every disease and sickness. When he saw the crowds, he had compassion on them, because they were harassed and helpless, like sheep without a shepherd. Then he said to his disciples, "The harvest is plentiful but the workers are few. Ask the Lord of the harvest, therefore, to send out workers into his harvest field."

(Matt. 9:35–38)

Music is a language of prayer in which words are inadequate to express our deepest thoughts. A melodic and harmonic salve, music used in times of grief alleviates suffering of the mind, body, and spirit. Music is a key to unlocking the realm of the spiritual world, when rhythm transports the inner realm to external experience. In music

141

we find the potential to minister to a basic human need: alleviation from suffering. Our bodies, souls, and spirits cry out in desperate hours for health and wholeness.

Suffering is universal. In every culture, tribe, and city, people struggle for liberation and healing from poverty, sickness, and injustice. In the New Testament there are two concepts of healing or liberation. One is of social liberation from suffering and evil, the other of illness. In the chapter on prophecy, we saw that music functions to preach for liberation from social injustice. In this chapter we will consider music's role in the treatment of illness. Healing, the restoration of wholeness, takes place on four different levels: body, mind, soul, and community (relationships).

First, we will define the term *healing* and place it within the context of what the Bible has to say about music in healing with examples from the Old and New Testaments. Second, we will discover how music affects the mind, body, and soul of the individual. Third, we will look briefly at the relatively new field of music therapy. Finally, we will discuss ways in which music can be incorporated into the ministry of the local kingdom community.

The Sound of the Harvest . . .

My father was a Southern Baptist preacher with an empathetic heart for the sick and poor. He grew up on a farm in southern Illinois during the Great Depression and understood the needs and concerns of the poor, the marginalized, and victims of life's tragic events. As a pastor of a small country church, he took great pleasure in talking, counseling, and listening. I remember a particular Wednesday night prayer service. It stands out in my mind today because of its healing focus.

In the congregation was one of our neighbors. I don't remember her name, but I do remember that because of her rather large size, she suffered from phlebitis, gout, and a very bad heart. She always walked with great difficulty, and the climb up the church steps always took an eternity, especially to a boy of ten who enjoyed jumping two steps at a time to the top. One morning, she asked the church to pray for her. The following Wednesday night I accompanied my father to her house for special prayer. I don't remember everything that was said, but I do remember a gentle kindness and humble spirit as a score of committed prayers crowded into her small living room. We began by singing a special hymn of prayer,

What a friend we have in Jesus
All our sins and grief to bear
What a privilege to carry
Everything to God in prayer

(Charles Converse)

My father voiced concern for "the sick lady" and then he asked us all to kneel. Kneeling was a favorite public prayer posture for my father in his early years, especially before he suffered from gout and heart problems. During the prayer I noticed how he placed his hand on her fleshy arm in comfort. While I don't remember much else about the service, I do remember the song, the posture, and the touch of healing prayer.

"Take everything to the Lord in prayer" to a ten-year-old boy from North Carolina was to be stretched and expanded in later years. I encountered a worldview that believed in the spirit world. When joined with a Pentecostal theology of the gifts of the Spirit, music's powerful spiritual dimension became real.

Twenty years later, I entered an inland village church in Kenya. Though the cultural setting was much different, the common concerns for the sick and the use of prayer for healing "in the name of Jesus" were the same. It was a cool evening in the coastal village, and many gathered from near and far to participate in the all-night service. At approximately 3:00 A.M., the celebrative singing changed moods. A young song leader moved to the center of the meeting and spontaneously led the group in songs about spiritual power:

Chase Satan, the great liar, chase him away.

As the congregation sang under the open sky, three women moved to the center and began shaking and moaning, possessed by evil spirits. The more intense the singing of the congregation became,

143

the more strongly the reaction of spirits inside the women. From the periphery of the group appeared a man in a long robe.

While the singing continued, in a low, hushed tone, he began to pray fervently, calling on the name of Jesus to break the power of Satan over the lives of the women. Then, placing his hand on the forehead of each, he loudly called on the demon to leave the women. Each one calmed as he prayed. The congregation then began to sing a song of thanksgiving that these women had been relieved of the evil spirits through the power of Jesus.

. . . And the Beat of the Street

Mary Saurman and her husband are music therapists. Over the years they have researched the effects of music on the human body. In one study they confirmed that people between the ages of seventeen and twenty-five learned to prefer certain music. They called this a *generational vantage point* (Saurman, 1995) because young people develop a preference for the music of their generation.

In their study of music and heart rates, they also found that when people listened to music of their generational vantage point, their blood pressure and heart rate remained the same or decreased— they were in a relaxed physical state. In contrast, when they listened to music in a contrasting style, or one with negative associations, their heart rate and blood pressure would increase considerably. Surprisingly, some young people actually relax when they listen to heavy metal rock music. One can see how parents, who may not like this music, conflicting with their teenagers who do, could have different emotional responses to the same music.

In an interesting case, Saurman describes how she helped a young expectant teenager give birth to her first child. The young woman was distraught, with considerable anxiety, high blood pressure, and a rapid heart rate. She was in danger of losing her child. Saurman convinced the nurses in the delivery room to allow the birth-mother to listen to heavy metal music, her favorite. Within minutes, the heart rate and blood pressure of the birth-mother, and the unborn child, decreased. The delivery was successful.

Healing

Music has an important role as healer when it brings about a holistic wellness that includes the body, mind, soul, and community. Before looking at the healing nature of music, however, we need to lay a foundation for the concepts of health and healing.

In English, we frequently use the term "healing" to mean a restoration of health. The Greek word of the New Testament, *therapeuo*, from which we get the word "therapy," means to serve, or to heal, cure, and restore to health. The World Health Organization has defined health not only in terms of freedom from disease but also as "a state of complete physical, mental and social well-being" (*World Health Report*, 1997). This definition is very close to the principles of the Bible.

The concept of healing weaves throughout both the Old and New Testaments in the ultimate redemption of humankind in a right relationship with God. Related to the holistic view of health, the body, mind, soul, and community were not separated. It is in this context that Jesus healed the sick and diseased, and cast out demons, declaring divine power over Satan.

Jesus was concerned with the salvation and healing of the whole person in order to inaugurate the kingdom of God in a new type of community (Harper, 1986, p. 145). For this reason, the word "salvation" is often used interchangeably with healing. Health in the New Testament was not the mere absence of pain or sickness (Harper, 1986, p. 143). The supreme mission of Jesus was to heal this gravely disturbed relationship and restore men and women to their real vocation, a close fellowship with God (Harper, 1986, p. 153). Was music part of Jesus' healing ministry?

Jesus lived in a Jewish culture influenced by the Roman world. While music was used in ceremonies and rituals, Jesus did not use music himself in healing. This does not mean he did not sing or dance, for we can imagine he enjoyed participating in social activities. However, in the story of the ruler with a dead child found in Matthew 9, Jesus entered the ruler's house and sent away the "flute players and noisy crowd," who were probably conducting a wake in honor of the child. After they left Jesus entered the room, took the

145

child by the hand, and she got up. Does this mean that music was not to be used?

Jesus was aware of music and quoted a common children's song as a concrete example of the present generation who failed to respond to the message of John the Baptist.

> We played the flute for you,
> and you did not dance;
> we sang a dirge,
> and you did not mourn.

(Matt. 11:17)

While Jesus' acts were not performed through music, there is an example from James where music was at least associated with the church's healing ministry.

> Is any one of you in trouble? He should pray. Is anyone happy? Let him sing songs of praise. Is any one of you sick? He should call the elders of the church to pray over him and anoint him with oil in the name of the Lord. And the prayer offered in faith will make the sick person well; the Lord will raise him up. (James 5:13–15)

In this example we see that it is the power of God through prayer that heals. Based on these passages, we could conclude that music has no role in healing. However, the focus is not on the divine power of music, but on its role as a tool in the healing process, much like anointing oil or the spittle Jesus placed on the blind man's eyes.

How we attain this restoration to health has much to do with our cultural worldview and belief system. One way of deciding a world-view of health is in the explanation for Saul's evil spirit. Was this really an evil spirit, or merely a metaphor for an emotional disturbance?

There are two different worldview explanations for this spirit. First, in a holistic worldview, there is no division between the spirit world and the physical world. As you saw in the second case study, prayer has healing power to not just bring comfort but to also cast out evil spirits, which move about freely between the seen and unseen worlds. God used the music of the harp to bring calm.

Second, in a scientific worldview, people separate the physical and spiritual worlds and rely on rational and scientific proof as explanations of events. There is a mistrust or unbelief of supernatural events. People with this worldview may conjecture that the spirit was a deep state of anxiety or depression.

Having looked at the definition and meaning of healing, we want to combine both a holistic and scientific approach to music as potential healer. In the descriptions below we will see, through both scientific research and anthropological study, how music affects the body, mind, soul, and community (see Figure 5.1).

In the scientific worldview, research is the basis for proving the validity of a hypothesis. Music's effects on the body and brain are becoming evident through such research conducted in the United States, Canada, and Europe. Many cultures do not share the same scientific worldview, however. A holistic worldview that includes the belief in the spirit world has long used music as a key to unlocking the power of this world.

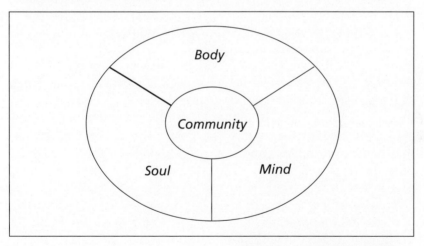

Figure 5.1. Holistic Health

Music and the Body

Music making is rooted in the human body. From the rhythmical heartbeat of a mother that surrounds a child in the womb, to the

147

constant sounds of our environment that enter our auditory senses, our body responds and our mind orders a flood of rhythms, pitches, and words.

We need this external stimulus. Prisoners in solitary confinement become lethargic and withdraw into their memories with a hunger for sight, sound, and touch out of a "stimulus hunger" for the world outside their cell (Storr, 1992, p. 28). People living in highly populated and technological environments may complain of "stimulus overload," where they have difficulty ordering the myriad of distractions that overwhelm them. Each of us responds differently to our environment, based on personality, experience, and culture. Depending on the person, our physiological response to music can be one of arousal or calm.

One of the unique responses of human beings to music is that it causes *arousal*. Arousal is "a condition of heightened alertness, awareness, interest, and excitement: a generally enhanced state of being" (Storr, 1992, p. 24). This is different than an emotional response. As a result of arousal, when external stimuli of music enters the brain through our ears, the results are physiological changes.

Music first affects our involuntary and autonomic nervous system. If there is interest and concentration on the part of the listener, music arouses a state of being with heightened alertness, awareness, interest, and excitement. This arousal is maximized in times of grief, anger, or other emotions. During this time, there are actual physiological changes in our bodies: "the electrical resistance of the skin is diminished; the pupil of the eye dilates; the respiratory rate may become either faster or slower; blood pressure tends to rise, as does the heart rate. There is an increase in muscular tone, which may be accompanied by physical restlessness" (Storr, 1992, p. 25).

This arousal response has two important results. First, it often leads to "action potentials" like the need to tap one's foot to music or some other rhythmic response. If you doubt this, watch a group of children who listen to music. They have an uncontrollable urge to dance. This rhythmic action potential helps us order time both within and without our bodies. Another result of this arousal can be provocation of powerful emotions, though the emotions may not be the same for any two people. While these responses may seem unconscious, our brains are at work responding in a number of ways.

I dislike traffic sounds at night because they disturb my sleep. My friend finds comfort in their constant flow.

If music has the power to arouse a person, it also serves as a calming agent by relieving the anxiety of the body and mind. It serves as a healing agent. Here are some physiological examples based on contemporary medical research:

- Listening to music helped reduce anxiety among patients undergoing colon cancer screening by reducing blood pressure and pulse rates *(Health News and Review)*.
- Music reduces autonomic reactivity (skin conductance, blood pressure, and pulse rate) and increases performance (speed and accuracy). In a study conducted on fifty male surgeons who listened to music while operating, researchers at the State University of New York found that music improved their performance, especially when they listened to music of their choice. In other words, just any music will not help. While Pachelbel's *Canon in D* did have an intermediate effect on the surgeons, using no music had no effect (Allen and Blascovitch, 1994).
- Researchers found that premature babies in an intensive care unit who listened to lullabies (through miniature Walkmans) had higher levels of oxygen in their blood and their heart and breathing rates were closer to normal than babies who did not (Munson, 1995, p. 42).
- People recovering from an injury have a speedier recovery though music. Music helps "ease, enliven and speed recovery." People listening to music are able to exercise longer with a greater range of motion. Music therapist Roberta Wigle of the University of Michigan Medical Center found the best music for "injury rehabilitation" has a heavy rhythm (like rock music) because it "stimulates movement and masks minor pain" *(Men's Health)*.

While experts by no means agree on the exact power of music in the healing process, there is mounting scientific evidence to support what many people have known intuitively: music has an impact on the mind and body. Humans respond to music through arousal or calm. This response is dependent on two things: music preference and a heightened emotional state. Considering the potential power of music, understanding how we listen to music can help in our music making.

Music and the Brain

The brain is divided into two hemispheres. While there is a great deal of sharing of information and joint functioning, by and large, the left brain is used for speech and the right brain is used for music (Storr, 1992, p. 35). That means that we use our left brain for logic and abstract objective thinking, while our right brain is used for emotional functions (see Figure 5.2). We do not, however, only hear words on the left and music on the right. What is important is the cerebral function when listening to music. We have the choice to think critically about music using our left brain, or to listen with our emotions using the right side of our brain. Because of music's power of arousal, when listening to music without our left brain "engaged," we can lose critical judgment and allow our emotions to persuade us. At the same time, if we listen to music with our left brain engaged, we may fail to feel any emotion or enjoyment of the music. Ideally, we need both sides of our brain.

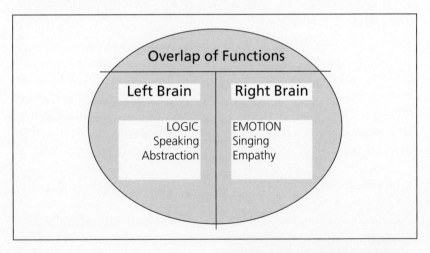

Figure 5.2. Brain Functions

As the apostle Paul admonished, "I will sing with my spirit, but I will also sing with my mind" (1 Cor. 14:15). Two of the greatest gifts we can give to young people are critical listening and singing. We develop and practice critical listening when the left brain is functioning in dialogue with the music. We express our emotions through singing, thus exercising our right brain.

Music and the Soul

An ethnomusicology student and I were discussing fieldwork in cultures where demon possession occurs regularly. She became somewhat anxious during the conversation and asked, "Aren't you worried that you will be possessed also?" Her concern was not unique. Later, I was sitting with a group of young people in The Netherlands discussing rock music. During the conversation they raised two questions commonly asked around the world: Can music be evil? If I listen to rock music, will I be possessed by an evil spirit? In order to answer these questions we will first look at this spiritual phenomenon from anthropological studies. Second, we will consider the Christian worldview.

Many people living outside the scientific worldview recognize an unconscious world of spirits and demons, often as intercessors. People of the Navajo Nation in the Southwestern United States perform an Enemyway ceremony to cleanse and cure members of the Navajo Nation after they have been among strangers because of the spirits of the non-Navajos who have died in the foreign place (Titon, 1996, p. 40). In Latin America, as well as many other parts of the world, shamans "travel back and forth between this world and a supernatural realm of souls and spirits" (Titon, 1996, p. 481). In a sense they do battle against the darts and arrows of shamans of the spirit world.

Christians also recognize the concept of mediation in the ultimate power of the Holy Spirit.

> In the same way, the Spirit helps us in our weakness. We do not know what we ought to pray for, but the Spirit himself intercedes for us with groans that words cannot express. And he who searches our hearts

knows the mind of the Spirit, because the Spirit intercedes for the saints in accordance with God's will.

(Rom. 8:26–27)

While a shaman is a human who seeks to influence the spirits for the benefit of human beings, the Holy Spirit is God himself, whose intercession for us fulfills a very different purpose—the sovereign will of God. Many Christians fail to understand the holistic spiritual power within the kingdom of God. Not discovered through reason or logic, this spiritual nature so often referred to in the Gospels and Epistles remains hidden or unrealized (Harper, 1986, p. 122). Yet "It is impossible to do full justice to the doctrine of the kingdom of God if we ignore the charismatic character of it" (Harper, 1986, p. 166).

Is demon possession possible? Can alien beings enter the physical shell of human bodies? History and Scripture show us the answer is yes, though many Christians with scientific worldviews would deny it. Recent studies by anthropologists, who traditionally might not accept this phenomenon, are exploring the possibility. Anthropologist Felicitas D. Goodman (1988) conducted a cross-cultural study including Brazilian, Mayan, Japanese, and Haitian cultures. Her conclusion was that

> On the psychological level, we have come to know the notion underlying all possession, namely, that the body is a shell, inhabited by a soul, and that this shell may on occasion be surrendered to an intrusive alien entity. The nature of this being and the circumstances of entry are culturally structured, so culture is another important basic term. On the physiological level, there is the altered state of consciousness of ecstasy and the emergence of brain maps. Ritual acts as a bridge that connects the events on the psychological and the physiological levels, leading to experience. That ties in with healing, especially in our context with the cure of injurious possession by the ritual of exorcism.

(Goodman, 1988a, p. 24)

Goodman calls music, and the related activities of drumming, singing, candles, and fragrances, *sensory cues*, which assist one in entering an ecstatic state (Goodman, 1988a, p. 11). Rhythmic activity is a "driving" force in inducing an altered state. In addition to the ecstatic state, other altered states of consciousness are trance, sleep, hypnotic state, and meditation. In her study of glossolalia, Goodman found that vocalization was part of this ecstatic state, which affected blood pressure and heart rate and influenced the nervous system for people to feel relaxed (Goodman, 1988a, p. 9). In glossolalia, accent, rhythm, and intonation patterns are *suprasegmental* parts of language. They "float above the segments of language" (Goodman, 1988, p. 6). Music, then, is a key to unlocking or opening the person to the spiritual realm. Music is also a sign within ritual (worship) practices that signals that there is a time for these states to take place.

This is what appears to have happened with the women who were possessed by demons in the example at the beginning of this chapter. Culturally, when a particular song or rhythm is used, there is a signal that healing was to take place. From the Goodman study, it appears that music is not the power, but the switch that allows people through culturally determined rituals to enter into psychological and spiritual states. However, not all people would agree with Goodman.

Centuries ago, Plato held the belief that music held the power to corrupt the character of young people. In *The Republic,* he outlined the importance of teaching the right kind of music based on Greek musical scales. Certain scales produced good character, while others did not. Though these scales are not in use today, a belief in the inherent goodness and evil of music continues in much of the Eurocentric world—a view, by the way, which is not held in all societies. In the former view, people will not listen to music (and will not even allow it in the church) because it was created evil. In the view described by Goodman, music has no power in and of itself, but triggers certain behavior in individuals. A recent U.S. court case illustrates the conflict between the holistic and dualistic musical worldview.

In *The Gift of Fear,* Gavin De Becker details the nature of violence in American society and offers guidelines for predicting such behavior. In one study, he describes a case in which he was called to testify. James Vance and a friend purchased the album *Stained Glass* by the music group Judas Priest from a local music shop. After listening to the profane lyrics they entered into a suicide pact, ran to Saint

Augustine Church, and attempted to carry out their pact. Vance's friend succeeded, but Vance's attempt left him grotesquely disfigured until he died weeks later.

As Becker describes, parents in these situations either blame themselves or find someone to blame. Vance's parents sued the music store owners for not warning the eighteen-year-olds about the satanic and violent nature of the music. "The court eventually decided that the proprietors of the record store could not have predicted the shootings" (Becker, 1997, p. 217).

At face value, the satanic and violent music was the evil influence that led to the shootings. Beneath the incident, as de Becker describes, the culprit was not the music but other contributing factors. While similar incidents may involve addiction to media products, a greater contributor to such violence is an addiction to alcohol and drugs. Far greater than music, these factors are "proven and intended to affect the perceptions and behavior of all people who ingest them" (Becker, 1997, p. 215).

Both young men had consumed a large amount of alcohol and drugs prior to the incident. According to Becker, Vance and his friend had a fascination with violence and guns. They also felt ignored and not part of the social world in which they lived. So while music became the focus for the reported event, there were deeper psychological and sociological issues.

Becker draws some important conclusions for consideration in the use of music and media. First, the greatest culprit seems to be the lack of human interaction, which is often prevented by too much media. "The content of media products matters, but the amount may matter more, whether it is watching too much television, playing video games too much, listening to too much rock music, or for that matter too much classical music" (Becker, 1997, p. 216). Second, violence within the home also precipitates violence in teenagers. Third, a lack of good parenting results in failure to learn basic life skills, "the ability to motivate ourselves, to persist against frustration, to delay gratification, to regulate moods, to hope, to empathize, and to control impulse" (Becker, 1997, p. 218).

Music is often no more than a way to express the emotional state of the individual. Ask any person who has been involved in a serious bout of depression or drug addiction. Not long ago I interviewed

154

a young woman who was living in a halfway house for former drug addicts. I asked about her music listening habits, "Oh, I used to listen to heavy metal, even Curt Cobain, but I never really listened to the words. The music expressed my feelings at the moment—like background music. But when I accepted Christ, I began to hear the words and they were not what I wanted in my life. They didn't express my new lifestyle. Sometimes I still listen, but they are not as meaningful as the Christian songs. The Christian songs give me peace. I like the words."

This brings me back to two questions. Is music evil? Can I be possessed by a spirit? To the first question we can give a qualified no. Music has no power in and of itself, even with its action potential. The evil or good of music is a result of the human heart and conditioning of culture. "For out of the overflow of the heart the mouth speaks" (Matt. 12:34). This does not mean that listening to music with unredeeming qualities is prudent. As food for the body, music has benefits for the soul. It is the association with evil contexts that creates problems for many people.

People do not realize just how much music informs our lives. In one study, a psychologist discovered that many people "produce music for themselves" throughout the day, using melodies they already knew, as much as one to two hours of each day. Storr concludes that music is a "permanent part of mental activity. . . . If music becomes a permanent part of our mental furniture, it must exert an influence on our lives" (Storr, 1992, pp. 123, 126).

In 1 Corinthians 8, Paul focuses on food sacrificed to idols. He gave complete freedom to those who had spiritual maturity and a clear conscience. The caution, however, came when this freedom became a stumbling block to weaker Christians. Similarly, I am free to listen to any music composed by gifted humans, because I know that it has no power over me. However, in some contexts, it is not always beneficial. For example, I have listened to recordings by alternative rock groups who use obscene words and satanic lyrics. I listen as a professor, trying to understand the world of music. Personally, I would not find it profitable or healthy to attend a live concert by these groups because of the presence of drugs and other illicit activities.

155

As far as the second question regarding demon possession, I have to admit that my scientific worldview makes it very difficult for me to believe in demon possession. I might want to agree with the theological dispensation that the gifts of the Spirit ended with the first-century Christians. However, after living many years among people who believe in their existence, and on more than one occasion having faced what I consider to be evil forces, I have to admit the possibility of demon possession, especially in light of such overwhelming New Testament evidence. Music plays a part in this experience. Our response does not have to be one of fear but of victory. For the power of Christ offers freedom and liberation from oppressive spiritual forces. But there is also another caution which has to do with our emotions. When minds are not engaged or conscious of the context and meaning in the music, and when the human heart is prone toward evil, music has emotional power equal to that of any evil spirit.

Commenting on Hitler's use of bands to warm up his audience before speaking, psychologist Anthony Storr comments that "music can powerfully contribute to the loss of critical judgment, the blind surrender to the feelings of the moment, which is so dangerously characteristic of crowd behavior" (Storr, 1992, p. 46). So to answer the question: all music is profitable, but must be used with prudence.

Music can affect the body, mind, and soul of a person, but, a person is also part of a larger community. As we have seen, during the ministry of Jesus there were no divisions between the bodily and the social, the emotional and the spiritual. Instead, healing always involved a network of relationships within a community (Green, 1995, p. 28).

Music and the Community

At the very center of wellness is the community. From the beginning of creation, God intended that we should live in harmony and in the company of other human beings. Our very physical survival requires that we organize into social groups to meet the daily demands of life and hardships in our environment. A healthy community is able to cooperatively work together as a living organism to meet the needs of the group.

The primary example from the Christian perspective is the local church. A community of believers should support and pray for one another. Yet an unhealthy community, filled with jealousy, strife, dissension, and disagreement, is unable to function for the benefit of all. The result is conflict, alienation, and marginalization of members. Music can fulfill a healing role through a variety of functions.

First, music creates a friendly space—a place to feel at home. The welcome and joyful expressions of Christians in worship communicate inclusion. Nondefensive postures of song, such as sharing a hymnal, signal a welcome attitude. In times of sorrow, music soothes a congregation but also allows the congregation to express their grief in an outward expression.

Second, music creates rapport with a community. When music is a common language to those who enter the community there is a sense of oneness or sameness. Even if our languages may be different, the act of sharing music reveals an openness toward others. If you have ever been new to a community—a class of children, a group of young people, or a congregation of adults—you know the immediate rapport that is established between the performer and the group, merely by revealing your gift. Related to rapport is trust. We give and receive trust as we reveal our self to others. Music exposes the inner dimensions of a person. In many African societies, marital interests are enhanced not by the outward beauty of a person, but by the way a person expresses himself or herself in song and dance.

Third, music creates order. Human beings often have anxiety over uncertainty and feel uncomfortable with ambiguity. We almost crave ritual. Music is a temporal activity. That is, it is created and performed within time. Rhythm, music's organizer and energizer, helps create order, consistency, and framework for the community.

Finally, music provides an opportunity to cooperate and relate to others. Congregational singing, on a very basic level, involves the cooperation of many voices to create one voice in praise and worship. Orchestral enthusiasts enjoy hearing separate instruments blend to perform a single composition. Another interesting example comes from the gamelon performers, in Indonesia where musicians may have only one or two notes to contribute to the piece of music, much like a handbell choir. A strong sense of order, cooperation, and timeliness is absolutely essential for a whole community of individuals. In each of these examples, the emphasis is not on the music per se, but on how it functions to foster community. Under the best of circumstances a healthy community suffers when its individual members undergo psychological, physiological, or spiritual suffering.

We will now look at two models for music as healer. The first model, based on a scientific approach, uses music in professional therapeutic situations. In the second model, we will discuss a healing music ministry.

Music Therapy

Almost universally, music and healing are bonded in the rites, rituals, and practices of healing. This special relationship of music to human experience is more mysterious than mystical (Gaston, 1968, p. 10). While holistic cultures have long practiced the art of music in healing, it has only been in this century that mechanistic cultures and scientific research have documented music's relationship to the alleviation of suffering and applied that research to medical science. What my father knew intuitively and what the coastal worshipers practiced religiously is now taken seriously by medical health professionals.

Following World War I and World War II, in the United States, many professional and amateur musicians entered veterans' hospitals to help in the alleviation of pain and suffering through their music. Wounded physically and emotionally, these veterans benefited from the music. In 1944, Michigan State University began an academic program to train musicians for this new discipline. Soon after, in 1950, the world's first association of music therapists was founded. Today, the American Music Therapy Association (AMTA) is the largest among a number of music therapy associations around the world.

Music therapists undergo rigorous academic musical training and practical supervision through internships. In the United States, music therapists complete undergraduate training at an approved university and six months of a supervised internship. They must also pass a national examination before being listed as registered music therapists (RMTs) through the Certification Board for music therapists. (There are similar accrediting organizations in Europe and Canada.)

In the United States, music therapy is now an accepted tool for alleviating suffering in hospitals, nursing homes, special education programs, and psychiatric facilities. According to the AMTA, the following are some ways music and music therapy alleviate suffering psychologically and biologically (AMTA, 1998):

1. Reduces stress
2. Supports physical exercise
3. Assists with child labor and delivery
4. Alleviates pain in conjunction with anesthesia or pain medication
5. Elevates mood and counteracts depression
6. Promotes movement for physical rehabilitation
7. Calms, sedates, or induces sleep
8. Counteracts apprehension or fear
9. Lessens muscle tension
10. Increases physical, mental, and social/emotional functioning
11. Improves communication skills and physical coordination skills

In his foundational book, *Music in Therapy,* E. Thayer Gaston describes major reasons music is so important to our lives. Music therapy emerged first as a behavioral science, the objective being to change or alter unhealthy behavior. In recent years, music therapists have moved even further into the hard scientific realm of physiological research. Gaston provides eight principles of music as it relates to our whole person.

1. All people have a need for esthetic expression and experience. Music utilizes human senses and, as an expression and exten-

159

sion of human creativity, contributes to the human experience. Humans are uniquely able to organize their external stimuli of sound through music composition and performance—it is truly a gift of God. "Rhythm is the organizer and energizer" (Gaston, 1968, p. 17) and has served as the way in which people order sound and impassion their music making. From the gentle pulse of a lullaby to the driving rhythm of rock 'n' roll, rhythm permeates our lives, makes work easier, and provides a bonding element in the unification of community.

2. Each cultural group determines its own mode or music of expression. How we choose to order sound differs across cultures. This personal and cultural esthetic preference provides not just musical activity but also identity and memories. Our childhood and adult musical associations are a primary reason music styles are important to us.

3. Music and religion are integrally related. As we saw in the chapter on worship, music is a unifying force in directing us toward God. Christians, however, are not the only religious group to use music. Every major religious tradition orders religious expression with sound.

4. Music is communication. Music with text communicates a verbal message. However, the majority of meaning is communicated nonverbally. That is, the expression through melody, rhythm, structure of musical form, and manner of performance communicates our deeper beliefs and values. "Music is a most intimate type of nonverbal communication deeply cherished and nurtured by mankind" (Gaston, 1968, p. 24).

5. Music is structured reality. Through musical activity people are able to experience the world around them, especially with other people in group activities. We desire experiences that make us feel centered and part of the physical world.

6. Music is derived from emotion. Music is an external expression of internal emotions: love, joy, and kindness, as well as angst, anger, and other negative emotions. In some cases, musical expression of the emotions is a cathartic or releasing act. In all ways, when emotions are expressed honestly as part

of a community context, people can feel a real membership within that community because of what was shared.

7. Music is a source of gratification. Music builds self-esteem and positive group relationships. Young children, adolescents, and adults know the sense of accomplishment of making music with others. This also contributes to strong community relationships.

8. Music potency is strongest in the group. Music draws people together and helps in developing positive interpersonal relationships. Solo performers certainly can be admired for their skill; however, in most societies, music making is a group activity.

Based on these principles, music therapy is finding success in three genres of medical study: (1) pain, anxiety, and depression; (2) mental, emotional, and physical handicaps; and (3) neurological disorders (Mazie, 1992). Now considered health professionals, music therapists assess strengths and needs of individuals suffering from physical, psychological, cognitive, and social disorders. Following assessment, they design a treatment, often in cooperation with other medical professionals, which includes creating, singing, moving to music, and listening to music (AMTA, 1997). Music therapists also involve themselves in medical research. There are also many Christian musicians who have and are choosing this as a vocation.

In our scientific and dichotomized world, we develop professional status and often want to leave the specialist to do even the things we are capable of doing. Music in a healing ministry is no exception. It does not take a music therapy degree to sing to a sick friend at home or in the hospital or to select music that ministers to a grieving family. Christian healing begins in the local kingdom community. Whenever the community relegates the gifts of the Spirit totally to a professional class of therapists, or virtuoso healers, they miss the blessing of ministry. "When we embody God's healing presence to others through touch, concern, or liturgy, we take part in God's activity of healing the world" (Koenig, 1997, p. 147). As I illustrated in the opening case studies, with my father and the demon exorcist, music naturally functions as healer within the holistic ministry of the local church.

Music Ministry

Millennia ago the writer of Ecclesiastes expressed the times of our lives.

> There is a time for everything, and a season for every activity under
>   heaven:
> a time to be born and a time to die,
> a time to plant and a time to uproot.
> a time to kill and a time to heal,
> a time to tear down and a time to build,
> a time to weep and a time to laugh,
> a time to mourn and a time to dance . . .
>
> (Eccles. 3:1–4)

Sadly, according to Joy Berger, who ministers to the dying on a daily basis, one of the reasons so many leave the church is because in their seasons of pain and grief they find no consolation in the church. In an honest criticism, many churches are so focused on joyous praise and outreach evangelism, hurting members of the congregation are left without a healer. Congregations are often unaware of the hurt, pain, and suffering of the members, or else respond with condemnation, bringing on the emotions of shame and guilt (Berger, 1998).

The greatest hymnal ever written, the Book of Psalms, often speaks more to the doubt, despair, and confusion of the writers than their praise. It is in the darker moments of life that the church must minister out of love.

Ken Blue (1987), in his book *Authority to Heal,* provides some observations and principles we might draw on in proactively incorporating music in the healing ministry of the local congregation. Blue believes that there are three basic values that are common to all Christian healing communities.

The first value requires a belief that God wills to heal the sick, that he desires wholeness rather than sickness for his people. God can act in situations where medicine may not have domain. It means that God may chose to heal instantly, if he so chooses, as in the demon exorcism of the first case study. But it may also mean that healing is a much longer process, one that includes healthy lifestyles for our bodies, a devotional life for our spirits, clear and rational thinking for our minds, and forgiveness of our communities. These things do not require professionals, and any musician can utilize music in this healthy lifestyle.

The second value is sincere compassion for those in pain. This often comes from an attitude of love and an empathy for those in pain. Two stories illustrate this point.

As a young psychologist, Vivian Nix-Early worked as a music therapy intern in a New York City drug rehabilitation center. Her task was to assist substance abuse patients in regaining a sense of wholeness and self-discipline. Her first assignment was to help a group of thirty young men. Hardened by years of drugs and petty crime on city streets, their appearance and young male sexual drives would intimidate any young woman. As Nix-Early entered a room of cold stares, the leader of this group, distant and defensive, eyed this attractive young black woman as he asked the question they all wanted to know: "Are you one of us?"

She strengthened herself silently as she stood face to face with the group's leader. In provocation he asked, "If you were my girlfriend before, and you saw me in here now, would you still love me?" Nix-Early instinctively knew that the wrong answer would preclude any help she might have to offer. She replied, "If there was a lot to love then, there's a lot to love now!" A grin appeared on his face as he responded, "What do you want us to sing?" So for the next several months, Nix-Early led the group in "Corner Boy Songs" the young men would have sung on the streets of New York in the 1970s. Their self-esteem, which had been diminished by years of disenfranchisement from society, began to strengthen.

Do you love me? Do you love me unconditionally? This was the question Jesus asked of Peter. It is the basic question we ask each other in our relationships. It is the question we answer before music can ever be used in healing situations. *Agape* love is absolutely essential in the first stage of helping others—building trust. Trust is the reliability of positive intent, with or without music.

Jesus' healing ministry was in line with his teaching on compassion and loving one's neighbor. This *agape* love was expressed concretely through concern about another's whole life needs through the healing of physical, emotional, and spiritual illness. One salient reason many people find hope in Jesus was his incarnation into human flesh and suffering in every way that humans have suffered. Often it is through suffering that we are able to empathize with others and become a part of their healing process.

If you entered the hospital on any afternoon, you might hear the voices of a hospital staff choir singing to a patient. You might see a young cancer patient. Not yet a teen and so upset by the needles regularly jabbed into her thin arm for blood samples, she refused to speak. Then a cheerful music therapist, Deforia Lane, entered the room with a cart full of musical instruments. Through music, Lane and the young patient have developed a relationship where the young girl can now sing, thus distracting her attention from the painful jabs of needles. This empathy has not come without payment, however. Lane says that, "Because I've suffered—I understand." She is able to empathize with her patients because she herself has suffered with two bouts of cancer. Jesus suffered for us and with us in his crisis with the cross. It is from our own crosses that we find a healing ministry (*Music and Medicine*, 1994).

The third value is the personal investment and risk-taking of those who pray and would heal with music (Blue, 1987, pp. 122–23). This principle is expressed best by returning to the opening story of the demon possession. At the close of the service the entire congregation gathered around the women and sang a beautiful song, "Lord be with me, be with me. In a world of problems, be with me." This concept, "being with me," is the sum total of the gospel of Jesus' incarnation. In the circumstances of our lives, when the times are darkest, "being with" is a comfort. It takes time, energy, and commitment to others in a busy world.

Dr. Berger relates a story of her healing ministry that illustrates "being with me." In the hospice where she ministers, there was a middle-aged woman named Sara dying with cancer. Her body was weak from disease and years of cocaine and crack use. Her dreadlocks in disarray, she knew little joy. Using principles of a healing ministry, Dr. Berger used music to get to know Sara, to enter into her life-story and be present with her in her pain. One might assume from Sara's appearance and environment that she preferred African American rap or gospel. Recalling a tucked away story from Sara's childhood, Dr. Berger also offered Catholic chant. Sara's enthusiastic response led into her spontaneous singing of "Ave Maria." As they continued to talk and sing, Sara began to unveil the deep pains of her life.

In childhood, Sara had been abandoned by her mother and placed in a Catholic orphanage. During those years she was immersed in plainsong, chant, and Catholic liturgy. From a time of security in her life, she reached back for the songs of comfort in her last days. Dr. Berger, using her portable piano, sang numerous songs with her—in many different styles—to validate her whole life story and simply walk with her in her final days. Additionally, she left a cassette player and tapes for spiritual support during the fearful nights.

One of Sara's favorite Christmas songs was "O Come, O Come Emmanuel," a Latin chant originating from the twelfth century. Using the text as they sang, Sara began to find comfort and hope through the tumultuous past, her painful present, and her unknown future. "O come, O come Emmanuel, And ransom captive Israel, That mourns in lonely exile," reminded her of both the exile from her mother, and the oppressive griefs of slavery of her own ancestors endured while looking for freedom as a captive people. She also reflected on being held "captive" by this awful cancer. "Disperse the gloomy clouds of night, and death's dark shadows put to flight." Another life-treasure emerged when Sara told of having enjoyed ballet while in the orphanage. So on the refrain, Dr. Berger invited her to dance with her arms, for her legs at this time would not respond. In a graceful movement, her arms swayed slowly to "Rejoice! Rejoice! Emmanuel shall come to thee O Israel!" She ended by bringing both hands to rest over her heart. Through visits until her death, the simple melody of "O come, O come Emmanuel" became her continued prayer and assurance of "Emmanuel, God is with me, right now, and forever" (Berger, 1998).

Believing that God heals, that he is with us in our darkest hours and weakest moments of doubt, a healing ministry calls for people to empathize and love. Musicians, being with the hurting of this world, express an incarnational ministry. While we cannot outline a universal strategy for a healing ministry, I will suggest some possibilities in relation to the body, the mind, the soul, and the community.

Ministry to the Body

Growing up in a conservative Christian environment, there was one rule we inherited from a Calvinistic theology: Christians don't dance. In fact, any movement of the body in worship must be circumspect. The human body should be controlled, lest it become too sensual, attract a partner, and lead to all kinds of sin. It was in African worship that I was liberated from this notion. African Christians are free to dance their joys as well as their sorrows.

Many people live sedentary lives. Our bodies become stiff and sore with age. Our minds often follow in lethargic praise. Yet, the young cannot contain their boundless energy. Even congregations that frown on "liturgical movement" and rhythmic praise forget their own movement within the worship event. These liturgical movements minister to the body as much as they do to the soul.

Some congregations enjoy clapping, even dancing, as congregational movement. While at times I have felt I was participating in worship aerobics, there are times when this bodily praise allows a release of confined energy in a cathartic healing. But not all movement has to be dance. Some of the most beautiful worship movement comes in the form of processionals and postures in prayer.

Ministry to the Mind

In the introduction, I discussed psychological captivity, in which an ethnic group can be held captive to the stereotypes of a more powerful majority. Many Christians around the world have been liberated from trying to be Christians, not in the image of God, but in the image of a dominant culture not their own. Singing songs of one's own cultural and ethnic identity promotes a healthy self-image and relieves the anxiety of having to conform to another's expectations.

Music helps us focus our thoughts by providing a rhythmic order. Many come to the worship community from a disheveled and fragmented context. Singing songs and hymns provides an opportunity to focus on God.

Music can unlock powerful and healing memories of our past. Remembering is healing when the association of songs and hymns meets us in the present. As we saw in the story of Dr. Berger and Sara, the power of God's presence meets us in the stories of our life's moments. These are not always hymns and spiritual songs either. Sometimes a children's song, country music, even a rock song brings to mind special moments in our lives—which become sacred to our experience.

Ministry to the Soul

Music in prayer is a discipline in the Christian life. Music expresses the inner thoughts and feelings of the soul that words cannot express alone. We cry, weep, beckon, call out, and intercede for healing, order, and comfort. The soothing and orderly rhythm calms us in distress. But music can also have a cathartic function, providing release from anxiety over uncertainty.

God has given us "songs in the night" (Job 35:10), when our pain and distress come most often in the loneliness of our days. Music heals when it creates order, wholeness, calm, and peace. If it is true that "The one who sings prays twice," then our praying is multiplied in our most intimate moments with God.

Richard Foster, author of *Prayer: Finding the Heart's True Home,* states, "On a purely human level music is one of the most powerful mediums because it appeals to both emotion and volition, both imagination and reason. When we tie music to prayer, we have a powerful combination. Singing also adds vivacity, buoyancy, and gaiety to our prayers" (Foster, 1992, p. 110).

There are several ways Christians can use music in the discipline of prayer. First in private song and prayer, we can read the hymnal as prayers. We can sing them alone. We can even sing spontaneous songs—making up words to fit the occasion. Second, public song and prayer is a congregational discipline. Collective prayer hymns provide the congregation an opportunity to focus on a single concern in faith. For the brave congregation, spontaneous congregation song can be a time of outward groaning, mourning, or petition.

Benedictions are another form of musical prayer. I remember as a youth singing a cappella benedictions following the Lord's Supper. Many families sing a prayer of thanksgiving before meals in a very effective manner. Finally, many psalms are prayers.

Ministry to the Community

Collective singing builds community. The sense of community is heightened whenever many voices are united. Few people can watch television and not see the terrible acts of violence that affect every society. It is at these terrible moments of community loss that grief overwhelms and pulls us into collective sadness. It is in times of collective grief that singing can express our lamentations. There are also times of collective joy. Expressing our collective joy equally binds the community together. The joy calls out beyond the sanctuary into the street.

As Egyptian Wafeek Wahby tells the story, Nabil was on the verge of suicide. "Nothing is worth living for," he kept telling himself. Suffering a series of setbacks, he had lost the will to live. Wandering the streets of Cario, Nabil was drawn to the sounds of joy and enthusiasm. He walked into the city church as the congregation welcomed him in song. It was a sound that "touches and melts them as individuals into a more unified body, washing their souls and refreshing their minds." Nabil would be healed by this singing community (Wahby, 1992, p. 53).

As the seasons change, so do the needs of a community. An effective healing ministry helps the community and its members live in the present with an understanding of the healing power of God. There is no more important service of worship for the collective congregation than the Eucharist. At no other time is the church so focused on "being with" God. It is in this same spirit of remembrance that funerals become a central point of healing for the families and friends of those who have passed away.

Principles

Drawing from this study and the work of Berger, there are several principles for a church healing ministry. While I will address these to musicians, they have implications for clergy, staff, and laity as well.

Principle One. Music in healing is not a technique but a ministry. In an interesting critique, Berger maintains that musicians have a love-fear relationship with music. For those who have high aesthetic standards and do not value the functional nature of music, they fear the power of music to unlock the inner self. By keeping music on a pedestal and focusing on the technical excellence of music, the focus is switched from the function to the art. In the stories above, we saw musicians use their gift functionally to minister to people. They had a love for people, and took the time to be with them. This type of musical people-skills also requires a very broad background in all styles of music coupled with an improvisatory gift. This is a portable ministry, where the music has to go to the person.

Principle Two. Musicians should know their own self. By that I mean that the musician must know how he or she responds to music, and make an effort not to transfer their own hurting to the one in need. For example, a musician may find that a hymn or classical piece of music ministers to them, and thus feel that it would minister to the bereaved. By selecting their own music, they do not allow the hurting to find their own voice. There are many types of music, and any of these kinds (including the music of the secular world) can become sacred to personal experience. It is in times of grief and loneliness that these songs can validate a person's experience and signal the presence of God.

Principle Three. Musicians should know their choir and congregations. At the heart of ministry is people, not music. In the midst of planning, rehearsals, and performance, it is easy to allow relationships to become secondary. When Mr. and Mrs. Jones sit in the second row and share a hymnal for forty years, and Mr. Jones dies, Mrs. Jones must experience a loss that should be ministered to through music. Past the visual presence, a healing minister will know the types of music important to his or her choir members outside the setting of the sanctuary.

169

Principle Four. Musicians and pastors should meet the needs of the suffering and bereaved. As we saw in the ministry experience of Berger, she met Sara in her space and gave validity to her past experience, which included music. Berger suggests a simple question: What is your all-time favorite song in times of celebration and joy, or sorrow and grief, or comfort and hope? These songs are then used in services. Depending on the context, even country western and rock music can be used to bring healing to the sacred experience that people have with God.

Principle Five. Musicians need a holistic ministry. This ministry takes place in the sanctuary, the church building, and the home. Music is great entertainment that has its own healing powers, primarily to provide relief from day-to-day activities. This "fun" nature of music is part of a healing ministry. This should never become the focus of ministry, but one cannot deny that if God is Lord of all creation, there is a place for this in ministry.

Below, are examples of how music is used in ministry outside the sanctuary:

- A cassette and video ministry of recorded music for meditation and relaxation
- A weekly aerobics class for exercise
- Folk dance classes
- A church sacred dance group

Summary

In this chapter we have surveyed the healing role of music within the kingdom. As whole beings living in faith relationships, music aids in alleviating physical, mental, and spiritual suffering on both personal and community levels. We looked at both scientific and holistic worldviews as we considered the ability of music to affect the mind, body, and soul. Music therapy is a scientific approach to healing and is a growing profession. In many of the world's cultures, music is used intuitively in healing rites, including evil spirit exorcism, by peoples with a worldview that recognizes the spirit world. From a biblical perspective, we discovered that the ultimate goal of a healing ministry is to bring the world into a complete relationship with God.

We contrasted Plato's belief that music can be either good or evil with the view that music functions as a key to unlock feelings and thoughts through expressive behavior. These opposing beliefs affect the way people approach secular music of the street. Taking the latter approach, we have outlined basic principles for developing a music ministry of healing.

An effective ministry of healing should have four basic foundational elements: a belief in the power of spiritual healing; a love for others; empathy for those who are suffering; and a commitment to act.

Questions for Discussion

1. How has music functioned as healer in your own life? In the lives of your family?
2. Does your church have a healing ministry? Is music part of this ministry?
3. What ways could you minister to others through music, without music therapy certification?

Exercises

1. Visit several churches in your area. Conduct a survey to see the various ways in which they consciously use music in a healing ministry.
2. Visit local hospitals and hospices. Discuss with the administration ways in which Christian musicians could be involved in aiding their healing ministry through music and the arts.
3. Interview a music therapist regarding his or her training and work. Ask advice on ways the noncertified music therapist can use music and the arts in a healing ministry.

Music as Preacher

For Isaiah says, "Lord, who has believed our message?" Consequently, faith comes from hearing the message, and the message is heard through the word of Christ.

(Rom. 10:16–17)

And this gospel of the kingdom will be preached in the whole world as a testimony to all nations, and then the end will come.

(Matt. 24:14)

Music is theological; it talks about God and our relationship to him and our world, and answers one basic question: What is the good life, and how does one attain it? When Mary, Jesus' mother, sang the "Magnificat," and Madonna, popular vocalist, sang "Material World," they both were expressing their worldviews, belief systems, and theologies. This theology held in song has power. Music was preaching for Martin Luther; music was a testimony to John Newton, the writer of "Amazing Grace"; and music was the "soul of the Civil Rights Movement" to Martin Luther King Jr. Hymnbooks are the theological compendium of the literate church. Congregational song is the oral theology of the Emerging World church. Popular songs are the theological creed of secular society.

This chapter is about music as preacher. The theology of music is active and reflective preaching in the oral and symbolic language of the masses. The meaning of music for Christians is two sides of the same coin. On one side of the coin, music reflects what Christians believe. On the other side, it reinforces or teaches these same concepts about God. In this chapter, we will look at how missiologists and theologians analyze the texts of music to understand the former idea: How does music reflect the idea of God? We will consider two ideas in this chapter. First, we will discuss the nature of theological study. Second, we will see how music is the theological index of the church with case studies from around the world.

The Sound of the Harvest . . .

It was a battle of words fought with singing in the street. Rounding the corner, crusty sailors from the dock and simple peasants from the countryside joined vocal forces as they headed straight for the great cathedral, singing at the top of their lungs, "There was a time when he was not—There was a time when he was not."

Banned from meeting in church buildings sometime in the fourth century, this group, known as the Arians, met on Saturdays and Sundays to sing their belief in the city streets and open porticoes of Constantinople. A noisy bunch, they attracted many followers—so much so that the Orthodox bishop Chrysostom became concerned about their growing numbers.

The bishop organized an opposing nightly processional from the cathedral to combat their musical propaganda. Marching and singing in a parade of music, candles, and crosses, they headed for a battle of hymns. Meeting in the street, voice met voice as singers stood face to face until lyric expression turned to shoving and pushing. Violence broke out in a clash of clubs and crosses. Some wounded and others dead, order was eventually restored, with the Arians banned from the city (Bailey, 1950). What was so important to sing about?

> All Laud to God the Father be;
> All Praise, eternal Son, to thee;
> All glory, as is ever meet,
> To God the holy Paraclete.
>
> St. Ambrose, 340–97; tr. Robert Bridges, 1899
> (The Clarendon Press, Oxford, in the 1940 hymnal)

...And the Beat of the Street

He was the king. The crowds pressed close to touch the hem of his garment. Some fainted from the power of his presence. Others chanted of his healing power, reciting his miracles—the love for children, feeding the poor. They had witnessed his healing of the world, the feeding of hungry children. And in a great flash of light they had witnessed his ascending into the heavens above. Who was this person? No, this was not Jesus the Christ. This was Michael Jackson in a video award presentation at the 1992 American Music Awards.

What Is Theological Study?

When we mention the word "theology," you might conjure up the image of a pontificating old seminary professor lost amidst dusty books and ungraded term papers thrown haphazardly about the floor of his office. The term possibly has more to do with singing theologians in the street than you might imagine, however. The Greek word *theologia,* from which we get "theology," was possibly an early hymn of praise to God with words like, "Praise God from whom all blessings flow, praise him all creatures here below. Praise him above you heavenly hosts. Praise Father, Son and Holy Ghost." This doxology, like the

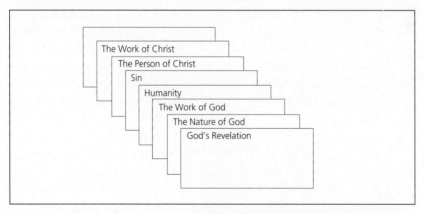

The Work of Christ
The Person of Christ
Sin
Humanity
The Work of God
The Nature of God
God's Revelation

Figure 6.1. Systematic Theology

175

verse of St. Ambrose, was stating a theological truth about the Holy Trinity. It was out of the controversy described in the first story that we still sing a doxology—a musical-theological statement of belief.

Theology is talk about God. In this chapter we look at two basic approaches to theological study. The first is a systematic and historical theology (see Figure 6.1). Drawn from Scripture this theological approach is a basic model. Like a filing cabinet of belief categories, this study provides the classical doctrines of the church. A systematic theology seeks to understand the truth of God and asks three basic questions: What is the nature of God? What is the condition of humankind? What is the way to salvation or liberation from this condition? These questions can be answered in three words: God, sin, and redemption.

The focus of systematic theological study is to clarify specific understandings about the nature of God and the redemptive history found in Scripture. It is a statement of doctrinal beliefs. We often sing these doctrines from our hymnal. As hymnologist Hugh McElrath points out, even Christians who are opposed to creeds sing their creed (or what they believe) in their hymns (McElrath, 1990). Most hymnals follow a systematic and doctrinal theology, in part, because many have been written by preachers and theologians. When a hymnal committee gathers to revise the hymnbook, pastors, musicians, and theologians work together to provide a balanced filing cabinet of music theology.

A second approach is a lyric and active theology. Drawn from the daily musical expressions of common people, this is the theology of the masses. It is the songs that tell about the daily life of people and their relationship to God in local expressions. So which approach do we need? Both! A systematic or doctrinal theology helps us understand truth in relation to Scripture. It gives us a map of truth. However, statements of belief can grow cold and impersonal without the sheer joy of living a relational faith. Living theology, on the other hand, tells us how people live out that truth on a daily basis.

The music of the kingdom also reflects both theological approaches. Objective hymns often focus on doctrinal beliefs, while subjective songs of personal testimony witness to God's interaction with the person. However, the meaning of a living theology can become lost without grounding in biblically based doctrine. This was the problem in the second story. The symbols and metaphors rooted in the doctrine of the Son of God and his resurrection were outside "orthodox" belief, and had lost their meaning, even creating confusion.

Hymnologists, people who study hymns, are looking closer at the expressions of God and church doctrine of hymns around the world. Ethnomusicologists, those who study the music of the non-Western classical traditions with the aid of anthropology, now recognize the religious and spiritual aspect of culture. Musicians are studying the lyrics of music and asking the question, "What does this song say about God and the song writer's sermon?"

This has even moved toward the music outside religious music. Non-church music is studied for its theology—how it talks about God or the good life. This investigation asks two basic questions of the song: What does the song say the good life is? How does it suggest one attains the good life? This can be a problem with a loss of meaning in popular music because meanings of symbols change with time and culture. If you think you were fooled by the opening Michael Jackson example, so were my students. When asked to debate whether Michael Jackson could be the returning Christ, students incredibly found biblical and visual symbols to support their arguments on both sides. How could they be confused, you might ask? First of all, it was an exercise where I asked the students to look at the video from a non-Christian perspective, one in which someone who didn't know about the Bible might view it. However, the video had amazing symbolic references to Scripture. Some fans waved palm branches as Michael marched with the armies of the world as in Christ's triumphal entry in the second coming. Other fans held signs, "He is the King." The narrator told of Michael healing the world through his generous giving, while the music in the background featured the now famous, "We are the world."

This simple and disturbing exercise is used in one of my classes to demonstrate the power of music and media in shaping religious thought in our technological society. This power, however, has long been respected in oral societies where music is a medium of communication. It is easy, though uncomfortable, to understand the confusion these students had in debating the question. On one

177

hand, they were all Christian students and believed strongly in the divinity of Christ. On the other hand, their uncritical listening and viewing of music and media led to mistaking the secular for the sacred. In what Neil Postman calls "The Great Symbol Drain," the more a symbol is used, the less potent its meaning (Postman, 1993).

The informational and technological age has done more than "speed" the transmission of messages. It has blurred their meaning in the process. William Knoke (1996) refers to the new age as a "placeless society," where everything is everywhere all the time, there is sacred place—it is everywhere, or nowhere. This age calls people of the kingdom to reinterpret and make relevant the redemptive story in every generation and culture. It also challenges us to understand the messages we see and hear.

How to Study/Analyze Music Texts

In Figure 6.2 we present a model for analyzing and interpreting the meaning of song texts. First, song texts provide a window on the theological world of diverse peoples and their theological understanding. Second, cross-cultural ministers cannot understand the theology of the song without knowledge of the context. This is both the immediate context and the broader cultural context of the song and those who make and sing it. Is there a framework that is universal, and yet fairly easy to grasp to provide all of us with "critical listening skills" in the spiritual and theological things of life? How could a theologian, a musician, and a lay church member find common ground in discussing "the theology of music"?

There are three basic steps in analyzing text. In the first step, the music is *analyzed*. This is a nonjudgmental stage where we ask the question, What is the message of the song actually preaching? In the second stage, the song is *compared* to both cultural norms and biblical standards. In the third stage, we *draw conclusions* about the directives of the message. What is it actually preaching? Before discussing this process in detail, we will look at the nature of song texts and how to collect a sample for study.

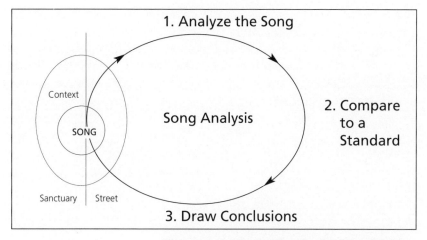

Figure 6.2. Music Theological Analysis

Song Texts

Songs are manifestations of the will. We sing to identify, express, or proclaim our viewpoint and loyalties. Songs function as guideposts to the deeper issues of life (King, 1989, p. 180). They provide information that is otherwise inaccessible—the hidden or unconscious worldview. They are a map of a worldview, telling the "basic assumptions the people have about the nature of reality and of right and wrong" (Hiebert, 1976, p. 49).

Texts are the content of songs. While the form of the song provides information about the broader culture, it is the text that provides information about a person's belief system. When we give a "thin" description about music our understanding merely describes what is being said. In understanding the theology and worldview of music, we want to strive for a "thick" description, which excavates, or exegetes, the meaning of the song within the culture of the composer/singer/listener (Geertz, 1973).

Song texts can be difficult to understand because of their *poetic nature*. There are several considerations here. First, songs use poetic language that changes conventional linguistic structures. Musical poets alter conversational and academic language to match the music—what is often referred to as "poetic freedom." For example,

179

this is very common in rap music, where the rhythmic structure of the song forces a modification of standard English.

Second, musical poets use imagery and metaphor or descriptive pictures that give a concrete view of an abstract concept. These images can be coded and culturally bound, so that, without understanding their historical and cultural context, it is impossible to know the intended meaning. For example, how would you describe the word "God"? One African student hymn writer used the term "Gyunke." The gyunke is a large tree of his village where people gather to talk, and rest from the heat of the day. He described how the gyunke had many characteristics like the God of the Bible, strength, comfort, and rest. This is no different than the psalm writers, who used their own cultural context to describe the nature of God, concretely.

Finally, composer poets use idiomatic expressions and "connotative" words that cannot be understood outside the culture without investigation. For example, in a contemporary Christian song by the group Reality Check, one would not know whether the song was Christian or non-Christian by the words of their song, "Losing Myself." There is no mention of God and the repeating words of the chorus, "take me away where I can feel you move me," certainly could refer to romantic love. However, listening closely one can hear a single line that says, "I want to get away . . . where I can pray." The final phrase of the song suggests God with, "I want to walk in your light." Yet light could mean the Eternal light of God, or the light of one's romantic love. Without a context and interpretation the message would be misunderstood.

In the mediated communication age of music television and Internet music our task is further expanded and yet simplified. Composers are able to select images that visually explain verbal meaning. A story is created. These visual symbols show what words cannot tell and provide an economy of meaning. As illustrated with Michael Jackson and "The Great Symbol Drain," symbols (including word and visual symbols) lose their original meanings as they are dissipated. The story must be retold and explained to new generations in order to maintain integrity. For example, the cross, which originated as a battle standard for the emperor Constantine, eventually became a symbol of the church. As a Christian symbol, it represents the death, burial, and resurrection of Christ. Yet coopted and worn upside down by some musicians, or worn in secular and profane contexts, it loses its meaning and is no longer the sacred symbol of the sanctuary. Without retelling the story of the symbol, its meaning may be lost.

Some song forms, especially the traditional Western hymn, provide an *objective* perspective on theology. The linear construction, using a developed analytical and abstract thought, provides an excellent base for church doctrine. It explains basic concepts based on a long tradition of theological thought—often written by preachers and theologians. In the objective hymn, "The Church's One Foundation" we sing, "The church's one foundation is Jesus Christ her Lord." This is a doctrinal statement.

Some songs, like the gospel hymn, are more *subjective* in character. They tell a concrete story and are often personal in nature. Choruses may be subjective in character also, and because of their proverbial and reflective nature are more difficult to understand. In this case they must be compared to the context in which they were sung. One of my favorite choruses is subjective in nature. "Be with me, be with me, Jesus, in a world of problems be with me." Yet, being with me here implies more than a visit, but continual love and support.

So how does someone sing his or her religion? To understand the meaning of music, we must uncover or "exegete" the text. Because texts of music are written within cultural, historical, political, and even economic contexts, their meaning must first be discovered within that context. This can be a difficult task even within one's own culture, but it becomes infinitely more complex when we try to understand the music of cultures different than our own. We need an accurate translation.

Ideally, we would like to know exactly what the insider, or creator and singer of the song means. This is called an *emic* view. Yet it is not always possible to know this insider view, because the composer may not be available, the culture through history has changed, or we may desire an outside perspective. Outsider, or *etic*, views can provide a fresh and sometimes needed critical analysis of music. The limitation with the etic perspective is that the outsider may miss subtle meanings of language and intention.

In another African chorus, "Kuku Managoma na Aganga", the translation reads, "All my chickens had gone to the witchdoctor." What could that possibly mean? As an outsider you wouldn't know until you investigated the culture and context and found that chickens were payments for treatment to a traditional doctor who did not heal. In other words, "I was wasting my money on solutions that did not work. I turned to Jesus who helped me."

We turn now to a basic guide for exegeting and analyzing musical texts. In order to begin an analysis of song text, you will need a sample. There are two types of samples: quantitative and qualitative.

Quantitative and Qualitative Analysis

We first start with a sample. In a quantitative sample you collect songs from a geographical area or an existing collection of music. You then categorize the major themes (King, 1989). This is fairly easily done with a hymnal because it has both index and a table of contents. Major theological and doctrinal concerns are already categorized. However, in oral cultures one must collect songs from the places where they are most used by a majority of the population.

A qualitative analysis discovers the meaning of specific words and concepts. For example, in a quantitative sample we may discover that a church places great emphasis on the kingdom of God. But what does the kingdom of God actually mean to that congregation? It is only through a qualitative analysis that we can actually know what that means.

Part of this analysis also has to do with the frequency of performance (King, 1989, p. 296). The space given to a song is not merely its presence in a hymnal but also how frequently it is sung. Many congregations have hundreds of hymns printed in the hymnal, but favor only a select few. Likewise, popular radio stations have what they call Top Ten songs, which they play frequently. In addition to the space given to salient songs, we find that within the song collection there are certain words and phrases that take prominence. Noting these is a good place to start in understanding basic concepts about worldview and theology.

Here is a classic example of music theological analysis. Shortly after World War II there arose a prophet named Silas Eto from the Methodist Church Mission in the Western Solomon Islands of Melanesia. Within a short time over three thousand people left the Methodist faith to follow Silas Eto in what many called "Etoism." Silas Eto was an interesting character. He had been tutored in the Methodist faith by a peculiar missionary woman, who reportedly prayed under her house hanging upside down like a bat. It is doubtful that Eto prayed like a bat, but he seemed as resistant to authority as his mentor, and his own grandfather had been a magic-man. Local people seemed to fear and respect him. In one case he put a taboo on the selling of coconuts. When one man ignored the taboo, his child later died, thus reinforcing the fear and instilling respect for his "spiritual" powers (Tippett, 1967).

As a missiologist, A. R. Tippett was interested in church growth. He wanted to know both the theology of Etoism and what might have precipitated this new schismatic religious movement. While there are a number of sociological, economic, political, and missiological causes, music played an important role. In a *comparative* analysis, Tippett sought to find out what music Etoists were singing, and then compared this oral theology to the theological index of the Methodist hymns in use on the island. By making both a quantitative and qualitative analysis of the hymns he was able to reach several conclusions, which I will briefly describe.

Tippett was able to gather the hymns and anthems the Etoists were singing in their worship services. Tippett states that "Without this collection of hymns a systematic statement of belief would have been impossible" (Tippett, 1967, p. 253). In a *chronological* analysis he discovered that the role of Eto as leader evolved, that Etoism was dynamic and not static. Through his analysis, Tippett discovered that the hymns outlined Eto "lyric" theology. The most salient discovery for Tippett was that in most of the hymns Eto, who was referred to in the hymns as the *Holy Mama*, had taken on the role of both Christ and the Holy Spirit.

In the analysis of Methodist hymnody used by the missionaries and local Christians, Tippett discovered that the hymn collection tended to become the theological frame of reference for this emerging Christian (Methodist) community. In their hymnal, there

183

appeared to be several contributing factors that led to the revolt. First, because there was an absence of any systematic catechist teaching in the mission, the hymns formed the basis of theological belief. Second, because the hymnal had not been designed around doctrinal themes but the preferences of a missionary's favorite hymns, there was a gap in theological understanding. A third contributing factor was that in over sixty years prior to the schism, not one indigenous hymn appeared, reflecting the paternalistic nature of the mission. Local people had not found or expressed their own theological voice. It took a prophet to give them one. We now look at this process in more detail using examples from other hymnologists.

Describing

After a sample is collected, the first stage is to describe the selection of music. Once you have selected a song or body of music, you exegete the text. You are then ready to begin descriptive analysis. Your basic goal is to describe what is being said. A good description is nonjudgmental. This may be merely writing out the text. In the case of oral traditions, you transcribe and translate the text into a language for analysis.

The second stage of description involves interpreting the text. Key terms are noted, along with idiomatic expressions. In the case of music television, visceral symbols are also noted. Third, a contextual analysis explains the context of the song performance. It also gives relevant background information. You want to know information about the purpose of the song within an event, and something of the sociological and cultural context of the congregation. Finally, an understanding of the song would not be complete without some background about the composer. The composer's story provides information regarding the purpose for writing, personal spiritual pilgrimage, and context for making the song. Once this information is gathered, you are ready to compare the text with other standards.

This example comes from Ethiopia. In our chapter of prophecy we learned of a courageous Ethiopian prophet by the name of Tesfaye Gabbiso. His life and music have been an inspiration to literally masses of people, from urban street to village hillside. Distributed on cassette, this oral theology has been both a source of comfort and an evangelistic tool. What makes his music so successful?

Lila Balisky wanted to discover the theology of Tesfaye. Using a *quantitative* approach, by collecting his 101 songs, and a *qualitative* analysis of their content, she concluded that there were several theological themes important to the Ethiopians. Briefly here are the five themes.

First, Tesfaye's songs are filled with "images of the natural world." Ethiopia is an incredibly beautiful country that has remained primarily pastoralist and agricultural. Like the psalmists, with whom he has much in common, his songs describe this life. For example one phrase sings, "Like a lost calf jumping on the mount of life, in blessed bliss I said to Jesus, 'Thank you'" (Balisky, 1997, p. 451).

Second, Old Testament narrative and characters are used to identify historical theology within Ethiopia's own past. The story of Shadrach, Meshach, and Abednego's trial by fire is especially poignant for the trials of Christians in the past years. Third, in a related theme, Tesfaye draws on the doctrine of the physical suffering of Christ on the cross. Fourth, expressing "the confidence of the Ethiopian church in the God who fixes broken hearts, who defeats the enemy with the big stick, 'giving his people power upon power,'" Tesfaye preaches a deliverance theme. This is, again, especially potent because of the persecution the church suffered under the communist ruler Mengistu. Finally, throughout all his music, Scripture serves as the foundational element. His "Lord's Prayer" has renewed and invigorated the meaning and life of the church as a whole (Balisky, 1997, p. 455).

Maybe as important to the music, which to Ethiopian ears is quite beautiful and contemporary, Tesfaye's own life of suffering in prison under religious persecution and his spiritually disciplined lifestyle give authenticity to his music.

185

Comparing

To accept the initial description without any critical thinking would be foolish at worst, naive at best. We must compare the sample against some criteria to understand both its relevance and importance. We want a normative comparison. Once we understand what is being said we then begin to compare it to three basic standards. The first is a cultural standard, the second a stylistic standard, and the third a biblical standard.

In a cultural standard, you need to research something of the culture from which it originates. For example, in studying a song from the urban context, you will need to interview the urban composers who created the song. It is here that key words are important. Dictionaries of slang or idiomatic expressions are hard to find. So, first-person explanations are important. Then you compare your sample to other song styles within that culture.

In a stylistic comparison, you want to discover how well the selected song compares to other songs by the same composer. Are there recurring themes or words? In a biblical comparison, you begin to look at how the text conforms to biblical teaching. It is here that a comparison to your systematic filing box helps. The Bible is your guide.

This example is a comparison of two hymnals to determine change. William H. Katra wanted an index of theological change taking place in Cuernavaca, Mexico, in the Catholic Church. Prior to Vatican II (1963–65) the Mass of the Catholic Church around the world was in Latin. As a result of decisions made at that time, local communities were freed to express the liturgy of worship in vernacular languages. As a *longitudinal study* of change Katra wanted to observe the influence of Latin America's liberation theology in a local diocese. He chose to study a hymnal published in 1984 under the leadership of Bishop Sergio Méndez Arceo, *Cantemos en communidad* (We Sing in Community).

His first step was a *quantitative analysis* of the number and type of hymns in the hymnal. The hymnal contained three hundred new hymns. Katra found that while two-thirds of the hymns treated traditional subjects of "consolation, adoration, praise, and the celebration of inner spiritual experience," one-third of the hymns reflected a change taking place in Cuernavaca and other parts of Latin America.

The hymnal included music of the local people, and even a number of popular songs. While previous hymnals were written for didactic (teaching) functions for the church hierarchy, the later additions focused on lay concerns. The expression of the hymnal seemed to be moving from a systematic theology, where one is in "the process of assimilating oneself to doctrinal norms or internalizing an approved intellectual construct." It was more of a living theology, where "Faith is living a relationship between self and divinity, between individual and community . . . bringing the word of God to true relevance in one's own life" (Katra, 1987, p. 529).

Through a *qualitative study* of the content of the hymns, two basic words stand out to illustrate his theological change: commitment and spirituality. Commitment, prior to Vatican II and liberation thought, often meant "activity in celebration of the Lord," whereas commitment now "cannot be considered in isolation from urgent social problems and the sufferings of others" (Katra, 1987, p. 530). A second term is "spirituality." Salvation in the afterlife is no longer the central preoccupation of the practicing Christian, but rather "liberation" in one's lived situation. By comparing the new hymnal to the old, as in the example of the Solomon Islands songs of Eto, Katra was able to observe changes in the church's singing belief. In order to understand how the songs conform to Scripture, one would consult scripture and theological studies and then be in a position to draw conclusions.

Drawing Conclusions

This part of the analysis has to do with drawing conclusions about your findings. If one were to follow the theological teachings of song, would it lead to a redemptive conclusion? It is here that you can take a broad answer to the question, What is the good life and how does this song suggest I attain it? Since not all songs are personal directives or answers to life's problems, the song may give directions or comment on social and doctrinal concerns.

Roberta King is an ethnomusicologist who wanted to discover how music communicated theology within a young Christian community among the Senufo of Cote d'Ivoire in West Africa. Central to her concern was the diachronic, or historical, development of worldview and theology Christians were singing. This was particularly interesting because she had the opportunity to enter a community young and growing in its Christian faith. Over several years she led new song workshops among the Christians. In this process, she was interested in observing not only the success of these new songs, but what changes in their music theology might become evident.

King conducted a "before and after," or chronological, study. In the initial songs she found several basic themes that concerned the Senufo Christians. These included aspects of traditional life, like sorcery, worship, traditional initiations, and funeral ceremonies. Other important areas included relationships with spirits, relationships with people, and personal problems. Each of these areas of concern revealed people's worldview assumptions about life (King, 1989, p. 204).

Her second study had to do with systematic theological concerns. Using both qualitative and quantitative methods she concluded that there were five basic theological categories: (1) the names of God, (2) the characteristics or attributes of God, (3) what God has done in the past, (4) what God does in the believer's life, and (5) the believer's relationship to God. In addition, there was a concern for heaven, Satan, and worship (King, 1989). Using this information, conducting subsequent song writing workshops, and analyzing their results, she concluded the following. First, the study of song texts is indeed a tool for charting theological concepts. Second, by using song texts that are frequently sung, one can perceive "a people's understandings, misunderstandings, and lack of understanding about God" (King, 1989, p. 296). Third, using this information, music becomes a tool to shape and form a person and community's theology. Starting from a relative nonexistent background in the Christian faith, the Senufo Christians grew in their understanding, depth, and theological wisdom about God.

Making Decisions

Finally, what do we do with this information? In this final stage, a judgment is made about the song in a *prescription*. Much like a doctor prescribes a medicine or treatment, the music theologian, along with local believers, decides whether the song should be incorporated, adapted, or excluded from Christian practice. We will discuss this approach in more detail in the next chapter.

The Hymn as Theological Compendium

Hymns, songs, and spiritual songs are theology. If you take a printed hymnal and turn to the index, you will find what hymnologist Hugh McElrath refers to as a compendium of theology (McElrath, 1990). This is not a total systematic theology, but it gives some indication of the theological beliefs and concerns of the community that produced it.

A decade ago, I was training choir masters in Africa. For over a year I noticed that these musicians carried a little green notebook. Most did not read music, and printed music was virtually unavailable. Yet, inside the little green books was the entire repertoire of their choirs. Each song in the book pointed to an oral or living theology.

Songs point to specific theological issues of concern to the kingdom community. One choir had a favorite anthem that they sang at the church convention for several years. Entitled "Oh! Namibia," it was both a lament over apartheid and a prayer to God for the liberation of Namibia/Southwest Africa from the South African government. Long before the rest of the world was concerned about the injustice of apartheid, these Baptist young people were singing a liberation theology.

As a compendium of theology, an index of hymnody also reflects changing worldviews and denominational development in the history of the church. War, changing views of women, and trinitarian theology are among the issues hymns address as they reflect personal and societal concerns (McElrath, 1990). From music fights in the streets of the time of Arius, through disagreements about the hymnody of Calvin and Luther, to the contemporary struggle in Christian churches between contemporary hymn and "praise and worship" music, the church's history and theological controversy are read and sung in hymns.

Music as Theological Index of the City

As you read in the first case study, two choirs marched through the streets of Constantinople, singing the songs of Arius and Chrysostom. As they met in front of the cathedral, they began a fight which continues to this day. The battle for theological thought is not fought in a sanctuary, but in the city streets where lines of understanding are sometimes clear and at other times blurred. For several years, people in the contemporary Christian music industry have debated the purpose and language of this Christian street music. Is it Christian when there is no mention of Christ? A similar debate rages in many parts of the world by Christians who consider listening to any music, other than "Christian" music, a sinful practice.

In an attempt to blend ethnomusicology, sociology, and theology Jon Michael Spencer coined the term "theomusicology" (Spencer, 1991). Building on the ancient thought of St. Augustine and contemporary theologian Robert Markus, Spencer developed a model for understanding the music theologies of the sacred church and the secular city. Primarily adapted to the African American context, the model has implications for all contemporary music. By understanding the theological contexts and perspectives of contemporary cultures, one is better able to evaluate worldview and eventually contextualize the timeless message of Christ.

While all music does not express a Christian theology, all music expresses the theological worldview of those who make it, sing it, play it, and perform it. Spencer proposes that music is found in three realms of life: the sacred, the secular, and the profane.

First, in the sacred realm, or using St. Augustine's term, the City of God, Christians are led by the Spirit and consciousness of God. The profane world, or as St. Augustine referred to it, the City of Man, is the profane realm of life void of any vision of God. However,

Spencer points out that these neat boundaries are not so clear in the real world. We are destined to mingle and mix until judgment. The Christian's call is to be "in the world, but not of the world." Spencer has amplified traditional Western dualistic categories where many Christians view the world as sacred or secular—good or evil. In the middle, according to Spencer, we have a category where music is potentially influenced by both the sacred and the profane; this is the place of the secular.

Using examples from African American music, Spencer presents a convincing argument of how the music of the secular has been influenced or "informed" by the sacred. This happens most often when musicians borrow sacred, or church, terminology and apply it to secular subjects. There is also a similar movement from the secular to the sacred, where musical beats of the street enter the sanctuary.

At the beginning of the chapter we said that there are three basic issues of Christian theology: creation, sin, redemption. There are three questions theologians ask of religious belief systems: What is the ultimate good? What is the nature of humankind? What is the way to salvation of liberation? (Netland, 1991). From a Christian perspective the answers will generally state the basic doctrines of the nature of God, humankind's sinfulness and fall, and redemption through Jesus Christ. Similar criteria are used for secular music.

In evaluating music of the street, outside the spiritual reality of the sacred sanctuary, the question usually is more philosophical in nature. What is the good life, and how do I attain it? A country and western musician may sing of losing his girlfriend, best hunting dog, best friend, and even his house, but he has his truck. This implies that the good life is found in a faithful pickup truck. Music of the sanctuary or the street may have excellent musical qualities, but from a theological perspective, it should and will offer answers to these basic questions. Music is usually enjoyed and sung because it expresses a belief and answers a question—it satisfies a theological longing. The ultimate question we must ask of any music is this: Does this song have value for the kingdom? This leads to another question: For whom and what purpose? God is the God of all creation. While some Christians may want to sing only within the church context and in the language of the sanctuary, others enjoy the music outside of the sanctuary within their daily lives. They express a loving God who is Lord of all their life. By understanding the meanings of song texts, all are better able to make judgments regarding the direction of the song's sermon and value for their daily life and worship experience.

Summary

The purpose of this chapter has been to discover how music is theological, or how it talks about God. Music involves two sides of the same coin—on one side it reflects a message, and on the other it teaches. In this chapter we were concerned with the reflective aspect. We first discussed the importance of Christians developing critical listening skills for listening to music. Understanding what a song is saying about God is important to a Christian worldview. From a Christian perspective a systematic and historical theology concerns three areas: creation, sin, and redemption.

We defined theology using two metaphors. Systematic and historical theology, more like a science, is a map for reality—truth in doctrinal statements. It is from this discipline that we have a fairly unified understanding about salvation history and church doctrine. A second type of theology is an oral or lyric theology, and grows from the masses in expressive, active, and everyday language—how people talk about God.

We then saw how different missiologists and theologians applied theological study to the music traditions in different cultures. This included the world of popular music which preaches different answers to life's questions. Through these studies we learned that music is an index of theological change and a compendium of theology.

When looking at music of other faith belief systems we ask the basic questions: What is the nature of God? What is the condition of humankind? What is the way to salvation/liberation? When studying music outside the religious sphere we can ask the question: What does this song propose is the good life, and how does it instruct us to attain that good life?

There are three basic steps to doing music theology. In the first, we described the music through seeking the basic description of music texts. In the second, we compared the music to biblical and cultural standards. Finally, we drew conclusions about values of music. We now turn our attention to the opposite side of the coin.

Questions for Discussion

1. Can you describe the difference between a systematic theology and an active theology?
2. Look at Figure 6.1. Do you know hymns that might fit in these categories?
3. Does your preacher refer to hymns when he or she is preaching? Does this help you remember his sermon?
4. Are you ever confused by symbols popular musicians use? Which ones are they?
5. Can you think of a popular song that uses language from the church context?
6. Do you believe contemporary Christian musicians should always use "church" language?

Exercises

Using the chart below, analyze familiar music for its theological content. There are several options.

1. Analyze and compare the quantitative theological content of hymnals from different church denominations. By comparing the way in which the hymnal is organized, and the topics used, you can draw initial conclusions about the doctrinal and theological emphasis for worship.

2. In a qualitative analysis, you could select a chorus, hymn, or popular song, and following the suggested questions in the chart, analyze the theological message of the song. Answer the basic question: What does this song offer as the good life, and how does it suggest we attain it?

3. Take a hymn with outdated language. Try to rewrite (contextualize) the text in a singable contemporary version using language from popular culture.

This final project is a group effort to understand how music of society treats certain themes and offers solutions. Following the tripartite analysis of Spencer, you want to select music from the sacred, secular, and profane. Divide the class into groups and select a relevant topic or theological concern (e.g. The African-America Family, The Disabled, Love, Peace, Warfare and Violence, Justice and Community, Missions and Evangelism, Ecumenism, Humanism, etc.).

1. Define your topic. It should be specific and focused, providing access to music of the church and society in a variety of styles.

2. Refer to biblical passages that will provide a biblical concept of your topic. What is the sacred symbol of your topic? What concrete biblical stories illustrate the abstract concept?

3. Next, begin listening to music on the radio, searching hymnals, and interviewing musicians for songs that address your topic.

4. Collect these and analyze them.

5. Finally, explain your reasoning for including these songs in the sacred-secular-profane categories. Conclude with an analysis of the conflicts involved through music communication. What strategies can be used through music to communicate faith in our secular and profane world?

6. In your class presentation be sure to provide recorded and printed examples of texts to support your ideas.

Theological Music Analysis Outline

Stages of Analysis	Process Step	Basic Questions
Analyze This is a nonjudgmental description of the song/style.	Collection	• Quantitative collection requires a representative sample of the music • Qualitative analysis looks at key words and concepts (a piece of music).
	Translation	• If the song/collection is in a secondary or co-cultural language translate into your own. Isolate key terms and idiomatic expressions.
	Interpretation	• Write a readable text with an explanation of meaning in local equivalents.
	Context	• What is the performance and cultural context? • What is the purpose or function of the song? • Who is the audience and what are the sociological or cultural understandings of the songs?
	Composer/Performer	• Describe the "story" behind the song, e.g., composer's intent, life, struggles.
Compare Using your descriptive analysis of the song/style, compare against other standards.	Cultural Standard	• Describe where this song or style fits within the total music of the culture. Within the culture is it considered good? How does it represent a cultural standard? Does the song recognize and address cultural concerns? Does it offer an innovation or maintenance of tradition?
	Stylistic Standard	• Within itself, is the selection(s) considered of highest standard? Is it sung well and often?
	Biblical Standard	• Search the song to see if it addresses biblical concerns in a positive way. This may be more themes than quotes and may use more popular language. Does it reflect biblical teaching? At a secondary level this might address specific denominational doctrines.

Theological Music Analysis Outline (continued)

Stages of Analysis	Process Step	Basic Questions
Draw Conclusions In this part you take the analysis to the level of making predictions about the reasoning. If you followed the teaching, what consequences would result? Is it redemptive in the broader scale of life?	Personal Directive	• If the person were to follow the directive of the song, where does it lead or what consequences result?
	Social Directive	• Describe what this song/style is asking of society.
	Doctrinal Directive	• Does it amplify a doctrinal issue?
	Redemptive Nature	• How does this song direct the listener to answer the basic theological questions of the good life?
Prescribe On a personal level you use critical judgment regarding your involvement with the music. In the broader analysis hymn and song committee evaluate for kingdom use in the functions of the community.	Incorporate	• Based upon your analysis, does this song/style have value for the kingdom?
	Adapt	• Based upon your analysis could some adjustment be made to find it acceptable for kingdom use? What would you change?
	Exclude	• Is this totally out of line with biblical teaching and acceptable standards and thus of no use in the kingdom?

196

7

Music as Teacher

Now write down for yourselves this song and teach it to the Israelites and have them sing it, so that it may be a witness for me against them. . . . This song will testify against them, because it will not be forgotten by their descendants.

(Deut. 31:19–21b)

God's instruction to Moses was not merely an opportunity for the people of Israel to practice singing. Israelite society was an oral society. Like most of the world's people, the Israelites remembered the past through narrative story and historical song. While it was written down, the majority of the people remembered it orally. Even in today's educational environment, where literacy is a valued critical skill, media technology has hurled modern-day people back in time to an aural dimension, where seeing and hearing provide the majority of information about life.

Living in a superstructure of mediated culture, the contemporary person is exposed to the news and entertainment of the world. The values of every conceivable faith, religion, and political orientation are available at the click of a television dial or a keystroke at a computer terminal keyboard. While television and film tell popular narratives, the singing bards of music television, online websites, and commercial CDs now teach and reinforce the cultural and spiritual values of a technologically driven culture. What are these values? In his book, *Learn to Discern* (1992), Robert G. DeMoss Jr. discusses five: materialism (ownership of possessions), existentialism (living for the moment), individualism (the importance of self), hedonism (the pursuit of pleasure), and secularism (God is not important) (pp. 103–4). If future generations are to understand a Christian world-view, then the music of the next generation must teach like the Israelite's song.

Music functions as teacher when it transfers knowledge and values from generation to generation. When people think of music in education, they refer to the teaching of music. In this chapter, we look at how music is a facilitator of learning, transmitting both religious belief and cultural values. First, we will discover how music enculturates values. Second, we will survey contemporary learning theories of music's potential for teaching biblical knowledge and Christian values. Finally, we'll consider some basic principles and offer suggestions for using music in the church and home.

The Sound of the Harvest . . .

A booming voice flowed through the wall that separated our class-rooms. I was losing my students. No longer listening to me, they were drawn to the growing chorus of voices filling the classroom hallways. My first response was to stop my lecture and complain about the noise. The music department had moved across campus, Why were people singing in our building? I thought. How could these students be having fun and learning at the same time?

I was determined to visit this class and find out who and what had taken control of my students. I discovered that the booming voice was that of Old Testament professor James Pollard Sr. With a stature equal to his booming voice, Pollard has long valued the power of music to stimulate students and reinforce the subject. More than anything, however, Pollard believes that learning should be fun. Using the traditional chorus, "Father Abraham," his students were learning about Old Testament genealogy—and enjoying it!

Christian teachers, however, are not the only capable teachers. The teachers of the street are equally adept at taking away the fear of evil through music. Mediated communication engages young minds, stimulates their interest, and reinforces the values of the street.

... And the Beat of the Street

Carol had two sons and was concerned for their spiritual and mental development. She made a choice. If the world was coming into her house, she would be a gatekeeper and control the traffic from the street.

When television was introduced into her small developing country, government censorship limited the number of programs from the United States. There were often complaints about the control of information and the rights of the populace to be part of a global society. Eventually that freedom brought a responsibility Carol shared with every other home around the world that was now connected to satellite TV.

Like many parents, she often wished for the encapsulated nurture of her parents' homestead. Narratives and songs were the sacred trust of the community's storytellers and singers. The storytellers of the village, much like Pollard, weaved song throughout a story that had a moral teaching of the community. Many of the storytellers were entrusted with the historical memory of the past. Today there was no sacred teaching tool. Musical storytellers from a thousand homesteads waited at her door in the form of music television, sitcoms, and soap operas.

Music and Learning

Before we look specifically at the function of music as teacher of biblical and faith concerns, we need to make several distinctions about music and learning. First, music as an expressive behavior of culture both reflects and reinforces the values of the people who compose, sing, play, dance, and teach music within culture. It informs us about culture and forms the culture. In the first chapter,

we defined culture as the way people see the world, organize themselves, and go about life. A culture is learned or enculturated on two
different levels. Cross-cultural writer Larry A. Samovar (1998) makes
the distinction between conscious and unconscious culture learning. Culture is learned consciously at a cognitive level. This happens
primarily at school and home.

Students are "schooled" or educated with the salient aspects of
cultural values by the selection of heroes in history and rules for
daily living. Music also educates at a conscious level. For example,
a country's national anthem consciously instills the values hoped,
dreamed, and acted through the words of the song. This conscious
learning through music is the easiest to identify; however, the unconscious or what anthropologists call the "hidden" level of culture,
often goes unnoticed. The hidden learning of culture takes place
through music, art, conversation, proverbs, and stories from daily
life. An excellent example is children's games. It is not just the game
or the singing that accompanies the game that teaches values, but
it is how the game is played that creates the "right" cultural way to
value and relate to others.

When I was a child, I played the game "Red Rover." In this game,
we divided into two lines. We called people from the other line to try
and break through our line. It was a competitive game where we
tried to "win" the most people to our side. In contrast, many African
children's games are more "cooperative" and performed in a circle.
There is no winner or loser, but all children are encouraged to cooperate and demonstrate their unique contribution through group
song and dance. The unconscious learning of cultural behaviors,
attitudes, and values is not just the realm of children.

In the technological world, hidden values are taught through television programs, music television, news programs, and other
media. The increase in information technology has caused many to
be concerned about the ubiquitous nature of values from many
communities so that we have become polycentric with these moral
values. This same way of seeing the world through information technology has led to a decrease in importance of literacy and an increase
in the importance of aural communication.

Orality and Literacy

The world, for centuries, has been divided into two types of people: those who read and those who do not. Literacy, and the emphasis on reading, has been the focus of religious sacred texts and the transmission of knowledge of societies through great libraries. Orality, or communication through music, stories, and proverbs, has been the holder of religious belief and transmission of wisdom and history for a majority of the world's people.

As Hiebert points out, "People do not have to learn to read to become Christians or grow in the faith" (Hiebert, 1985, p. 32). As a case in point, he refers to work by Luke and Carmen, who found that Christians in South India have a "lyric theology" in which they store their beliefs in songs. These Christians memorize Bible verses in song, and use dramas to illustrate the application of faith in the open market of their villages. This distinction can be seen more clearly as cultures come in contact.

Triet was a survivor. Born in a small village in a remote part of Laos, Triet learned about life through the oral stories and songs of his village. In the evenings the family would congregate in the stilted house above the watered rice fields and converse long into the night. Neighbors moved freely in and out of the house in a fluid community. The French occupation passed almost unnoticed until Laos gained its independence in 1949. Soon after, factions began to form, including a new communist influence. By 1960, the Ho Chi Minh Trail was bustling with the activity of armed conflict and supply between China and North Vietnam.

Triet's first test of survival came in the wave of heavy U.S. bombing of the Ho Chi Minh Trail. Centuries of life's rhythms ended. Rice was no longer cultivated, and to find food Triet's growing family became refugees of the war. Triet chose to help the United States against the Communists and, for the decade of the seventies, would suffer for his decision. At the close of the war that involved all of Southeast Asia, Communists summarily executed any pro-American supporters. Following other relatives, Triet led his family to Thailand, where for several years they lived a meager existence in controlled refugee camps without running water or electricity. When an

201

opportunity came to immigrate to a community in Kentucky, there was no reservation. Triet's life would take new survival skills and continued adjustment. In Kentucky, however, a local church had other expectations.

When the Kentucky city of Margaret accepted the refugees into a housing project on the outskirts of the city, the Sunday school director was eager to incorporate these new immigrants into the life of the church. Her primary focus was the children. Triet decided to accompany his wife and children one Sunday. During the opening session the teachers invited the parents to join the children and then later leave to attend the "adult" Sunday school classes.

It was a wonderful cross-cultural moment. The Kentucky Sunday school teachers anticipated the incorporation of children into American Christian life, and the Laotians welcomed the opportunity to practice their English and meet new friends. When the teachers invited the children to sit in a circle on the floor, Triet, his wife, and his mother, along with other parents joined the children in the circle on the floor. After all, in their traditional life, families learned together. They tried to sing the songs and appeared to enjoy the story of Jesus. After the opening, the teachers announced that the parents could go to the adult Sunday school and the children would continue with stories. Triet and his adult cohorts remained seated. They enjoyed the stories with their families and wanted to hear more. The teachers didn't understand. In their minds, adults studied from books.

As this story points out, oral cultures and literate cultures are often in conflict. While there are many values to literacy, there are also several contributing factors to orality among many of the world's cultures. The first, as we saw with Triet, has to do with *cultural tradition.* Orality is part of the cultural system of many tribal peoples, who "use oral methods of communication and think in concrete-functional [through relational stories] terms" (Hiebert, 1995, p. 151). Even within a traditionally oral society, reading is not always possible or desirable.

Second, there are also *socioeconomic* reasons for limited literacy (including music) among the world's people. Before the invention of the Gutenburg Press by Johann Gutenburg in the fifteenth century, copying manuscripts by hand was a laborious process. Even with the mass production of the Bible and other writings, printing is an expensive process. Textbooks and printed music are thus out of reach for many of the world's poor. Printed music products like music textbooks, choir anthems, and musical scores remain the private domain of those who can afford them.

Another reason to maintain oral transmission is *political.* In many countries, printed information is monitored and censored by local authorities. In countries where Christianity is illegal, oral communication, including music, is an effective way of transmitting information, beliefs, and values. A second political reason has to do with maintaining identity amidst political crisis.

Betraying secrets means betraying one's identity and leads to being ostracized from the community. In *Bury Me Standing: The Gypsies and Their Journey* (1995), Isabel Fonesca tells the story of a Roma, or Gypsy singer, named Papusza. Papusza was a traditional Roma musician. Highly respected for her art, Papusza composed and sang long ballads drawn from improvised storytelling and simple folk songs of Roma tradition. In 1952, the Polish government enforced a program of forced settlement called the Great Halt. This Great Halt would stop the nomadic wandering of this marginalized people. Several years earlier, a Polish poet recognized Papusza's talent and published a number of her ballads about the wandering and suffering her people had experienced during World War II when they faced the same persecution as the Jews in Europe. For the next several decades laws were enacted to settle the Romani people and improve their lives. No one asked the Gypsies, however, who were opposed to the idea because of losing their nomadic lifestyle. The result was a bureaucratic dependency on European social structures.

Unfortunately, the Roma people believed that the untimely publication of the poems contributed to their situation. They believed Papusza had collaborated with the government. Despite her efforts to have publication stopped, she was put on trial by the Polish Roma and pronounced unclean, which meant her banishment from the group. "Papusza never sang again" (Fonesca, 1995, p. 9).

Technology has created a new learning environment. With the introduction of information technology there has occurred a literacy jump. People no longer need to read papers, books, and magazines for information. While there is a freeing of the control of information, there is a resulting problem. All messages compete on an equal basis.

In this environment, information is ubiquitous and carries the values of a dominant economic culture. The unconscious learning of values comes from commercial teachers. Young people can identify the slogan of a sport shoe manufacturer or fast-food restaurant more readily than they can a biblical truth, partly because songs today contain values related more to consumerism and materialism than deeper relational values. There is a growing educational concern for this subconscious learning.

In the musical community, we find a similar division over literacy and orality: those who read music and those who don't. Just as there may be a literate bias against those who read by those who don't, the literate musician is often biased against the one who doesn't read music. The result has been the mistrust or lack of respect for oral traditions. As there are differences in orality and literacy, music faces a similar division for learning. Literacy-oriented kingdom communities have preferred "written" music in the form of printed music, such as hymns, choral anthems, and musical scores. Oral-oriented kingdom communities have utilized orality in the form of spontaneous song, and lyric theology. The distinction I make is not to choose one over the other, but to help the Christian teacher appreciate the possibilities and appropriateness of different traditions. By understanding the power of music to encapsulate values, and as a tool for transmitting beliefs and values, the teacher's "toolbag" carries greater effectiveness.

Many educators limit themselves to the teaching of music in the formal school context. In this setting, music is seen as a separate subject of instruction, and music skills are taught apart from other academic disciplines (or subjects). Within the Western system, the subject of music primarily concerns the teaching of a Western classical or "high art" aesthetic view of music. Although this view is beginning to change, this orientation to music is best described in the goal to produce competent musicians who can sing, read, write, and compose music. Christopher Small states its limitations this way:

Art is more than the production of beautiful, or even the expressive, objects (including sound-objects such as symphonies and concerts) for others to contemplate and admire, but [art] is essentially a *process*, by which we explore our inner and outer environments and learn to live in them." (Small, 1977, p. 8)

The clear distinction here is that there is a difference between teaching music and using music to teach.

Music as Education

The Greek philosopher Plato believed that both sports and music were important to the balanced individual. He was opposed to the sole pursuit of music because it produced an individual who was soft and feeble, whereas the sole pursuit of sports (gymnastics) produced an individual who was violent and uncivilized (Storr, 1992, p. 43). His ancient teachings on music still impact Western thought. But he was not alone. The Chinese philosopher Confucius equally believed that music was important in the development of the individual and society. Music instruction was often required of nobility (Chen, 1996). Below we will outline recent research in which music is considered relevant to learning in the forms of music intelligence, learning styles, and culture.

Music Intelligence

In recent years the research of Harvard University professor Howard Gardner has confirmed the role of music as an intelligence. He defines intelligence as follows: "An intelligence entails the ability to solve problems or fashion products that are of consequence in a particular cultural setting or community" (Gardner, 1993, p. 15). In his works he describes at least seven learning intelligences: music, bodily-kinesthetic, logical-mathematical, linguistic, spatial, interpersonal, and intrapersonal (Gardner, 1993).

Gardner's multiple intelligence theory has several implications for the function of music as teacher. First, different people are gifted with biological intelligence in one or more areas. This gifting is found

205

across cultures. In other words, we find some people with unusual gifts of music in each culture, though they may express that gift within the music of their culture. Second, while music is not typically considered an "intellectual skill" like mathematics, we find that the making of music is a universal ability. Depending on the cultural primacy of "schooled" or conscious learning, music is a valued gift for learning.

Finally, the greatest implication for education is that focusing on only one aspect of an intelligence may limit the development of "whole" individuals and communities. For example, churches that focus on the analytical and logical aspects of faith may indeed have highly gifted and "intelligent" Christians, who are limited in their ability to relate interpersonally and intrapersonally. Equally missing may be the exclusion of intelligent artists who add an expressive dimension to the Christian faith. Ultimately, Christians should be encouraged to express more than one intelligence in their spiritual walk. This contributes to the wholeness of their understanding of the gospel. This also acknowledges various strengths people have in acquiring information.

Learning Styles

Learning is a lifelong process. Not only do we have to learn and memorize information, but we have to draw conclusions and apply them to our daily lives. For example, someone who reads Scripture and memorizes many passages, but cannot apply them to his or her daily life, as Jesus suggested, "hears but does not understand." Educator David Kolb developed a famous model of education that is used frequently in nontraditional or adult education. Based on the importance of a cycle of experience, "the cycle begins with experience, continues with reflection and later leads to action, which itself becomes a concrete experience for reflection" (Kelly, 1997). Kolb refined the process to include four elements in the cycle: experience, critical reflection, active participation, and abstract conceptualization. Of immediate importance to the use of music in learning is Kolb's development of learning styles. People have strengths and weaknesses in how they learn and apply information. Some learners are *activists,* who learn well through a subject of life experience. If you are an active learner you may wish to hear the music talked about in this book, or you may be thinking of your own past experience. Others are *reflectors,* who tend to reflect on a subject in deep thought and observation. If you are a reflective learner, you may be reading this book and deciding what is important, significant, different, or unique and have many questions. *Pragmatists* prefer active experimentation by getting directly involved in the subject. They like to experiment with the subject in new situations. If you are pragmatic you may be enjoying the case studies or be ready to try it out for yourself. Finally, *theorizers* tend to draw theoretical concepts and conclusions. If you are a theorizer, you may be reading this book and focusing on the theories, like this one.

The important point for our discussion is that music making is a concrete experience. As such, not all people approach the learning of music, or the use of music in learning, with the same perspective. For example, some groups with more active-oriented styles would like to sing about a subject. Reflective learners may prefer to hear a piece of music and think about its meaning. Pragmatists might enjoy experimenting with writing their own songs about a subject or hearing the stories behind the songs, while theorizers may enjoy doing research and critiquing projects.

In applying this theory to music you should consider the following. First, when you decide to use a song as teaching, not all people will hear it in the same way; each person may apply it to his or her life in a different process. Second, music as teaching works well with a variety of teaching strategies. For example, when teaching doctrinal issues and catechistic subjects, music may work well as a memory aid. Certain subjective hymns and stories may help people reflect on the subject or recall a past experience. However, application to life may require other strategies outside the immediate context.

Culture and Learning

Not all songs teach in the same way. We have already made a distinction between orality and literacy. Music can, even when written, function as orality when people do not read the words. However, there are several cultural distinctions that affect their outcome with different groups. We can apply these differences to the case study of Triet in Kentucky.

Literate cultures, particularly those of Europe, North America, and Canada, by and large are abstract thinkers. They think in concepts. Oral cultures tend to be concrete-relational thinkers. The difference is much like how this book is written. When I use stories, I am providing a concrete-relational approach to the subject. When I use conceptual terms (like "abstract and concrete") I am giving an abstract explanation. If you will think back to the previous chapter on theology, we can see a difference in approaches to the theology. A systematic theology tends to be abstract and talks about doctrines; a living and lyric theology tends to be more concrete and talks about relationships. This has some implications for selecting songs. Abstract thinkers like to use songs that teach doctrine. Objective hymns are a good example of this. Yet, to a concrete-relational thinker, subjective story songs are more relevant. In other words, they listen differently. In Triet's case, he was interested in stories whereas the adult Sunday school class to which the children's director wanted him to go focused on abstract teaching of biblical concepts.

A second consideration has to do with a cultural dimension Dutch researcher Geert Hostede called individualism/collectivism (Samovar, 1998). In individualistic cultures, individuals choose personal goals over group concerns. In collective cultures, group concerns take precedence over the individual ones. In the music context, we find that collective cultures enjoy group singing, whereas in individualistic cultures, solo performance is highly valued. In Triet's collective culture, the family learned together. They were not separated into many age groups like the Kentucky church.

A third cultural consideration has to do with linear and circular thinking. Linear thinkers prefer a lesson that follows a consistent progression from one idea to another. Circular thinkers, on the other hand, get side-tracked by related ideas. They get to the main point, but indirectly. This is what attracted Triet. Stories and songs are often indirect and circular ways of sharing a point. They may not follow a single progression. Lectures, on the other hand, follow a consistent progression from one point to the next.

A final cultural consideration is that of ambiguity. Abstract and linear people will enjoy a song if they can see the progression in a lesson plan. They do not like the ambiguity of enjoying a song that does not explicitly relate to the lesson or is totally new: I once talked with an Ethiopian who said he really enjoyed choruses because they gave him an idea and allowed him, in his mind, to apply it in many areas of his life. Like many people around the world he was eager to learn new songs, and did so rather quickly.

In this section we have looked at how people have different musical gifts, learning styles, and cultural orientations, which may affect how they listen to music. When planning music in learning activities, a teacher should be aware of these differences and plan accordingly.

Music as Teacher

As we saw in the opening example, Pollard's music provided immediate benefits for his teaching. On the first day of class, he introduced the lineage in the Old Testament with the song, "Father Abraham Had Many Sons." Repeating the song at each new point in his lecture, he accomplished several goals.

First, music *makes learning fun*. Nearly all people enjoy making music and this expressive activity can be a valuable learning aid for children, young people, and adults. While being a fun activity, music is also an unconscious teacher of community values. Pollard wanted his students to enjoy learning.

Second, Pollard *reinforces* the major point of the lecture by keeping it at the center. Abraham, Sarah, Hagar, Zipporah, and their descendants became living, singing people. Listening to and singing music are important activities in learning, particularly in oral societies. One musician's comment illustrates the point: "When the music and sermon match, people sing the sermon all week long." The same concept has been expressed through the history of the church. R. W. Dale in the preface of the 1874 *The English Hymn Book* stated, "Let me write the hymns and I care not who writes the theology" (Hawn, 1996, p. 43).

Third, music *engages* the mind. People are naturally drawn to the external stimuli of sound. Our active attention is given to song and our minds sort through mental categories for the memory and meaning contained within. Pollard engaged the students as they participated in his lecture. For many students, ancient biblical history is dry and boring. They cannot make a connection between history and their present experience, so the song bound their emotions and thought into a single moment of learning.

Fourth, music *stimulates* the body in a physical response. As we saw in the chapter on music as healer, there is an action potential in music. Pollard stimulated the students physically and mentally. This is what caused so much activity. They clapped, sang, and even danced. Whether early in the morning when most students are barely awake, or in the early afternoon when a warm room beckons sleep, music stimulates blood flow and awakens interest.

Fifth, music *takes away the fear* of the subject. Virtually any subject can be sung, and a subject that sings is within the possibility of every learner. Pollard likes music because a subject that sings cannot be the private domain of learned scholars and is therefore within the grasp of the most novice learner. Even a child can sing "Father Abraham." When presented by a capable teacher, the great lineage of humankind becomes real.

In addition to the ideas of Pollard, we can point out three others.

Music is a *mnemonic* device. In a mysterious way, musical rhythm and melody attached to words make it easier to memorize a subject. It may be that through this process the left and right brains are connected in a single task, but there is no doubt that information encapsulated in repetitive melodies and rhythms fosters retention. While children have used this method for memorizing the alphabet, linguists are tapping into this resource for learning a new language.

Music *provides structure.* When music encapsulates information, it provides a simple structure for remembering any information. Children all over the world over sing songs to learn alphabets, animals, and plants.

Music *complements other teaching methods.* The primary consideration of music as teaching has to do with its combination with text. However, music, when combined with drama, dance, sermon, or prayer, facilitates learning. For example, in Pollard's lecture, music became a central theme around which he hung basic historical concepts.

How has the church responded to music as teacher in the past? Unfortunately, music and the arts have had a rocky history. Because they are so closely related to popular culture, there has been mistrust by clergy and abuse by laity. We now look at several examples.

Music as Teacher in the Kingdom

Outsiders may be welcomed into an evangelizing community, but their non-Christian beliefs and behaviors are not. They are enculturated into the cultus of the church in much the same way a child first learns his or her culture. In a ritual process, nonbelievers pass through rites of passage from nonbeliever to new believer status. During their period of "indoctrination," when they learn basics of the faith, they are essentially in a stage of liminality (betwixt and between), when old habits, behaviors, and beliefs are refined by the new community. This has often resulted in conflicts, and places responsibility on the receiving community for good training. Music has a role to play in this process.

An example comes from the New Testament church at Ephesus. The Apostle Paul spent much time mentoring this church into maturity. He encouraged them in the faith: "Walk as children of light (for the fruit of the Spirit is in all goodness, righteousness and truth), finding out what is acceptable to the Lord" (Eph. 5:8–10). Paul understood the value of songs to both teach and create unity. By example, he used an early hymn to teach, "Awake, you who sleep, Arise from the dead, And Christ will give you light" (Eph. 5:14). Like Dr. Pollard, Paul used a common hymn to reinforce his teaching, building on what the church already knew. Paul also encouraged the church to use singing as a method for enculturation into the body: "And do not be drunk with wine, in which is dissipation; but be filled with the Spirit, speaking [teaching] to one another in psalms and hymns and spiritual songs" (Eph. 5:18–19). There is joy to be found in music making, and in the process we learn.

211

Today we know something of the beliefs and conflicts of the early church because of the music used to influence the masses of people who learned through orality. In the previous chapter you read of the controversy between Arius and Chrysostom, who combatted beliefs through singing. In the fifth century a council was held in Ephesus concerning a teaching called Nestorianism. Nestorius taught that Jesus was divine and therefore could not be born of a human woman. This questioned the doctrine of the human nature of Christ and led to what Catholics now call the doctrine of Mary Mother of God. We know this teaching spread far to the East because an eighth-century Nestorian hymn is still in existence in China. Though the hymn contained what the church conference deemed a heresy, it is held in high regard in China as evidence of the growth of the early church into Asia (Chen, 1995).

Once controversy is settled there is a formalization of doctrine. This is then passed to the next generation. In non-Orthodox churches, this becomes complex because music changes so much with the times. However, in Orthodox traditions, the theology is usually molded into a codified music. In North Africa, the Ethiopian Orthodox Church believed that in the sixth century A.D. a special saint by the name of Yared was taken into heaven by three birds. In heaven, he was given the liturgical songs (zēma) of the church, including a method of notation. When he returned to earth he sang the song for the king. Excited by the sound, the king let his spear slip from his grasp and it stabbed Saint Yared in the foot. These zēma are still sung today in the church and musicians are meticulously trained in the church music tradition (Shelemay, 1987, pp. 52–63).

One of the difficulties in enculturating new converts from different cultures has always been language. The first response was (and is) to teach the new converts the language of the dominant church community. Eventually, however, the new community finds an authentic voice. Early in the Modern Missionary Period, literacy was an important strategy in every "mission field." As a result, we find French, Spanish, and especially English in the global context. The translated Western hymn was characteristic of this process. Prior to Vatican II, much vernacular music was excluded as irrelevant, unimportant, or threatening to church tradition. An example of this process of conflict comes from Europe.

Beginning sometime in the Middle Ages, there arose a church tradition known as "miracle plays." At first, miracle plays were short reenactments of the Holy Days, using simple readings and songs. Possibly because of a concern to educate the nonliterate in the stories of the gospel, or merely a desire to use drama in celebration of the Holy Days of Christmas and Easter, these early liturgical dramas began in Latin. Over the centuries, they were performed in vernacular languages in long poetic monologues, eventually adding choruses and extensive scenery and covering many biblical subjects. Miracle plays enjoyed great success because they brought the Scriptures to life. They eventually moved outside the church context and led to modern-day theater, partly because of the growing abuses of the poets and performers, who added humor and "secular" embellishments.

Offended by the humor and vernacular expressions, the custom ended abruptly in France when, in 1548, the Parliament of Paris forbade the "Confreres de la Passion" because of opposition by Protestants. Though not opposed to congregational singing, Protestants criticized the Roman clergy, who had long limited the practice of congregational singing to priests. Protestant leaders provided their own alternative.

Martin Luther, who began the Reformation when he nailed his Ninety-Five Theses on the Wittenburg castle church in 1517, valued the use of vernacular music and instruments in kingdom ministry. Calvin and Zwingli found vernacular music expression too sensual for the high praise of God. Their innovations often included the destruction of musical instruments and beautiful church art. Because of their concern that music be simple and modest, they brought to the kingdom metrical (rhythmical) psalmody (Reynolds and Price, 1978, p. 27). While psalmody found wide use in the gardens of the worship sanctuary, it would not sing well in the street.

It took two preacher brothers in the eighteenth century to foster a Great Awakening that would set the stage for the Modern Missionary Movement. John Wesley was born to a humble English preacher. It was a miracle he even made it to adulthood, for in childhood he barely escaped a raging fire when local parishioners set flame to the church rectory. Under Anglican church tutelage, he grew up singing metrical psalms. As a young adult he volunteered for mis-

213

sionary service in the Americas and boarded a ship to Savannah, Georgia. After a short and relative unsuccessful stint as a missionary, John boarded a return ship to London.

During his journeys he came in contact with Moravian Brethren. These German Christians enjoyed singing hymns in the tradition of Martin Luther. John taught himself German and began translating these hymns, eventually publishing a hymnal that would get him in trouble with his Anglican brethren, who held tightly to the rule of psalm singing. In London, he began visiting with the Moravians and one night experienced a personal relationship with the living Christ, who forgave his sins. Joined by his brother Charles, a prolific hymn writer, they took this gospel to the streets. Preaching salvation to the masses of underclass poor, music became a primary teaching tool.

During this time in England, the wealthy upper and middle classes were considered "worldly, callous and immoral." Massive social injustice prevailed. Public hangings were entertainment, three out of four children died before their fifth birthday, and public morality was at the lowest of standards. Ignorance and illiteracy were fired by rampant addiction to alcohol. Eleven million gallons of cheap gin were consumed in 1750 alone. The sign on many gin-shops read, "Drunk for one penny. Dead-drunk, tuppence. Free Straw" (on which to sleep off the effects) (Bailey, 1950, p. 76).

Against fierce opposition from the Anglicans, who considered the Wesleys emissaries of Satan and called their followers "nasty, canting, dirty, lousy Methodists," John and Charles reached out to the poor outside the walls of the church with a personal gospel that would bring them out of poverty. On Wednesday evenings they gathered the converts in Methods classes to learn a deep faith. Charles Wesley's 6,500 hymns provided a systematic Methodist theology for singing at every meeting. Unlike the theology of Calvin, which focused on the election of God where God had chosen only certain ones to be "saved," the Wesleys followed the view of the Dutch Arminius, who believed that all had the will to accept God's "free grace." Not the sole contributors to theological hymnody, the Wesleys were joined by many others in lifting England to a new spiritual age that would find its way into European Imperial Expansion in Africa and Asia.

Subjective and personal hymns of the Great Awakening were the theological stock of missionaries, who translated them into scores of

languages on the "mission field." A systematic theological base for
Christians in Asia, Africa, and Latin America, the hymnal is presently
considered as sacred as the Bible to many Christians. Yet, though the
themes were based in Scripture, the musical and theological language
is rooted in a "foreign" culture. Christians in the emerging church,
indeed globally, continue to sing of a relevant faith for their changing
contexts. Based on a rich heritage, their new songs reinterpret salvation history to their context, teaching timeless truths in new languages.

Practical Music Teaching

In the previous chapter we discovered that music is theological.
The songs of the kingdom reflect what followers believe about God
and his interaction with humankind. We discussed ways to analyze,
compare, and predict the meanings of songs. There is a fourth stage
in this theological process, which we will call a didactic (teaching)
function. In this stage, Christian musicians prescribe or intentionally design music as theological teacher and moral reinforcer of
beliefs and values. This teaching function can take the form of either
a systematic pedagogy or a thematic pedagogy.

A Systematic Pedagogy

Recently I attended a Christian rock concert in the eastern United
States. Arriving a full hour before the performance began, I passed
the time with a young electrician who was supervising the concert
set-up. Our conversation quickly turned to his own spiritual experience. As a new believer, he shared about the worship in his nondenominational church and the growth of his faith. What made this
conversation so interesting was the lack of spiritual vocabulary. He
constantly filled his conversation with "I don't know what you call
it," or "I don't know how to express it," or "You know what I mean?"
Granted, I have the advantage of being a preacher's son with a seminary education, but I couldn't help but wonder how his worship
style, which focused primarily on "praise and worship," had stunted
his spiritual growth. While I appreciate the value of this style in

extending the kingdom, churches that limit their worship to evangelistic "seeker" purposes and the language of the street run the risk of a shallow, at best, and myopic, at worst, spirituality.

Hymns educate a community's religious growth by providing theological vocabulary. Take a hymnal and look at the topical index. What you see is a compendium of a community's theology. If you add the songs children and youth sing, anthems of the choir, and special groups or solos, you have a good indicator of what the church believes and values. The beauty of the many orthodox traditions is that they organize Scripture and song around a liturgical year, where a worshiping congregation moves through the Bible in word and song. When congregations limit their musical practice to a relatively few well-loved and favorite songs, their lyric theology expresses very narrow categories. On the other hand, liturgical traditions, conservative by nature, may fail to contemporize their music to meet the musical needs and language of a contemporary congregation. Singing provides people with theological metaphors for expressing the faith. When singing is part of worship and congregational activities, our ability to express our faith deepens and expands, thus giving us a common and growing language of faith.

Many churches encourage the teaching of doctrine and faith belief in weekly Bible study or Christian learners' class. This catechistic teaching is systematic and "graded" according to age groups. Following in the tradition of John and Charles Wesley, many organizations enlist musicians to compose songs in a pedagogy of faith. As many missionaries and local Christians have discovered, new songs in contemporary languages that speak to relevant life issues are continually needed for a growing and maturing faith. As we saw in the study on the Christians on the Solomon Islands by Tippett, a lack of a systematic music theology creates a gap that will be filled because basic questions about life and God are not answered.

An excellent tool for systematic teaching is a church hymnal. Many denominations publish their own hymnal based on the specific doctrine of their church. Publishing a hymnal can be very time-consuming, but it is worth the effort. Not only does it give identity to a local congregation or community of churches, but it provides the congregation with a singing faith and belief. Developing a hymnal or song collection does not have to be difficult. Many churches appoint a hymnal committee to publish their own. In oral societies, a published hymnal may not be possible or desirable. As in the example of Roberta King in the previous chapter, Christian ethnomusicologists aid growing Christian communities to expand their Christian music repertoire. As we will see in chapter nine, learning to compose new songs provides the Christian community with an authentic Christian voice.

A Thematic Pedagogy

Aside from a systematic music teaching, there also remains specific thematic issues that grow from every context. There are at least six areas where music can be an effective teacher in the kingdom. Singing is an excellent way to *learn Scripture.* One of the first activities in teaching new members of the community is learning the Scripture that serves as the basis for the faith. As we will discuss in Chapter 9, writing Scripture songs is an activity available to every community.

In an interesting and important study in how oral African societies learn and retain information, Herbert Klem (1982) discovered that among the Yoruba of the West African country of Nigeria, people who listened to songs of Scripture, as well as sang Scripture songs, retained information as well as those who just read Scripture.

A second area of music as teacher is for *specific theological* issues. There is no subject that cannot be addressed by Christian belief or the teaching power of music, though it takes a creative and capable musician and an appropriate context for singing. A number of issues have been addressed in this century: apartheid in South Africa, world poverty, and the environment.

A third area of music teaching lies in the area of *personal spiritual growth.* A number of years ago, while attending a youth camp in Africa, I was awakened by a fellow teacher singing. He carried two books with him, his Bible and his hymnal. He read his Bible to hear the Word of God. His hymnal made the Word practical in singing his devotional faith. In more contemporary contexts, the electronic hymnal is the CD and cassette player. Young people enjoy the teachings of modern composers sung by choirs, solo performers, and groups.

Outside of many development organizations around the world, many Christians are unaware of how music is used in teaching about *specific community needs*. Music, especially singing, is used around the world to teach about health care, farming techniques, and personal hygiene. For example, in many developing countries musicians will team up with a drama team and development professional. They design a music drama teaching basic elements of health care. Related to development is learning a second language. During my own second language acquisition, songs became an excellent way for me to learn many nouns, verbs, and sentence structures.

A final area of teaching that music affords is in *general kingdom awareness*. Teaching songs from Christians around the world expands our worldview by providing new perspectives of the people and the special issues they face, which may be different than our own.

Strategies for Selective Listening/Viewing

Like the Third World mother, in the case study above, who was concerned about what her children were learning from television, the unconscious worldview values of a dominant technological society are a major concern in all of the kingdom. Because the church in our present day does not, in many cases, play a major role in the social development of children and young people, they do not have a biblical worldview.

One of the recent concerns of many Christians has been the "secular" or nonworship and evangelism language of contemporary Christian music. There is real value in these young artists who sing about a Savior who is Lord over all their lives. They teach a Christian worldview. "While you may teach your child about the Lordship of Christ over all of life, they will soon learn that Christian music has little to do with the Lordship of Christ over all of life, and that for music having to do with love and romance, they would have to turn to someone such as Babyface or the Spice Girls for their tutoring" (Peacock, 1997). It is also important to recognize that not all nonchurch music is demonic and opposed to the kingdom. "Truth is truth," even when it is taught by those outside the kingdom. Just because someone is a Christian musician does not mean he or she understands fully the truths of Scripture. Therefore, it is important for parents, children, and teenagers to gain critical listening skills.

This suggests two strategies for the Christian. First, parents and their children need to develop critical listening skills. The mother, in the second story, had the right idea. Her course of action was twofold. She first decided to control information that came into the house. If she would not welcome a thief through the front door, why would she do the same to a "virtual" thief? The television was placed in a locked cabinet and opened only under her supervision. When the television was viewed, she sat through preselected programs with her children, taking the time to teach them about the concepts of the story.

The second strategy was more proactive. She purchased newly imported Christian music videos for children that used music and story as teaching tools for learning about the Bible and the Christian faith. Yet she was still concerned. While these imported media filled the need for Christian entertainment, they came cloaked in the cultural values of the West. At present, there were no locally produced programs that contextualized the Christian faith within her own culture. Her children would certainly learn more than just songs about the Bible. There is a desperate need around the world for culturally sensitive Christian musicians to create, write, and produce electronic media that speak to the needs of a culture, without the trappings of Western cultural values.

How to Teach with Songs

Much like the concerns of our chapter on proclamation, many of the principles are the same here. The difference is in the purpose. In teaching, there is a specific educational goal that teaches a concept, idea, or value. We will review a number of the stages, and place more emphasis on music selection.

1. Conduct Adequate Research—Listen

A good teacher tries to assess the needs of the students. After assessing both strong and weak areas, they can better plan a teaching strategy. For the most part, this does not have to be difficult. In a small class or church, a teacher will usually know the needs. However, as we saw in the theological analysis in the previous chapter, with large communities, it takes more work.

There are a growing number of Christian musicians who are studying ethnomusicology. Based in anthropology and musicology, this field of study provides excellent training in both theoretical and practical skills for cross-cultural musicians who wish to research, understand, and apply appropriate methods in teaching and training for the church around the world. In recent years, the Summer Institute of Linguistics coordinates and encourages training for cross-cultural workers in this field. They publish an excellent newsletter *EM News* (7500 West Camp Wisdom Road, Dallas TX 75236 USA), with both theory and practical materials. There are a growing number of Christian colleges and seminaries that also offer basic courses and degrees.

In the cross-cultural context, conducting research takes energy and time. One of the errors of the cross-cultural worker is to *assume* the needs of a community. Learning a language and spending time with people—listening—is important. In *Communicating for Development,* Karl-Johan Lundström says that "Communication that supports the full development of people must be participatory communication. Thus, anyone who comes to work with a community must first learn about the local culture and its way of communicating. Non-disruptive, lasting change must come through a society's own communication systems" (Lundström, 1990, p. 1).

2. Understand the Audience

A second important step is to understand the learning audience. You should have a basic understanding of their age, gender, ethnicity, language, socioeconomic status, even literacy and technological understanding. Understanding your audience helps you select a musical style that is comfortable for them. For example, many youth groups enjoy rap music. Placing a concept or biblical passage into rap is fun and educational for this generation, but it may not be well received by a group of octogenarians who enjoy the old hymns. The major concern is to find music that the group enjoys listening to and singing in their home context.

Lundström suggests that the first step in understanding involves learning the "internal communication system (ICS)." This internal communication system is observed by how people share information in (1) two-way communication, (2) one-way information flow, and (3) rituals and ceremonies. The ICS binds the community together and is their own unique system, much like the central nervous system of the human body. Information from the outside (external communication system) is evaluated by how it meets the needs of the society. Outsiders must "earn the right to be heard." Lundström suggests five ways to do this:

1. Participate in the society as a learner. Be open to the fact that you have much to learn *from* your host community, in addition to learning *about* their society.

2. Learn how the group communicates—its different signal systems and its normal channels of communication.

3. Try to understand the people's behavior and then identify the cultural themes and values of the group.

4. Begin to adapt the new information that you bring, so that it reflects some local insights and experiences. Then, at appropriate times, begin to introduce it, asking how the message might be further adapted.

5. Cooperate with people in the society who are able to adapt the message and determine the best way for it to be shared in the community. Enlist them in telling other people the new information (Lundström, 1990, p. 19).

Particularly in the cross-cultural context, the teacher is first of all a guest. It is important to participate in the life of the host community so that the hosts and guests can get to know one another. The guest must earn the right to be heard.

3. Utilize Music Effectively

Music is most appropriate for teaching when four things take place. First, there should be some kind of *participation*. Singing itself is participatory, so singing a song is an effective way to involve the learning group. In addition, an excellent way to involve the group is to have them compose a song. By doing this, you will be able to see how the group applies the learning concept. Another effective method of participation is to ask the class to contribute songs they enjoy that support the lesson focus. A second concern is to *integrate* the song into the larger lesson plan. Select songs that support the central focus of the lesson. We saw this in the teaching of Pollard. A third consideration is to *interpret* the song. Because people listen differently, some may be enjoying the music, while others may be thinking of the words. It may be necessary to explain the meaning of the words. Finally, *apply* the song to the teaching concept. In the formal worship context, preachers often take a familiar hymn and apply the text to their sermon. In the classroom, where there is freedom for discussion, students can find applications for their lives and larger society.

4. Select Songs

Songs for teaching should have four basic qualities. First, good teaching songs are *repetitive* so that they are easy to learn; or, they are longer songs that the group already knows. Second, the melody should be *easy to sing*. If a group is struggling to learn a difficult melody, their mental focus will be drawn away from the text. Third, *rhythm* is the energizer and structure of music. Select a song that uses rhythm both to draw in the class and to support the text. Finally, the text should be in a *language* that the audience can understand. For example, with young people archaic language is not enjoyable, and will distract the group from the main focus.

There are three song genres that work well with teaching, depending on the subject matter and familiarity with the song. First, short repetitive songs are excellent for introducing specific concepts. Second, strophic hymns work well when a group is familiar with the text. Third, self-composed songs provide an excellent way for the student, class, or group to learn by doing.

There are several ways in which a group can self-compose or arrange songs for teaching.

1. Use existing songs familiar to the group or easy to teach.
2. Use new words to familiar tunes.
3. Compose a new tune to an existing text.
4. Compose a new song.

5. Integrate Media

Music is an effective support medium for other types of communication. First, it works well in preaching, storytelling, drama, and movement. Second, as we mentioned earlier, technology has created a new way of listening. For many, unfortunately, participatory singing is not effective. Music cassettes and videos allow people to listen at their convenience as a form of entertainment. An interesting example comes from Hong Kong. The staff of the Baptist Media Center noticed the new craze of karaoke, where amateurs sing along with a recorded video. Using existing Christian songs, the center video taped music and dramatic story, so that youth groups could sing along.

6. Evaluate

Finally, evaluate the effectiveness of your music. In the participatory context, you will have immediate results. If the group enjoys the song, you will see that through their involvement. However, with electronic music the task will take more effort.

For example, for a number of years I directed a media center, where we produced radio programs. At the request of an international organization we produced an English program targeted for a country that was closed to Christians and where English was a second language. Using contemporary Christian music, the program was broadcast for over a year at considerable cost. At the end of the year we evaluated its effectiveness. We discovered several things that eventually led to its cancellation. First, we received very few letters in response to the program. Letters are one way of feedback or two way communication. Second, we discovered that the radio signal was very difficult to receive in the targeted area, so even if the program had been designed well, it was not heard.

Using these six principles, teachers have a process for developing lesson plans that effectively utilize music as teacher. Gifted teachers may apply these principles naturally. The ultimate evaluation comes when students begin to incorporate, not just the song, but the truths contained in the song in their daily lives.

Summary

In this chapter we have discussed music as teacher. We have seen that from a biblical basis the Israelites, an oral society, used music in carrying a sacred tradition. As with many of the world's people, music may have served the same function in the New Testament churches. From these beginnings, music as a tool of orality and literacy encapsulates and structures information for learning.

Howard's contemporary education theory suggests that music is more than an expressive art; it is also an intelligence. While some people in every culture are gifted specially in music, most people have a gift of music. Kingdom communities can expand both their teaching potential and their holistic ministry through music and the arts.

Throughout the history of the kingdom, in every age and denomination, music teaches values, doctrines, and beliefs. While much of this teaching is coincidental and unconscious, effective teaching requires a conscious strategy. Wherever people of the street seek sanctuary in the shelter of God's kingdom, music awaits as a welcome teacher and mentor. As should be evident by now, there is plenty of opportunity for Christian composers and musicians to become involved in a teaching ministry. Musicians often find music as an expression of their own special "message." Yet musicians who teach as well as express offer the kingdom a valuable gift to future generations of Christians.

224

Questions for Discussion

1. Can you identify cultural values you learned from a children's game?
2. Review the learning intelligences and styles. Can you identify your strengths and weaknesses?
3. In what ways could your church improve its use of music in teaching?

Exercises

1. Survey your church to discover how music is used to educate. You can interview Bible study teachers and pastors. Look for ways in which music would improve what is already taking place.
2. From your survey, select a topic you think is important for a specific age group. Using acceptable secular music, hymns, and songs, design a lesson plan in which music is used to teach the subject. Then, work with the teacher of the class to present the lesson plan to the class.
3. Try your creative writing skills by taking a popular song, and writing a text that teaches a biblical subject.

Part 2

Music
for the
Kingdom

The Voice

The LORD your God is with you, he is mighty to save. He will take great delight in you, he will quiet you with his love, he will rejoice over you with singing.

(Zeph. 3:17)

If God sings, what does his singing sound like? In the words of eminent church musician Donald P. Hustad, "even though [music] is created by humans, it is intended to be, in some sense, an expression of God." The singing of the church is "the voice of God" (Hustad 1993, p. 27). Created in his image, redeemed people offer sacrifices of praise through voices of allegiance. In the words of Charles Wesley, "O for a thousand tongues to sing my great Redeemer's praise, the glories of my God and King, the triumphs of God's grace." It is likely that Wesley intended these thousand tongues to express the penultimate unison song in Revelation, but in the present kingdom, they are a thousand languages of cultures who seek their unique voice for praise. Herein lies a conflict as old as the church. What music is appropriate for the church? What styles of singing are representative of God's voice? And who decides?

In this chapter we attempt to answer these questions with four sections. First, we will begin by looking at the human voice, the idea of singing style and organization. Second, we will consider the contexts of singing and the terms "sacred," "secular," and "worldly."

Third, we will consider the criteria for "good" music. Finally, we will look at a music decision model for the critical contextualization of worldly musical behaviors into the sanctuary of the church.

The Sound of the Harvest . . .

No one remembers her real name. They do know, however, that she loves to sing and that is how Mrs. No-Name and her husband were awarded new names. According to local testimony, Mrs. No-Name was involved with a local religion called voodoo. This combination of African spiritualism and Catholicism beckoned Mrs. No-Name into an obsession with voodoo. The big drum, racine beats, and nightly rituals tossed her about the day. In ebbs and tides of ecstasy, she moved frightfully between the realm of earth and the spirit world.

One day that changed as she met the person of Jesus. There was such spiritual freedom that she began to sing endlessly in joy. On Sunday mornings you could her voice above the entire congregation. During the week she would visit her neighbors and sing to them during prayer. She had a perpetual song of joy, so much so that everyone began to call her "Mrs. Voice." To this day she and her husband are known as Mr. and Mrs. Voice.

. . . And the Beat of the Street

June is a professional singer. Trained at the finest music schools, her voice is full and robust with the power to fill a great hall. A popular soloist at evangelistic meetings, she offers her musical testimony wherever she worships. One Sunday she visited a small country church in the Southern United States. There was great anticipation to hear her sing, for not only was her voice beautiful, but her lovely physical appearance, fine clothes, and refined manners gave evidence of a "cultured" background. She gracefully made her way to the church platform and reached for the microphone.

Recently, the church had installed the latest sound equipment. Large speakers protruded from the edges of the choir loft. Several microphone stands dotted the altar landscape while their cables crisscrossed about the front of the sanctuary. From the back of the auditorium, a sound technician placed in a cassette of a prerecorded sound track. After years of working with machines the technician had suffered a hearing loss, so the levels he chose usually were above the normal levels of the majority of the congregation.

Meanwhile, during the recorded instrumental introduction, June had tangled her foot in one of the microphone wires. Momentarily distracted, she began shaking her foot to dislodge the microphone cable. With her foot suspended above the floor, and the introduction coming to an end, the soloist quickly smiled toward the congregation and began her song. Apparently the microphone level had not been set prior to the service so there was an explosion of sound as she articulated her first words.

The congregation, like most congregations, was forgiving of these inconveniences. Yet, as each new phrase was offered, neither the soloist nor the sound technician noticed that sound levels were reaching excruciating proportions. Each time the verse would climax and the soloist's voice reached for higher and higher notes, the members of the congregation began to wince with pain. Assaulted with sound, it was the children who felt uninhibited enough to do the safest thing: they covered their ears with their hands.

The Human Voice

On the surface, both of these singers, in their respective cultures, had excellent voices. Their singing was committed to praising God and ministering to people. With the psalmist they fulfilled a basic biblical principle, "I will sing of the LORD's great love forever; with my mouth I will make your faithfulness known through all generations" (Ps. 89:1). Which of these singers do you think came closest to a biblical voice? With whom was God most pleased as giving a sacrifice of praise? Was one voice more appropriate for worship than another? Certainly Mrs. Voice expressed joy and uninhibited zeal.

231

June spent years training her voice and sang for large audiences through evangelistic events, recordings, and TV appearances. We might, at first, think that Mrs. Voice had the appropriate musical style, but I can imagine that some in her congregation got tired of hearing her voice above all the others. And while June had an obviously well trained voice, her lack of technical preparation and choice of "prerecorded" accompaniment obstructed the message she wanted to present. There are four considerations to answer these questions.

First, we look at the nature of the human voice and singing style. The human voice is the most intimate of musical instruments. It is the single most expressive way we can articulate and express our inner thoughts and feelings. From joy to sadness, anger to empathy, from the first cry of a newborn child to the last sigh of a dying person, the voice is our connection to the present world and our hope for a kingdom to come. We can beckon God, and, in the thought of Martin Luther, drive away Satan.

Amazingly, this emotional expression can come from deep emotional channels. Born of a desire to sing, sound is produced first through the expelled air of the lungs and supported by the diaphragm. A steady stream of air passes first through the vocal chords, which begin to vibrate and thus reshape the stream of air. If this vocal stream is unencumbered by a stop in the throat, tongue, or lips, a tone is amplified by natural resonators of the human body.

If we gave the voice that simple definition, all of us would sound alike. There would be little difficulty in deciding which music is appropriate for praise. As we will discover, it is our individual physiology, personal preference, cultural background, theological histories, and, recently, technological influences that complicate our mode of expression and aesthetic enjoyment.

We all have the same basic vocal instrument. With lungs, diaphragm, vocal chords, larynx, tongue, and teeth, there is not much that distinguishes our voices. The majority of difference comes from musical preference and training. We can imagine, however, that personal anatomical differences affect our sound. Our bodies result in differences because our vocal chords, oral and nasal cavities, tongues, teeth, and skulls are different sizes. Our body types shape the sound.

Our vocal sound also changes throughout our lifetime. During puberty vocal chords lengthen and chest sizes increase. Our voices stabilize. For this reason, most vocal coaches do not start training until a child has matured physically. Throughout history, however, many have preferred and enjoyed the sound of the child voice. During the late Middle Ages and Renaissance in Europe, young boys sang the higher voice parts of the choir. In order to maintain their service to the church, many young boys were castrated so that their voices would remain high. Known as *castrati* they made their way out of the church and into Western classical performance as well.

Aside from obvious physical differences, singers can control the sound of their voice in a number of ways. First, the amount of air that passes through the vocal chords changes the volume or loudness of sound. This is often called the "support" of singing. Prior to the advent of electronic sound amplification, most cultures valued vocal sound that could travel great distances, unamplified.

Second, almost without exception, a single note or tone is produced when air passes through the vocal chords. Not all cultures adhere to this natural part of singing, however. Each singer of the Gyuto Tibetan Tantric Choir, for example, has a unique and developed skill of producing three tones at the same time!

Third, the sound that moves from the vocal chords can be manipulated by controlling the rate at which the chords vibrate. Usually called *vibrato* or *tremolo*, this sound has waverings that accent the pure tone. Not all cultures appreciate vibrato, especially excessive vibrato, and prefer a *straight* tone, even to the point of controlling the wavering out of the tone.

In addition, vocal sound is varied through the openness of the throat. The larynx is an important organ for controlling the *pitch* and *range* of the vocal sound.

Another element in vocal sound is the tongue. Not only does this versatile muscle help articulate words, but its placement changes the "color" of the vocal sound. And finally, lips, teeth, and tongue help enhance diction and formulate vowel sounds.

By combining these elements of production we find a number of timbre or vocal styles, each of which tends to be preferred by different cultures and in different performance settings. Some singers tighten their necks and abdomens and belt out their songs over great distances.

Others sing in a strident falsetto in the upper range, while others love a full and wavy vibrato. Francis Bebey describes well the functional way many cultures use the voice as expressive communication:

> African voices adapt themselves to their musical context—a mellow tone to welcome a new bride; a husky voice to recount an indiscreet adventure; a satirical inflection for a teasing tone, with bubbling up to compensate for the mockery—they may be soft or harsh as circumstances demand. Any individual who has the urge to make his voice heard is given the liberty to do so; singing is not a specialized affair. Anyone can sing and, in practice, everyone does. (Bebey, 1975, p. 115)

Now compare the description of British opera critic Uma Suthersanen. She describes the voice of a soprano singing a role in Handel's opera *Ariodante:* "Her voice was full, beautiful, controlled, confident and, something I have not heard for a long time, remarkably fresh" (http://www.belcanto.com/97/1-9/reviews/ariod.htm). The first description was functional, based upon life's experiences; the second was an artistic description based on a beautiful sound in performance. Both depend on cultural context. Our understanding of vocal sound would not be complete without another factor.

Language also affects singing style. If you have ever tried to learn a new language, you know that you have to conform (and sometimes contort) your mouth in new ways to accommodate the words. Some international students who are learning English for the first time complain that Americans speak like they have rocks in their mouths. Several years ago, while attending a music concert in Vietnam, I had to adjust my musical ears to the very nasal and strident singing. In China, where the languages are tonal, the musical voice must conform to the nuances of verbal pitch. Pronounced or sung incorrectly, the meaning of the text would change.

Musical Style Part I

A culture's concepts, attitudes, and values are transferred into physical and verbal behavior. How someone sings reflects his or her culture. This singing style includes both vocal technique and vocal quality. Ethnomusicologist Alan Lomax developed a taxonomy (classification system) for analyzing musical style called cantometric analysis using thirty-seven different stylistic considerations (Lomax, 1976). For our purposes here, we will consider six such characteristics of concern for the singing of the kingdom: (1) centrality of Scripture, (2) lyric expression, (3) vocal embellishment, (4) nonverbal expression, (5) vocal/choral organization, and (6) instrumental accompaniment. (In the next chapter we will add to these stylistic characteristics.)

1. The Centrality of Scripture

At the core of vocal expression is the text related to Scripture. Scripture and the text it reflects prevent music from becoming an end in itself. Music, however, brings the text to life (Doran and Troeger, 1992, p. 52). There are two ways text and Scripture are important in Christian music. First, Scripture informs our selection of music and singing style. In other words, using Scripture as an authority for life, people draw conclusions about what kinds of singing are appropriate for their lives. Second, Scripture is central to the songs of Christians either as the *text* or as the basis for the text.

There is not one Christian denomination that does not in some way give central place to the Bible. As Holy Scripture for Christians, the Bible serves as the supreme and final authority in faith and life. This very centrality has led to many debates on life issues, and music is no exception. While singing is never debated as an appropriate form of personal, spiritual, or corporate worship expression, Christians through various faith and cultural traditions continue to debate and define the role of vocal style and instrumental accompaniment. Prior to the Protestant Reformation, when a central authority was accepted in matters of faith and practice, debates were limited to church conferences and edicts. However, since the Protestant Reformation, and especially in the late twentieth century when democratic governance, individualistic values, and global communication have so much influence, music has become the ball in a gigantic soccer match between purists and relativists.

If we look at the Bible itself, the majority of references to singing refer to proclaiming the good news and works of God. This does not mean, in my view, that only the Bible should be sung, as John Calvin demanded (he eradicated organs and nonbiblical hymns from worship). As we will see, it is impossible to sing any music in a "biblical cultural" style by virtue of translations, cultural styles, and nonverbal components. We can say, however, that text is the primary consideration in singing. Hence the voice is used to complement and interpret the text, as well as to serve the Christian community. Singing naturally does this.

2. Singing: Lyric Expression

Singing is a lyrical and symbolic expression. It is personal, intimate, vocal, and expressive language, in which words are not spoken but carried through lyrical, elongated sounds. As you can see, even describing what it is and what it is not can be difficult. We cannot read Scripture and remain unmoved by its meaning in our hearts, for religious expression is more than intellectual thought.

The voice is nothing more than an instrument until it is combined with words. Singing is the primary focus of praise in Scriptures. It is a communicative instrument. Curt Sachs suggested that music had its origin in both word and emotion. Logogenic music is born from the expression of words, while pathogenic music grows from emotional utterance.

Many of the arguments about singing in the church revolve around these two issues: How is the voice to sound and what quality should it have? How much freedom is there for words and music together? Additional arguments center on whether the voice should be accompanied.

In most religions, there is a fear that overexpressiveness in the worship setting can lead to a focus away from God and on more worldly matters. In such cases the word "music" or "singing" are not even used. For example, in Islam while a lyric expression is used to intone the Koran, the term "singing" is reserved for secular or worldly music. A minimum of expression is used to carry the sacred words. This one note to one word ratio is called *monosyllabic* and was used by the early church. This was certainly the stance of John Calvin during the Protestant Reformation and is still found in the Reformed tradition, where only Psalms are sung in worship. The earliest forms of Gregorian chant allowed one note to one word or syllable. It was not until later that *melismas,* or several notes to a word, were introduced into the singing. *Polyphony* (several melodies at once) and *harmony* (several notes sounded together) were added even later.

3. Vocal Embellishment: More Than Words

Humans cannot and will not be satisfied with an intellectual faith. We seek to express our emotions in regard to what we say. While intoning sacred words may help us focus on the words themselves, and this is important, humans have a desire to interact with and relate to words within their own experience and emotion.

One of the most interesting examples of this is how we came to get the religious word "alleluia." It is believed that the word made its way into our vocabulary through the ecstatic utterances of Middle Eastern culture. Called *vigelegele* in Swahili, it is a ululation of excitement made by flapping the tongue in rapid succession on the roof of the mouth. It is still used today in many cultures of Africa and the Middle East. In a reverse application, it is difficult to sing "alleluia" without some kind of vocal extension or melismatic expression in song.

Vocal embellishments, however, include much more than melismas. Many vocalists use extraneous sounds. Native Americans use what are called "vocables" to express emotion within a song. These repeated phrases like "yi-yi-yi-yi" accentuate the mood of the piece. A contemporary example might be a rock singer who sings, "I love you, oh-oh-oh, so much!" Many cultures around the world, particularly African cultures, will include grunts, yells, and other sounds as part of the song.

Is this right? We must ask the question, What is the intent/purpose of the singing? What is the context? And what is the result? While we cannot imagine singing the Ten Commandments at High Mass in the city cathedral, with *Thou shalt have no other Gods before me, oh, no-no-no, I say, hey, hey, hey!* we, at the same time, could not

237

expect a new believer who has experienced the utter joy of a relationship with Christ, to sing around her house, *I am now a believer* in a stoic melody.

4. Nonverbal Expressions: More Than Music

Much of what we believe to be right about music and worship, singing, or lyric expression has little to do with the actual singing itself. We seldom think about it and most often accept it unconsciously until some boundary of behavior is broken. We accept a synthesis of nonverbal codes when we sing. Most often known as body language, our singing involves clothes, space, touch, color, facial expressions, and even movement.

To the Westerner who visits an Eastern Orthodox Church, where the incantation of Scripture is considered holy, the extramusical and extratextual communication can be overwhelming. Flowing robes, burning incense, icons, and sacred movements can be very distracting. At the same time, an orthodox worshiper who visits an African American Pentecostal church that holds Scripture just as sacred is equally overwhelmed by the shouting, dancing, and singing of a robed choir and the enthusiastic congregational response.

We are accustomed to and mentally able to sort through the many symbols and nonverbal messages of our own culture. It is when we are faced with new external stimuli that we are literally shocked and confused by what we hear, see, and feel. Yet these nonverbal expressions are very much a part of singing. Consider the last time you sang in a worship service. Do you remember the clothes or robes the choir was wearing and the special movements to stand and sit, the conducting of the choir, the expressions on people's faces, the distance members stood from each other, the color of the robes, the volume of the music? We unconsciously learn these cultural codes, consider them as right, and attach them to the act of singing. Now try this experiment with your mental image. Change the gender of the singers, put on clownsuits, have them hold radios and swing from the ceiling in large chairs. Ridiculous, isn't it? Yet, if we were only concerned about the incantation of Scripture, the rest shouldn't matter. But it does.

5. Organizational Considerations

As we saw in the chapter about music in healing, we learned that one of music's natural powers is to create community. Not only do we have a natural tendency or desire to sing; we actually seek to sing with others. Up to this point we have discussed the soloist. However, the majority of Christians sing in relationship to other Christians—first in congregational singing, but also in choirs and groups.

Maybe from the singing around the campfire of a nomadic and hunter-gatherer tribe, or the need of one singer to join his or her voice with another, musical groups and collective singing is as old as humanity. The first appearance of group singing in Scripture is in Exodus, where we read of young women dancing and praising God with tambourines. In Leviticus we read of the first choirs that were organized for formal worship. They did not, however, sing in harmony.

In many cultures people enjoy singing in groups to make work easier and more enjoyable, to celebrate special occasions, and to mourn the passing of a life. Group singing has also entered religious life. Gifted singers have enjoyed spending extra time and energy composing, rehearsing, and performing music. Kings, queens, and dignitaries have commissioned special music for state affairs and entertainment.

In the Christian tradition, choirs first entered the liturgy in the Catholic Church, when a clergy class took over the role of congregational singing. These choirs sang special songs, but also helped in leading the congregation in worship. From cantor or sacred music schools, early musicians learned chants, notation, and music reading.

The church around the world owes its use of choirs to these traditions. The use of musical groups and worship bands is related directly to the popular music field. They have been sanctified (made "holy") by many churches for the ministry of the church. The traditions of organization are as varied as cultures. Solos predominate in the Western church. Group singing can be found in many collectivist cultures.

How these groups are organized depends on the culture. In many cultures, genders do not mix in groups. Women sing for women and men sing for men. Many may find this odd, but it is a reflection of cultural values. I can remember singing in all-male choirs in my youth. But these are not found as frequently, partly because of the American movement toward equality. However, many contemporary rock bands carry on the tradition through gender-specific groups.

Another division has to do with generation. In many cultures, children do not sing with adults and a graded choir system is used. For example, many large churches have several children's choirs, a youth choir, an adult choir, and even a choir for senior adults. Still another division has to do with ethnicity. Many people enjoy singing the music of their culture. Some choirs and groups form around a particular style of music. For example, there are choirs that sing exclusively choral anthems. Choral organizations vary greatly from culture to culture, and another stylistic characteristic has to do with whether the music should include instruments.

6. Singing and Accompaniment

In 1 Samuel, when David picked up his harp, he began a tradition that continues to this day—accompanying singing with an instrument. As we saw in the chapter on music as healer, we know that music has an action potential—the human body automatically wants to respond. When we sing, we have a natural tendency to move. When accompaniment is prerecorded and amplified through electronics, it may be difficult for us to understand the natural relationship between instruments and voice. While the voice is the most natural and personal extension of ourselves, the instrument is also an extension of our bodies. We use our hands and fingers, breath and body to support our singing.

In music of the kingdom we find this order most often. Text takes precedence over voice; voice takes precedence over accompaniment. While we are each drawn to different aspects of style—that which we see and hear first—we listen for a text (see Figure 8.1). In the Christian context, where the Word has such prominence as central to the faith, it is important that the Word be understood. While faith cannot be wholly understood apart from our actions, it does, nevertheless represent Christian values and beliefs in verbal symbols. While instruments have played an important role in music of those expressing the faith, instruments are secondary musical support and embellishments to a verbal language.

There is sometimes complaint from instrumentalists on this point. While I will discuss the role of instruments in Chapter 10, and I myself am a trumpet player, in the vast majority of music in global Christianity, the voice carries a verbal message central to the faith. This does not mean that instruments (and beautiful voices) are not valuable, but they require a gift, technology, and training that is specialized in comparison to common singing. It is, in my opinion, this common singing—the sound of spiritual harvests—which represents the song of God. Solo instruments can be this voice when associations are tied to familiar contexts; the solo voice when it expresses group consensus.

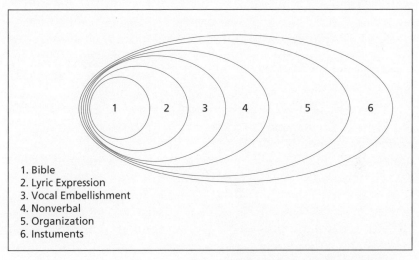

Figure 8.1. Music and Text

Instruments support singing. Instruments help us find appropriate pitches; they also undergird our singing, especially when we are learning something new or lack confidence in our singing. In many churches the organ actually leads the singing. Instruments can set the mood for singing and maintain the tempo. Instruments help introduce and place the text in a context. Yet what is a blessing can also be a bane.

When improperly tuned, singers lose the pitch. When too loud, the message is lost. When played with prideful intention, our worship shifts focus from God to player.

We will consider instruments in more detail in Chapter 10. However, for the purposes of discussing accompaniment, it is interesting that there have been two historical considerations. First, while instruments were used extensively in the Old Testament, they are absent in the New Testament, primarily because of immoral associations. It was not until the sixth century, when the church became a strong influence, that they were reintroduced into religious life. Second, when they were reintroduced, there was not the problem of covering the voice we find so prevalent with instruments in this century. Early instruments did not have powerful volume. As technology has developed, sound has been amplified, thus forcing voice and instrument to compete.

Consider June, our excellent singer at the beginning of the chapter. She had a problem with the microphone cable and the volume of sound coming from the speakers. While we often don't consider it an instrument, sound technology requires the same planning, rehearsal, and consideration we would give a keyboard accompanist.

I would be remiss if I did not mention one exception to these instrumental concerns. In a few cases, instruments themselves sing. Instruments are also very much like the voice and can sometimes speak. The *dundun* of Nigeria, also found throughout West Africa, is called a "talking drum." The *dundun* has an hourglass shape and tension strings are attached to the head so that when placed under the arm and tension is applied the pitches change. Several years ago I attended a Yoruba funeral in Abidjan, Cote d'Ivoire. It was a solemn occasion. Many people gathered to pay honor to a great man of the church. A choir and instrumental ensemble of guitars and drums accompanied solemn hymn singing. During the hymn, however, a *dundun* player kept beating out high and low tones in rhythm that, to my untrained ears, sounded out of place to the hymn. But as I looked around the audience I saw people nodding their heads in agreement to someone speaking a great truth. My translator then made it clear: the *dun-*

dun player is in essence a commentator who "prophesies" with his drum. Because Yoruba is a tonal language, the drum can imitate the tones of the language. Proverbs are highly valued as an indirect communication medium. Because proverbs are set formulas, they are easily played by a skilled *dundun* player. This player was merely adding comment to the ceremony: "A great elephant has fallen in the forest!"

In the Ear of the Hearer: Aesthetics and Culture

What is "good" singing? There are two considerations. First, some cultures have an objective and abstract standard for what is beautiful and good. Others have a more functional standard of "beauty." Neither is adequate for understanding the beautiful, and both have something to offer. Second, all societies have some standard for evaluating music. They categorize styles and then rank them in importance (Nettl, 1982, p. 305). First, let us consider concepts of good music based upon cultural values.

Spectator-oriented cultures influenced by the West, as mentioned in the introduction, tend to look at art abstractly. A beautiful voice is one that has a pleasing sound, perfect tone, and technical excellence. In English such words as beautiful, lovely, and marvelous are used to label the tone of voice. Even the fact that I am not referring to the singer, but to the voice, gives an indication of the objectification of a person's gift.

In many non-Western cultures, however, it is not the voice that matters, but its function and impact on the community. Words like hot, cool, and sweet are used to describe the nature of the song. A good singer in Swahili is called a Mwimbishaji, or one who causes others to sing. He or she is able to bring the heat to a congregation of singers as they join in singing and dancing.

In a spectator society people evaluate the music based on its sound and applaud recognition; non-Western and collective societies may show their approval in other ways. Yoruba people "spray" their musicians with gifts of money.

243

Every society has a standard for excellence in singing, or what they would consider to be a good voice. For example, individualist cultures value the soloist or single performer. One need only look at the music videos and music award programs to see that the major winners and divisions have to do with "best single" or outstanding "artist." Individual achievement is highly valued. This is based in part on our belief that we are individuals and that the individual is of greater value than the group. In contrast, in many collective cultures, groups and choirs are valued above individual performers. If individual performers are valued, it is for their contributions to the community at large. When these cultural values and beliefs intersect in cross-cultural contexts, there is sure to be conflict.

It was a Sunday morning at the Kariobangi Baptist Church in Nairobi, Kenya. The congregation had sung many songs and choruses that included call-and-response singing. There had been much excitement as evidenced by the smiles on the faces of the congregation. The pastor announced that there was a guest soloist from America. There seemed to be excitement at hearing this testimony in song. The visiting man stood to sing. As he began, people lowered their eyes and became quiet. While they may not have considered this singing bad, just different, they were not moved by the music because it was outside their belief and value system regarding "good" music. Early missionaries were not so kind in their response when first confronted with African culture considering the singing raucous and uncultured.

In the illustration above, cultural differences were important in explaining why the solo did not appeal to the congregation. It also illustrates our second point. All societies and cultures rank music based on its value to the society. Try this experiment. List five or six musical styles you heard last week. I might think: choral anthem, popular solo, marching band music, congregational hymn, television commercial music. Now take your list and prioritize, based on what you consider the best, most important music to the least. Whether we like to admit it or not, we make selections of music based on their value and importance *in our context.*

Sacred and Worldly Singing

Last year I was teaching world music at a large Christian international university. At a banquet the president of the school asked me what subjects I taught. "Among several cross-cultural subjects, I often teach world music," I replied. "What!" he responded. "You teach worldly music?"

As we saw in the chapter on music as theology, we naturally divide music in the Christian context into godly music and worldly music. How can we define sacred music and find its opposite of "worldly" music? While this may not be an issue in many urban churches that acculturate quickly to the global trends, it is a real issue in many traditionally based churches and cultures.

Several summers ago I was visiting a friend in South India. I was invited to speak at the local church. My host was kind enough to arrange a short music festival following the service, where the members performed Christian songs in folk and popular styles. This was an excellent time, I thought, to videotape the music. I was to find out differently. The church leadership considered the worship service holy and sacred. When approaching the platform, which only men could do, everyone had to remove their shoes. Even for the brief music festival, all folk and popular music had to be performed on the floor—not on the platform. My hosts tried to accommodate my wishes and came up with a solution. I could stand outside the church, looking in, and videotape through the window. I decided not to videotape, and enjoyed a wonderful service.

People naturally categorize and prioritize music based on culturally determined standards. The sacred/secular dichotomy, so often used by Christians, creates conflicts because we do not have an authoritative revelation or designation of what is sacred. Certain music is designated as "sacred" or the ordained music for church worship. In the Reformed tradition of Calvin, the psalms are the most sacred because they are God-breathed from the authority of Scripture. Both Pope Gregory of the Roman Catholic Church and Saint Yared of the Ethiopian Orthodox Church were divinely given music for church worship. And as St. Augustine reasoned, there is music for the people of God, all other music is of the world.

How, then, does the Christian or the Christian community decide on what music is within the boundaries of our faith? Much of our decision making has more to do with context—where music is performed. For example, several years ago a musician friend of mine set one of his traditional tribal circumcision songs with Christian words. In the city, where this is performed, the congregation enjoyed the lively rhythms and melody. However, when he tried to sing the same song in his village church, many were offended because of the associations to the earthy lyrics to which it was originally wedded.

A more appropriate category has to do with religious and nonreligious music, or music performed in the service of the church and that which is not. These musics are within a holistic music, given by a Holy God to every person (Hustad, 1993). Our problem is not so much with these categories as with the antireligious or profane music that is opposed to the Godly. How do we decide?

Principles for a Godly Voice

So what does God's singing sound like? Is there a universal standard of singing we can apply to all cultures? Should we all take voice lessons, or should we throw these standards to the wind and only sing as the function demands? Recently I gave a lecture entitled, "God don't make no bad music!" It was intended to be provocative, with a non-standard English title, and several people took the bait. In the halls I received comments, "No, God don't make no bad music, but people sure do." That is the point. Our judgments of singing are most often from a human perspective. What is God looking for? Rather than argue what songs are best, what singing style represents the voice of God, I believe God has given many songs to choose from—to grow and expand our repertoire—to express the fullness of his glory in making music, holistically.

There are four principles that can guide us in the kingdom. We all would agree that we are to sing. So I have used the acronym, *SING (Sacrifice, Intent, New Song, Godly Ministry)*, to present these principles.

Principle One: Sacrifice

The word "sacrifice" in Scripture has several meanings. First, in the redemptive story from Old Testament practice to the ultimate atonement for sins by Jesus on God's behalf, sacrifice means a way to repair a broken relationship with God for people who are separated from God (Heb. 8:1–4).

A second meaning, and the one we will apply to music, is that of a "sacrifice of praise." This meaning is alluded to in the psalms: "I will praise God's name in song and glorify him with thanksgiving. This will please the LORD more than an ox, more than a bull with its horns and hoofs" (Ps. 69:30–31). We are to "offer to God a sacrifice of praise—the fruit of lips that confess his name" (Heb. 13:15).

Sacrifice is an offering of gratitude and love, a life witness of our allegiance to him. Within this definition there are four concepts for offering our musical sacrifices of praise: the direction of the sacrifice, the excellence of the offering, the cost of the sacrifice, and the faithfulness in sacrifice. We can apply these in fulfilling the words of Jesus: "Love the Lord your God with all your heart and with all your strength, and with all your mind, and, love your neighbor as yourself" (Luke 10:27).

First, in loving God, our sacrifice of praise is first of all offered to God. Singing, and music making in general, is more than simple thanksgiving; it is a voice of allegiance. The focus of our music, whether in the sanctuary, the marketplace, or the concert hall, should bring glory to God in the totality of our living. Conversely, when our art and song become glorified they have redirected our worship from the Creator to that of the created. As theologian Ralph P. Martin describes in *Worship in the Early Church,* Jesus embodied a new order of worship in which "The sacrifice the Christian has to offer is the 'living sacrifice' of his person, yielded up in surrender and service for Christ. This is the 'reasonable worship.' The priestly office of the whole church, is no longer found at any earthly altar, for it is the offering of the sacrifice of praise and thanksgiving" (Martin, 1975, p. 23).

Second, in loving God, our offerings of highest love, gratitude, and praise demand our best. Our aesthetic standards of "good and bad" (excellence) are culturally determined. Within every culture, and

247

within each style of music, there are evaluative standards of the "best." Not to be confused with this cultural aesthetic standard, all music has at least limited potential for "goodness" by virtue of the creative gifts given to all people of all time. This moral goodness is found in the heart and actions of people. Just as people of faith have been made holy, so can the music they offer in praise. But is all music "good?" It is here we must begin to sing with our "minds," as Paul calls it (1 Cor. 14:15). All music is possible, but all music may not be profitable. Christian standards of excellence in sacrifice relate more to giving our best appropriately to the context in which it is made.

If we take the stewardship of God's gifts seriously, then we pursue excellence within the accepted norms of the musical culture in which we operate, whether that be gospel, classical, jazz, heavy metal, hip-hop, "high church," or indigenous forms. As any musician, in any style, will tell you: Excellence in making music is hard work. There is a sacrifice of time, talent, and energy in making our best music. Poorly rehearsed and prepared music offends like a trinket given to appease our guilt and placate a complaining relative. It falls far short of our best. Conversely, a sacrifice means moving beyond our musical comfort zones and striving with hard work and sweat for higher standards in whatever sounds we use to make music. Yet this excellence is always balanced in the love of our neighbors and community, who hold us accountable to God.

Third, in loving our neighbor, we recognize that life and worship in community may require a sacrifice of our culturally determined standards. We may, indeed, in order to love our neighbor, have to sacrifice our own standards for that of others who do not share our culture, training, or aesthetic standard. This sacrifice takes place within our own culture, but also in relation to cultures different than our own.

In the thought of C. S. Lewis, within one's own cultural standards there is a blessing when the classically trained musician "charitably" sacrifices his or her aesthetic standards for the sake of untrained parishioners who do not understand or who are not moved by the technical expertise. At the same time there is a sacrifice when the parishioner, unable to understand or appreciate the music of the trained musician, patiently renders a respect for the skill involved. Both these people have sacrificially loved their neighbors' music and

God is glorified. However, when the skilled musician "looks with contempt" in what he or she perceives as an ignorant congregation; or a sullen congregation entrenched in willful indignation refuses to offer a friendly space for another, God is not glorified. It is when musical tastes are sacrificed for another in love that they become a means of grace (Lewis, 1984).

This same attitude of grace affects our relationship to other cultures when ethnocentrism prohibits loving those who are our neighbors, but who may be culturally and ethnically different. Single historical and stylistic approaches to music reinforce cultural imperialism and myopia. When these cultural standards are valued for their own sake it produces a "ceremonial religion not only [accenting] pride in ritual performance but [creating] an unbridgeable social chasm between the practitioner and the outsider" (Kraybill, 1978, p. 183). In many congregations Western "classical" music is still regarded as "the highest art" while music of the diverse cultures outside the dominant culture is regarded as unacceptable for worship. But this also applies to any worshiping congregation who cannot welcome the music of other Christians. This attitude perpetuates and reinforces a paternalistic and often condescending approach to the diverse people who may sing the same song, yet one that is born in a different cultural garden.

Loving our neighbor with our music means a sacrificial faithfulness to God's purposes. When Jesus commanded "Go and make disciples" (Matt. 28:19–20) he was talking to all disciples—musicians included. A sacrifice of faithfulness beckons Christian music makers to live in the world as children of salt and light. The ministry of the sanctuary is a message for the street. Music making as faithful sacrifice is a journey, a discovery the church does along the way—on the street and in the marketplace. While I have not mentioned the many professional musicians who make their living in the artistic world outside the ministry of the church, these highly skilled craftspeople witness with their lives and music on a daily basis among many unbelievers. In many ways, their faithfulness is challenged and tested with an intensity those within the walls of the sanctuary would find uncomfortable at least, daunting at most. Theirs is a special gift to be appreciated and encouraged.

249

I will conclude this section with a short story that for me encapsulates the concept of sacrifice. Many years ago I was the minister in an affluent congregation. By all standards, the music and musicians were excellent. There was considerable pressure, though often unspoken, for the Sunday service music to be of highest standards. There was a bass in the choir who became the superlative example of sacrifice. Franky was what some people call "tone-deaf." He rarely sang on pitch and members sometimes complained after the service, "Your anthem sounded great, but I could hear that drone through the whole anthem. Can't someone teach him how to sing?"

At first I wished he would go away, but he wouldn't. He was early for every choir rehearsal and was so committed that he would call if he was going to be late or absent from the Sunday service. We were left with three options: adjust our standards, ask him to leave, or teach him to sing. We chose the later. As it turned out, Franky had what could be crossed-ears. He couldn't sing the pitches he heard with his ears. So starting from scratch he committed himself to match pitches. We all sacrificed and it was painfully slow. In rehearsal and performance, two of the better basses sat next to him and sang toward his ears. Between rehearsal and performances we would match pitches, starting from the only one he could sing. While Franky never learned to sing like an opera star, his singing was a sacrifice of praise. He devoted himself to God's service, he strove for personal excellence, and he contributed to the community in faithfulness. Despite how many felt at the time, I am sure God was pleased with his sacrifice of singing.

Principle Two: Intent

God is more concerned with the heart or motive for human creative expression than the manner of expression. Music is a gift of God to the believer. From the heart of faith comes Christian expression. You might be surprised that the Bible commands us to sing—and it also commands us *not* to sing. "Away with the noise of your song! I will not listen to the music of your harps" (Amos 5:23).

Music is a matter of the heart. God said it well to Ezekiel: "With their mouths they express devotion, but their hearts are greedy for unjust gain. Indeed, to them you are nothing more than one who sings love songs with a beautiful voice and plays an instrument well, for they hear your words but do not put them into practice" (Ezek. 33:31–32). If our music-making is to reflect the voice of God it must be authentic.

When Esther, the woman you met in the introduction, became a believer, she did not begin speaking in English (or Greek or Hebrew, for that matter). She began using her native language in new ways, first with the right motive and intention—to glorify God. Her song was an authentic expression of her faith expressed in the language of her cultural home. And she was tested. On a daily basis her song of faithfulness was watched and evaluated by her peers at the watering holes and harvest fields.

Recently I was conversing with a young person before a contemporary Christian music concert. I asked him what he thought about rock music in the church. He responded, "I've been watching, I want to know if they are the real deal." He wanted to know what every observer discerns in the musician: What is behind the singing? A Christian can sing good music with the wrong motives. Christian rock musicians can sing for the money, opera singers for the fame, and choirs for the glory of applause. At the same time, many Christian rockers can have an honest desire to glorify God, along with opera singers, choirs, and thousands of Esthers around the world. Understanding matters of the heart, however, is hard to discern, and ultimately rests with the Almighty. Asking Esther to learn a new language, sing from a hymnal, and refuse to dance may have been a test of her faithful intentions to the missionaries, but her authentic voice would have been lost.

Principle Three: A New Song

When Jesus told Nicodemus "You must be born again," he was speaking in spiritual terms (John 3:3). One is not reborn into an earthly kingdom, but a spiritual kingdom. As members of this new spiritual kingdom, our perspective changes, which in turn affects our behaviors—but not all our behaviors. Nicodemus did not start speaking another language, but he may have sung a new song. As we saw earlier, the essence of the Christian faith is not found in the musical forms, but the text. Our outward expressions, so long as they express love and goodness to all people (Gal. 6:10), are not as important as the newness of our spiritual song. Expressing this new song requires thinking in new ways, past our own prejudice. Though not a musical example, the story of Peter illustrates this process.

In the early church there was an argument over circumcision. Circumcision was a sign of a covenant with God, signifying being set apart as a holy nation. Peter was a dogmatic and authoritarian thinker, rigid in his beliefs and lacking tolerance for ambiguity. He was very resistant to modifying his beliefs about circumcision—those who were not circumcised could not be "inside" the boundaries of his faith. It was not until he had a dream, where not circumcision, but another bounded-set category, food, was revealed to be clean as a result of God's creation, that he was able to accept Cornelius and say, "God has shown me that I should not call any man impure or unclean" (Acts 10:28). Notice he did not say food.

Any musical genre is possible for the church. There are many new songs that express the birth of believers in languages and cultures from every part of the kingdom. Old songs often fail to speak to present realities. We need new songs to continually express the eternal and dynamic significance of the gospel to a present age. In fact, we are commanded throughout Scripture to "Sing a New Song."

This does not mean that we throw out old songs. Music from the kingdom's past helps us identify with the historical fullness of the kingdom. Musicians' greatest gift to the kingdom is the critical listening skills to evaluate the present, the prudence to remember the past, and the wisdom to extend the kingdom outside one's own frame of reference. Much of the music in the kingdom (especially inside the walls of the dominant culture) is not only exclusive—its form caters to a specific generation within a specific culture—but the music also perpetuates a myopic view of the kingdom. Vast numbers of worshipers are missing something of the Christian tradition that is two thousand years deep (and deeper if we count our Hebraic roots) and many cultures wide.

Most important is that our singing must be made new in a fresh commitment. One of the most difficult tasks of performing is singing the same songs with the same newness as when they were first learned. It is this newness that provides a ministry to the kingdom.

Principle Four: Godly Ministry

Behind every voice is a person. At the heart of a godly ministry is love for people. We respond out of love for people, not just their music, even though their music is a part of who they are. Music is a relational art. Two college music majors sat behind their desks in a sullen, smug, almost self-assured manner. "We don't mind listening to the music, but do we have to learn about the culture stuff?" Joe queried. "I'm a composer. Show me the theory so I can write music like that. I'll never travel to these places." Steve replied, "Well I guess it's okay, though I don't think I'll ever use it."

Both students have promising careers. Steve, an excellent instrumentalist, wanted to teach public high school and continue serving his church as minister of music. Joe was an electronic genius. Specializing in music composition through the computer, he enjoyed capturing (sampling) sounds and altering them in his composition.

"Joe, who do you compose your music for? Who'll be listening to it?" I asked. "Nobody, really," he answered. "I'm interested in creating excellent music for myself."

This indifference to others' culture may be more dangerous than paternalism, because it accepts all music without critical evaluation. At the same time, it ignores the fact that meaning is not in the music but in the people who share in its use. It is like saying, "I like their music, but I don't care much for them." At some point we must develop musical empathy, living (and suffering) with others to understand them and the music they make, in order to love and care for them. By developing musical empathy, and learning together, we develop relationships and are better equipped to share our faith. It is for, from, and in these relationships that music serves and ministers holistically, as priest, prophet, proclaimer, healer, preacher, and professor.

This brings us back to the theme of the book. Music serves a spiritual kingdom which includes our culture. Because music is an expression of culture, it also functions within culture for a purpose—

whether the highest art of the culture or practical singing to lighten the daily work. In a godly ministry, music does not lose the cultural function, but has a higher purpose (function) for the kingdom.

For example, from a ministry perspective, the expensive organ and large choir in a suburban church ministers in a priestly role, officiating the congregation into the presence of God. At the same time, however, it can in its cultural function validate the position in society of a powerful elite who (un)intentionally use this music making as a socioeconomic barrier of exclusion from the poor and marginalized. So do we rip up the carpets, tear down the organs, and disperse the choir? Yes and No.

If the music is being used to exclude others from the presence of God because it validates a powerful minority, then yes. It has become a cultural idol and must be dashed at the very altar of God. Wait a minute! Is this not what some Protestant Reformers did? We have said that music is not inherently evil—it is the intentions of people who make it. Their music, as a symbolic expression, needs to be changed, and the congregation needs to be held accountable by the kingdom at large through a change of heart. But I don't advocate ripping up someone's carpet. However, if as an honest sacrifice of praise, with a humble intention as an authentic cultural expression of faith; and if the church is in a redemptive and holistic relationship with the faithful of every social class, ethnicity and race, then no. It is one of many authentic and humble expressions of God's singing.

In the minds of some Christians functionalism is equated with utilitarianism—an "end justifies the means" rationale for what we do with music. The utilitarian sees music as a tool for ministry. And while I agree with this principle (and will discuss it in chapter ten) the same tool can also become a weapon. We can use music to achieve almost any purpose we want, if the hearers are willing to listen and are emotionally inclined to respond.

Manipulation is not ministry. Music is not a club to beat unbelievers into a submission of our faith. Music is more than what we can do with it. While I do not believe that music can be good in itself, apart from the cultural aesthetic we assign to it, I find a beauty that transcends my own understanding when I listen and participate in the lives of God's people who sing his song—whether in voice, instrument, dance, or art. While my understanding may be different than that of the person in another culture, God is bigger than our narrow categories and the Holy Spirit moves in ways I cannot understand. Music making (art) is a worthy and needed gift to the kingdom. It ministers, not because we manipulate the results, but because we seek to serve a God with whom we have a living relationship, and who desires a song that is faithful to him.

Principles

1. All people can and should sing.
2. Solos should be encouraged as testimony of active theology but not as a prideful display.
3. Exceptional musical gifts should be encouraged as a gift to the community.
4. How we sing, in vocal production, should be determined by the aesthetic of the local community.
5. What we sing should be determined by the active theological reflection of the individual and the community.
6. Because our music reflects who we are, musicians need to be involved in Bible study and personal ministry, to both broaden and deepen their spiritual expression through music.
7. Vocalists should develop their craft and seek to improve.
8. Vocalists should be encouraged in the prophetic responsibility they have within and outside the Christian community.
9. Worship should encourage the participation of the community in singing.

Conclusion

The voice of the church is more than singing. Yet the song is the first sound of the harvest. In this chapter we began with the sound of the voice and explored its broader meaning in the life of the kingdom. First, we reviewed the nature of the human voice in the production of singing. Second, we looked at six important elements in the style of singing: centrality of Scripture, lyric expression, vocal embellishment, nonverbal expression, vocal/choral organization, and instrumental accompaniment.

We saw how the element of style is determined by personal preference, culture, and history. These influences have determined our concepts of "good" music. We both categorize musical styles and prioritize their value based in part on their context of performance. This context is not bounded by impregnable walls because music finds its way into every space. Finally, we concluded with four principles for evaluating the "goodness" and value of music. In these principles Christians are to evaluate music based on: (1) an appropriate cultural standard of excellence, (2) the intentions of the performers, (3) a re-newness of the song, and (4) the resulting contribution to kingdom music ministry. We now turn our attention to another element of style and that is the forms of our singing.

Questions for Discussion

1. How would you define a beautiful voice?
2. Based on this material, who should sing solos in worship?

Exercises

1. View or listen to your favorite Christian singer, choir, or music group. Using the five aspects of singing in Figure 8.1, describe what makes them good?
2. Using the Bible as your guide, and also the statements of your own pastor or church organization, write a statement or definition of beautiful singing.
3. Using the SING model for godly singing, discuss how different types of music are expressive of God's purposes for the kingdom and an authentic voice of the people who make the music.

9

The Song

Speak to one another with psalms, hymns and spiritual songs. Sing and make music in your heart to the Lord, always giving thanks to God the Father for everything, in the name of our Lord Jesus Christ. Submit to one another out of reverence for Christ.

(Eph. 5:19–21)

Let the word of Christ dwell in you richly as you teach and admonish one another with all wisdom, and as you sing psalms, hymns and spiritual songs with gratitude in your hearts to God.

(Col. 3:16)

Praising God in song is eternal. The kingdom was born in song. The earliest gatherings of believers in community continued an age-old tradition, established before David. Canticles, psalms, and different musical forms provided a foundation for the early church. The last worship of Jesus even ended in a Jewish canticle (New Testament Psalm).

The kingdom will end in song. We read in Revelation that "Then I heard every creature in heaven and on earth and under the earth and on the sea, and all that is in them, singing: 'To him who sits on the throne and to the Lamb be praise and honor and glory and power, for ever and ever!'" (Rev. 5:13–14). We can only conjecture what that song may sound like, and we can only hope for a kingdom song today.

Ever since Pentecost in Acts, when the disciples' tongues were freed to speak the gospel in many languages, and maybe long before, the church has been divided over which songs we sing in the kingdom. There are two camps basically. On one side there are those who believe that if the Bible doesn't specifically forbid it, any music is a gift of the kingdom. In the other camp are those who believe that only the specific music mentioned in Scripture is suitable for the church. Most of this disagreement centers around the context of the sanctuary—the sacred space of worship. Even John Calvin, who was in the later camp, loved music in his home and was reported to play instruments. The question is: Do we maintain tradition or innovate? While we can agree to sing, the agreement ends there.

No three words in the New Testament have fueled more fires between Protestants; no three words have divided more pastors and musicians, and no three words have caused more confusion to emerging world Christians than "psalms, hymns, and spiritual songs." Some Christians have held tightly to a literal interpretation of singing only psalms as divinely inspired texts. Others practice musical glossolalia or songs of the Spirit. Still other Christians appear to accept any humanly composed music of the day. Is there an internal conflict in the Bible? Can citizens of the kingdom sing new songs as indicated in the psalms? Or, as in the New Testament, are we to sing only psalms, hymns, and spiritual songs?

In this chapter we want to explore the genre of music in the kingdom. While we will focus primarily on congregational singing within the context of worship, Christians utilize a wide variety of musical forms that originate from culture and tradition. First, we will explore the meaning of the three terms. Second, we will consider the nature and meaning of the new song, looking at the origins of music and the path they take as cultures change. Third, we will describe how to introduce songs within the Christian community. Finally, we will provide some principles for writing your own new songs.

The Sound of the Harvest . . .

Nestled behind an earthen dike by the North Sea, a church steeple rises from the center of a quiet village community that values *geselleg,* or coziness. Small shops and neatly trimmed lawns of village streets quickly blend into the fields of small farms. This is the rural Netherlands, and the most visible remains of its past is the windmill at the juncture of two residential streets. It's 10:00 A.M. on Sunday morning and scores of people move from their houses down the cobbled sidewalks to one of many Reformed churches. As visitors, we enter what Francis Shaeffer reportedly called a "black socks" church because of its orthodox adherence to John Calvin and the Protestant Reformation and the black clothing they wore. We cross into the foyer of the church and are told by the usher that we must wait outside the sanctuary. There is a green light above the pulpit that signals the elect of membership to enter. We wait. After all families are seated, the green light is turned off and we, the "nonelect," are ushered to the remaining pews.

The organ is suspended above the pulpit, providing a canopy that accentuates the importance of the "Word of God" that will be delivered. On this Sunday the preacher is not available so the "reader" reads a printed sermon, but not before the congregation follows a liturgy that includes their only congregational singing— psalms. Accompanied with simple chords, the congregation begins the slow, almost arhythmic chanting of sacred psalms in the Dutch language. My young host then leans over and says, "They sing so slow you could chew a mint between each note!" He later shared that he could not remain in the church and had transferred his membership to a local charismatic church. True to Calvin's intent, this service was void of any external emotion or symbols and icons, including the cross. For over two hours, worshipers sat in perfect and controlled silence, save the passing of mints midway through the service in order to facilitate the singing of the psalms.

259

...And the Beat of the Street

It is the gymnasium of a local high school. A prefabricated platform is being raised at one end of the basketball court while assistants begin setting up folding chairs on the gym floor. A group of musicians begin to roll in cases carrying amplifiers, speakers, microphones and yards of cable. Within an hour the gymnasium is transformed into a worship sanctuary of the Rhema Bible Church.

Former nightclub musicians before their conversion to Christianity, the worship team begins warming up by playing gentle rock rhythms. They then welcome the congregation to join in a praise chorus. For fifteen minutes the worship team leads the congregation to an emotional worship peak, and then the leader invites the Holy Spirit to lead the congregation. At this point people begin to "sing in the Spirit" in an improvised and free-flowing musical glossolalia. With hands waving in the air, some crying, others jumping and shouting, the congregation ebbs and flows in waves of musical sound. The worship leader then directs the congregation back to a praise chorus.

Psalms, Hymns, and Spiritual Songs

On my office desk is a tin-type of a distant relative. Exposed to the air for the past hundred years, the picture is faded, except for the center of my distant uncle's face. The only thing I know about this relative is a story my father shared before he died several years ago. The man in the picture was the brother of my great-great-grandmother. She was a Native American, and my father, as a boy, remembers her washing and ironing her traditional burial cloth. That's all I know. The rest I can only conjecture.

Kingdom music is a once living artifact very much like our relatives who leave us an inheritance. Some of the artifacts of inheritance fade and disappear with time, save for their memory. All of them are important, in some way, because they tell us our heritage. As the family tree grows, so does its music.

Our first inheritance is from Scripture. Three musical genres form a guiding principle of songs for the church: psalms, hymns, and spiritual songs. We consider their meaning within the context of the New Testament and draw some conclusions for application for today.

Psalms	Hymns	Spiritual Songs
Book I: 1–41	*Magnificat* Luke 1:46–55 (canticle)	Ephesians 5:19–21 (reference only)
Book II: 42–72	*Benedictus* Luke 2:29–32 (canticle)	Colossians 3:16 (reference only)
Book III: 73–89	*Gloria* Luke 2:14 (canticle)	
Book IV: 90–106	Ephesians 2:14–16	
Book V: 107–150	Philippians 2:6–11	
	Colossians 1:15–20	
	1 Timothy 3:16	
	Hebrews 1:3	
	1 Peter 3:18–22	
	Revelation 5:13b	

Psalms

Many people refer to the Book of Psalms as the hymnbook of the Bible and temple worship. The word "psalm" literally means one of the songs that has been included in a psalter. Psalms are a form of Hebrew poetry. The singing of psalms was more like an incantation, with a strong emphasis on the text. Psalms have their beginnings in tabernacle and temple worship. The collection we have today developed over many centuries and influenced the music of the early church.

While it is true that psalms were used in temple worship and are referred to throughout Scripture, it is fairly well established that the psalms may not have been the only music used in temple worship. The existence of Psalms in the Old Testament and canticles in the New Testaments also suggests that other psalms were sung as well. Even suggestions within the Book of Psalms to "sing a new song" imply that new psalms were constantly written and altered for worship. This alteration comes from both new texts for worship and the alteration of existing melodies to fit old psalms. *Makam*, which were more like short musical formulas than developed melodies, were used to accompany song texts (Elwell, 1988, 1502). We can also conclude from a reading of the Old Testament that the Israelites did not do all of their singing in worship, but that singing was involved in all aspects of life—including what we might call folk music today.

With the destruction of the temple in A.D. 70, psalms continued into the synagogue and then later into the services of the new Christian community. They may have been sung antiphonally (where one group sings a phrase and another responds) or responsorally (where a cantor sings a phrase and the full congregation responds). These psalms carried over into the early church with a sound not much different than the early liturgical chant.

Psalms are sacred to the church and are considered "divinely inspired." For this reason, the texts are rarely changed, though their musical settings have been altered into every musical style. It was Calvin, though a lover of many kinds of music, who believed that psalms were the only acceptable form of singing because they were "divinely composed" music. Even so, a form of psalms called "metrical psalmody" added humanly composed music to these psalms, much like a modern *makam*. In many psalters one tune can be used for a number of psalm texts. The description in the first case study is an example of Calvin's unison metrical psalm singing.

Hymns

On my desk is a copy of *Nyimbo za Sifa*. First published in 1964, it is one of the first printed hymnals of Western-translated hymns in Swahili for evangelicals. The bottom right-hand corner of the book has been literally thumbed through for ten years. The worn edges represent a symbolic gesture of love for the hymn. Hymnals are sacred books—almost as sacred as the Bible—used for both private devotion and public worship.

The earliest hymns in the New Testament are alluded to in Matthew 26:30 and Mark 14:26, when Christ and his disciples sang a hymn during the Last Supper. This was probably a Jewish Passover hymn. Later in Acts (16:25) we read of Paul and Silas singing hymns in prison.

A hymn is a humanly composed song. It is generally strophic (composed of verses) and in the early church focused on Christ and praise to God. The early church hymn was borrowed from Greek hymn forms. While many people today sing the hymn with harmony, this would not have been the case in early times, when worshipers would have sung in unison. Harmony as we know it in the western tradition is an outgrowth of polyphony from the tenth century in the Roman Church and the chorale tradition loved by Martin Luther in the sixteenth century.

From the beginning of the church, hymns have been used to teach and combat heresy. New hymns and songs have accompanied every development in the church as it spread throughout the world. New innovations to the hymn are a result of language, musical forms, and cultural context.

By far the greatest amount of hymnody has developed in the Western church (Europe, the United States, and Canada). This European hymnody is well documented. With the end of the Modern Missionary Period and the tremendous growth of Christianity in virtually every part of the world, hymns and hymnlike songs are an authentic expression of the faith. However, in non-Western countries, the hymn (defined here as congregational song) has taken on the character of the emerging church. This hymnody has gone through a process of development well-documented by a number of ethnomusicologists and missiologists.

Spiritual Songs

We don't really know what these New Testament spiritual songs actually were, but scholars have suggested that they may have been songs sung "in the Spirit." This singing may have been without words, like a musical glossolalia. Many charismatic churches practice what might resemble this genre today, as I illustrated in the second story above. It is possible that excesses in this style of singing is one reason Paul exhorted the church to "Sing with the spirit, and sing with the mind."

A second suggestion is that these spiritual songs are much like short choruses found in many churches around the world and popular in the "praise and worship" services of many contemporary Christian communities. However, they would have been sung in a Middle Eastern style and would not sound like many of today's choruses.

In conclusion, if we read these verses as "psalms, hymns, *or* spiritual songs," then we must limit ourselves to these genres only. If we take a very orthodox approach to music, we would, as some are doing today, return to or maintain the chant of the Orthodox Church, which is void of any music development from the past 1,500 years. If we take a noncharismatic theological position, then we sing "psalms, hymns, *and* choruses" (interpreting the spiritual song as a short chorus). Contemporary charismatics would take issue with this and freely enjoy singing "in the Spirit" through psalms, hymns, and spiritual songs.

The first option—the rule-oriented approach to singing—has a number of cross-cultural problems. First, we really do not know for sure what the early music sounded like. Because Western music notation was not used, we have no immediate extant hymn, psalm, or spiritual tune. Even if one were discovered, it is doubtful that it would be used, even by the most fundamentalist of believers, because of the difficulty in teaching music to new congregations and the unpleasurable aesthetic experience. However, recent research by Suzanne Haik-Vantoura (1991) has given interesting insights into actual tunes used with Old Testament texts. Interpreting the musical notation that accompanies the Masoretic Hebrew text these melodies have been suggested and recorded in the singing of psalms. Might our singing change?

If we take this passage in the broader context of Paul's concerns we can find a principle for the songs of the church. Paul was concerned that early Christians teach, admonish, and express joy in building up one another in a community of faith. His use of these terms denoted the types of music in use in his time. Therefore, we might conclude that all music is possible for the community, as long as it accomplishes these values. How, then, do we apply Paul's principle to build the community of faith through the use of psalms, hymns, and spiritual songs?

If we take the latter approach, then all musics are possible for the kingdom. These words, in the modern context, become biblical songs, humanly composed music, and spiritual songs. The music of the kingdom also includes more than congregational song. Within the worship context, instrumental music is used to bond segments of worship together.

A second consideration, other than the words and forms, is the difference in singing style (which we discussed in the previous chapter). The roots of Christian song go back millennia, to the culture of Israel. While there is much scholars do not know about the music of ancient Israel and early Christian worship, all would recognize the importance of music in traditional life and worship. As we noted in the chapter about music as theology, oral societies place more importance on "hearing" as opposed to "seeing" (Foley, 1996, p. 25). This emphasis gives music a special importance to our discussion.

First, music of the Jewish religious tradition is *logogenic*. Musicologist Curt Sachs coined this term based on the origin of melodies that grew from the cantillation of sacred texts. This would be in contrast to songs that are born of emotion, or pathogenic music, possibly the ecstatic utterances of the spiritual song.

Second, we cannot understand the meaning of a song unless we place it in its cultural context. In review, this includes especially the concept of the aesthetics of "beautiful" singing. In our contemporary world, so influenced by performance-based music that focuses on "quality" of vocal singing, the music of biblical times was highly functional (accompanying a cultural, social, or religious activity) and the singing has often been described as raucous (loud and noisy). In other words, the importance was not on making beautiful music, but rather, on making music for a purpose.

The sound of the singing would have been radically different than today's recorded standards of singing. Research indicates that religions of the time believed that God could be beckoned by a strong and loud voice (Elwell, 1988, p. 1501). For many Western people of the "arts," words like "beautiful" are used to describe "good" music. However, in biblical times and non-Western cultures of today, words like "sweet," "hot," or "strong" are applied to the quality of the music.

Third, while our written texts about music codify the oral tradition, in its own oral time music would have been changed and altered to suit the event.

Fourth, Edward Foley also suggests that the music of Israel and the early church reflects the architectural environment as a major influence on the music.

A Kingdom Inheritance

Historical influences change how we utilize biblical music. The primary music of the kingdom throughout the ages has been congregational song. Yet we can find many traditions, especially the Orthodox and Catholic, where there is very little congregational participation and the singing of sacred texts is the domain of the cantor or choir. The reasons for this are much different than contemporary reliance on solo music, which has its roots in the performance-oriented culture of the West. In Orthodox traditions, and the early development of the Catholic Church, sacred texts or Scripture were cared for by a vocational music clergy, much like the vocational class of temple musicians in the Old Testament. The invention of the printing press in the fifteenth century made it possible for the basically oral Scripture to then be in the hands of everyone. It was freed from the authority of the clergy. The contemporary solo tradition, on the other hand, is a development growing from the individualism and performance orientation of Western culture.

Today we have a heritage of a variety of musical genre, forms, and styles. From the Catholic and Orthodox traditions we have chants and a host of medieval and Renaissance choral styles. From the Lutherans we inherited the German chorale and the cantatas of J. S. Bach. From the Calvinists we inherited the metrical psalms. Between the seventeenth and twentieth centuries the hymn has provided a virtual inheritance of gold in theology, doctrine, and song. From the Anglicans we can appreciate not only hymns but great choral anthems. From the Wesleys we have the roots of gospel hymn, gospel anthem, and gospel choir arrangements. In the twentieth century the family has become so large it is difficult to enumerate the heritage; almost every conceivable music is a storehouse of family treasures, including solo song, Christian rock, and forms that haven't even appeared yet.

As our inheritance has a depth of history, it also has a width of ethnicity. Like a grand banquet table at a family gathering, songs of the harvest are spread before the kingdom—though not without some conflict. Since 1950, in a time sometimes called the "Emerging Church Period," songs have come from every part of the world. Some have very long and interesting histories.

Asia

Hymn singing in China goes back four thousand years, when groups would sing praise to leaders in religious ceremonies. The Yue Ji (Book of Music), part of a Book of Rites from Confucius, set a standard and theory for political, social, cultural, and spiritual formation. During the Zhou dynasty (1027–256) nobility were often required to study music. Buddhist and Taoists chanted with instruments in the Han dynasty (205–220).

The first Christian hymn appeared in China possibly as early as the eighth century, when Christianity was introduced by Nestorians in the Tang dynasty. It was not until 1807, however, that Robert Morrison of the London Missionary Society brought the first Western hymns and translated them into local languages. As early as 1861, Scottish missionary W. C. Burns published hymns in vernacular style.

C. T. Chao in 1931 later began to publish Chinese hymns, though to many the Chinese hymns sound "Western." They combine elements of style differently than the Western concept. Today long songs (hymns, both translated and Chinese) and short songs (choruses and Scripture songs) are loved by over 15 million Christians on the mainland of China, although almost 90 percent of the hymns are of Western origin (Chen, 1996, p. 5).

Theologian Chen Zemin says that "Some hymn leaders and choir conductors, especially in the city churches have a tendency to regard Chinese tunes as 'secular,' 'pagan,' or even 'vulgar' and 'not Christian enough,' therefore not suitable for worship. Even the use of Chinese instruments as accompaniment or solo is thought to not be sacred enough. . . . But in the rural areas where not all of the worshippers have cultivated this kind of 'mind-set' often show a special

267

liking for Chinese hymns . . . accompanied by the *er-hu* [er-hu (bowed spike fiddle) and pipa (zither).]" (Chen, 1995, p. 5).

Many kingdom expressions come from the Philippines, India, Myanmar, Indonesia, and other countries in the geographical area we call Asia. A Taiwanese ethnomusicologist, Ito Loh (b. 1936), has collected and edited many of these in a hymnal entitled *Sound the Bamboo* (1990), which was a trial hymnal for the Christian Conference of Asia. The styles of songs are drawn from many Asian cultures. In the hymnal he includes instructions for performance with traditional instruments, original languages, and melodies ornamented in local styles. Loh has divided these hymns into four categories: (1) Western styles like the hymn; (2) traditional styles adapting traditional melodies; (3) syncretistic styles, which use folk idioms with traditional Western harmony; and (4) international and contextual styles, which use both native and modern musical idioms (Hawn, 1996, p. 6).

Latin America

In Latin America there is a similar history of crisis or conflict regarding the Western translated hymn and "new songs" as they are often called. Primarily before 1980, the majority of hymnals published contained Western-translated hymns. However, today there appear to be several genres of new songs (Gutiérrez-Achón, 1996, p. 101).

The new songs have both cultural and linguistic roots in Hispanic cultures. In the hymn style there are some notable composers—Pablo Sosa, Cesáreo Gabaraín, Rosa Martha Zárate, and many others. The hymns often begin with an *estribillo* or chorus and are repeated at the end of each verse (Gutiérrez-Achón, 1996, p. 101). The *corito*, or short song, is also popular and is found in many rural churches. It derives from folk styles of singing. Each music has the unique character of its birthing culture, with many songs and hymns from Brazil, Peru, Chili, and the Caribbean.

The Catholic Church since Vatican II has contributed. One particular Mass, called the Nicaraguan Mass, was a source of inspiration during the civil war in the 1980s. In urban areas, one particular composer's music is heard transnationally, the praise and worship music of Marcos Witt. Marcus Witt was born to a missionary family and was reared in Mexico. A fluent Spanish speaker, he now lectures, writes music, and leads worship in all of Latin America. His worship and praise music in a contemporary Spanish style is easy for many urban dwellers to sing. His own production company, CanZion Producciones, has made his recordings widely available.

Africa

Between 1737 and 1850 many Protestant missionaries arrived on the continent, bringing Western hymnody (Warnock, 1983, p. viii). Though throughout their tenure, many missionaries condemned African music, some did not. However, by and large, until the late 1950s, the majority of music for the kingdom in Africa was of Western origin. One of the most famous African hymns was written by South African Enoch Sontonga in 1897. At the request of his school principal, where he taught music, he composed the song that would later become the National Anthem of South Africa, "Nkosi Sikelel' iAfrika." African hymns borrow the form and harmony of the Western hymn, but are infused with African melodies and rhythms, which make them quite exciting.

Much of Africa's kingdom music, however, is not found in hymnals, but in the hearts, voices, and bodies of African people who would not be bound by Western forms. As you saw in the story of Esther in the introduction, much of Africa's music was born out of necessity and, in many cases, defiance. The African Independent Church movement is almost as old as the Missionary Period. These movements created their own "spiritual songs."

Two unique problems in fostering a trans-African music has to do with the lack of a universal language and the orality of Africa's many cultures. With nearly three thousand vernacular languages, we find almost as many musical styles. Missionary musician Joyce Scott has an interesting and helpful classification system. She divides African music into three types. *Home music* (what I call songs of the harvest) is the unique songs and spiritual songs of particular ethnic groups. *Town music* is a hybrid music found in the urban areas that combines African music idioms (syncopation, instruments, voice style) with Western guitars and other instruments, and forms and harmonies of the Western gospel songs. This is used by many choirs, and today has emerged in more popular styles influenced by Western contemporary Christian music. Her third category is *Western city music*. This music is basically transplanted Western classical music, but also direct transfer of Western popular music and modern church music like praise and chorus songs (Scott, 1990, p. 7).

However, not all African kingdom music was imported from the West. As we saw, the Ethiopian Orthodox Church believed that in the sixth century A.D. a special saint by the name of Yared was taken into heaven by three birds. In heaven, he was given the liturgical music of the church, including a method of notation.

Ethiopia is in North Africa and very near the Middle East. Though I will not include here, it is important to realize that the rich music of the Middle East, which contributed so faithfully to the early church, is still alive. Though in many countries Christians do not have the same freedom to worship, music continues to play a central role in the life and worship of the area, as you saw from the story by Wafeek Wahby in the chapter on healing.

The African Diaspora

By far the most influential and prolific musical influence in the kingdom is a result of the more than 13 million Africans who were sold into slavery between the sixteenth and nineteenth centuries. "Even without extant records we know that Africans in diaspora made use of the musical gifts, which could not be chained by human bondage. They even continued with a variety of uses of music, effectively blending sacred with secular, as they bonded and created new songs in a strange and alien land" (Costen, 1993, p. 93). In the United States spirituals influenced and mingled with the blues and then emerged as gospel songs. Metered music, improvised hymns, modern and contemporary gospel all owe their heritage to a suffering but singing people. This same process would influence music in the Caribbean, Latin America, and Brazil. The greatest contribution of Africa to kingdom music around the globe may be its distinct syncopated rhythm and the spirit of praise and joy it embodies.

Native Peoples

Often marginalized by colonial and imperial powers, the native peoples of many countries have their own unique voice. Native American songs exist in many Indian nations of the United States. Also, among tribes in the Amazon, the Aborigines of Australia, the Dani of Iryan Jaya of Indonesia, and many other places, music for the kingdom is being created and sung.

A Song History

No song is totally new. Ethnomusicologist Bruno Nettl suggests that songs have a history (Nettl, 1982, p. 194). Applying his diagram technique you can see the history of Esther's spiritual harvest song (Figure 9.1). Esther's music was born outside the sanctuary. Her traditional music was ethnic African, but because of centuries of trading with Arabs, the melodies and vocal style had Arabic music characteristics in a style the local people called *kiringongo*. The dotted line represents the message within the Western translated hymn (WTH). So while she maintained her indigenous style, the gospel was contextualized by her new song. In the town music example, however, there is more of a fusion. Syncopation, call and response, and African vocal style remain. From the Western translated hymn of the nineteenth century, the gospel message, four-part harmonies, and form of the hymn contributes to the song. Later, the composer of town music may add electric guitars and Western vocal styles from popular music. The text speaks of the gospel within the contemporary African context.

271

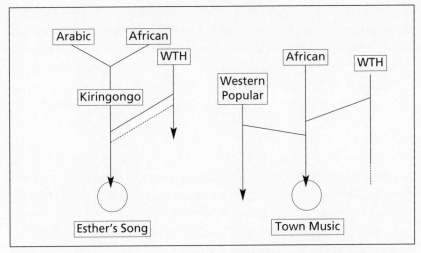

Figure 9.1. A Song History

How does all this come about? Why do some songs survive while others seem to fade or are transformed?

Musical Style Part II

While psalms, hymns, and spiritual songs refer to *genre* of music, they can be sung with different *style*. In other words, just by changing an element of style, the same genre can have a different sound. Elements of style give a piece of music its character. This is particularly noticeable across cultures, where the same song can be sung in different ways. It is important for musicians and pastors to understand elements of style, because when introducing new songs for the church, in many cases, all one has to do is to change the offensive element to have the style welcomed by a congregation.

In the 1960s what most U.S. Christians objected to in the music of Elvis Presley was not the harmony. The same harmony was found in the hymn. It was not the text, because the same texts could be found in much secular country music. They did not object to the melody, which was very similar to the gospel songs they sang in church on Sunday morning. Nor did they object to the guitar. What they objected to was his body movement, which included wild hip swinging and "making eyes" at the young girls who attended his concerts. Many, of course would also object to the performance context.

Sometimes understanding the meaning of style can be quite deceiving. A number of years ago I taught a course in ethnomusicology in Canada. It was early Sunday morning and I decided to watch television before beginning my day. One channel was televising a worship service in Chinese. The people were sitting in neat rows of pews. The organ was sweetly accompanying what sounded like a Western hymn. The table in the front of the pulpit held a nice bouquet of flowers. So I listened for a while and enjoyed what I saw and heard. Then as the credits rolled across the screen, I was shocked. This was a Buddhist service! When comparing musical styles, close attention has to be paid to many elements, especially language! (see the table below).

Music Style Comparison of a Hymn

Elements of Style	19th Century European	African
Melody	Chromatic	Pentatonic
Harmony	Expanded	I-IV-V-I
Rhythm	Even	Syncopated
Vocal Quality	Vibrato	Straight tone
Form	Strophic	Strophic with Call and Response
Movement	Stationary singing	Group Movement
Text	English	Swahili (Translated)
Instruments	Organ and Piano	Drums and Guitar
Clothing	Coat and Tie	Coat & Tie
Facial Expressions	Stoic	Expressive
Context	Sanctuary	Street Service

Sing a New Song

Where does music come from? There are as many explanations as there are cultures, and ethnomusicologists do not totally agree. Here are some interesting possibilities.

In the late nineteenth century anthropologists speculated that music's origins followed Charles Darwin's theories and was *evolutionary*. Early song was born around the campfire at night. Esther, the singer you met earlier, might have described how her ancestors grunted and chatted around the fire until conversation became song. The covered cooking pot became a drum as clapping moved from hand to leather. Maybe her male ancestors returned from hunting and began plucking the string of the bow in a melodious twang or blowing into the horn of the antelope killed in the hunt.

The problem with this theory is that it was based on an ethnocentric view. Westerners believed that their music had developed beyond the music of tribal peoples and therefore was superior to theirs partly because of technical abilities and a notation system. Many people are unaware that there are highly complex written theoretical systems of music in India, China, Indonesia, and the Middle East (Guilbault, 1991, pp. 117–39).

Many cultures have *mythical* explanations like that of the Zomi people of Myanmar, a hill tribe group of former Burma. As the story goes, there was once a woman with a single beautiful daughter. She was so beautiful that hundreds of young men sought her hand in marriage. The mother could not decide among them and so organized a contest. The one young man who could eat a whole cow would have her daughter in marriage. Try as they might, not a single suitor could eat a whole cow. Now in a distant village lived an ugly and evil ogre, who heard of the contest. Eating cows was his business, so he disguised himself as a handsome young fellow and proceeded to the home of the mother. "I can eat the cows, O fair mother." And with this he ate a cow in one gulp. The mother was filled with joy and handed over her daughter to the ogre—who then commenced to eat the beautiful daughter whole. The mother was so sad she began to sing a song of mourning. And to this day in Zomi culture mourning songs are sung at every funeral (Sum, 1995, p. 5).

Some cultures point to *political* origins. The Chinese have a legend about Ling Lun. About 2700 B.C. the emperor Hung-di sent Ling Lun into the mountains to find bamboo. Ling Lun was to cut the pipes from which fundamental musical pitches could be derived. Thus the Chinese would have proper pitches and a connection with the forces of nature.

Music could also have abstract *theoretical* origins. It was Arnold Schoenberg in the mid-twentieth century who organized the chromatic scale of Western music into what he called a dodecaphonic scale. He selected an order and then did not repeat a note in the twelve-tone series until all had been played or sung. It produced a rather cacophonous sound, and has faded from most performances save for the academic concerts of Western music historical enthusiasts. Yet, the scientific and more cognitive origins of music persist. When asked where his music comes from, one contemporary Christian composer stated, "Music is nothing more than mathematics. Notes, rhythms, and harmonies can be reduced to a mathematical language and when combined together produce music."

If you ask Esther, she would probably tell you that song is a gift of the Holy Spirit. And I don't doubt her! In reality, however, it takes all of these definitions to understand the origins of music. The Holy Spirit gives the inspiration for a new song and provides a revelation of experience, yet it communicates in the languages of humanity. As expressive culture, music reflects history and the stories it carries, our scientific and spiritual worldviews, and the emotion of our hearts and thoughts of our minds. Music elides, collides, and is constantly transformed into new styles, based on the confluence of people and their music.

Music Transitions and Innovation

Why is it that some music flourishes and other types don't? For example, the Western translated hymn still survives in some places, but by and large, the praise and worship chorus thrives in nearly every part of the kingdom. While each song's history is different, there are three basic considerations for our discussion based on the thoughts of Bruno Nettl (1982). First, hybrids and mixes of music are a result of "relative complexity" and "degree of compatibility." I'll explain using two selections from the Western tradition, Benjamin Britten's *Requiem* and the chorus, "God Is so Good."

Even at a very minimal observation, Britten's *Requiem* is seldom performed outside even the most high church concert traditions. On the other hand, "God Is So Good" is one of the first choruses translated into a local vernacular language. Why? It all boils down to complexity and compatibility. Britten's *Requiem* is very complex, with many intricate harmonies and rhythms requiring a high degree of artistic and technical sophistication. Also, its basic theoretical base is not very compatible with non-western traditions, even the most complex. On the other hand, "God Is So Good" is both simple and compatible with many music systems. This is one reason "Amazing Grace" is also very popular around the world, as opposed to more complex hymns. The pentatonic melody is easy to sing. And the text is compatible with the experience of many Christians.

A second consideration is the motivation to change. As in the Christian independence movements of Africa, Orthodox traditions, and a few elitist "artistic" congregations, some groups want to keep their own identity. They therefore are very resistant to new music or music of other cultures. At the opposite extreme, there is a complete Westernization by some ethnic churches. Somewhere in between these two extremes is the principle Nettl refers to as modernization, whereby the culture merely adapts, as needed, to the changing environment of new technologies. As the broader culture changes, its influences are felt in the church.

A third consideration is how this process takes place. In the case of many mission fields in the nineteenth century, there was a complete break with tradition. The Western hymn or liturgy supplanted and excluded any local expression. As in the case of Esther, spontaneous singing gave birth to a new tradition totally outside the existing Christian community.

Finally, we will consider in more depth a process suggested by Ito Loh (Hawn, 1996; Gutiérrez-Achón, 1996) and researched by myself and others in different cultures. This process of innovation involves *introduction, adaptation, transformation* (sometimes referred to as inculturation or contextualization), and *authentic expression*.

Music innovation, or change in music behavior, involves a constant battle between maintaining continuity while implementing change. Innovations are actually a two-way street. On the one hand, when missionaries introduce the gospel cross-culturally to other cultures they transplant the gospel *to the street* in the form of the hymn, among other cultural artifacts. On the other side, Christian musical innovators try to introduce elements *from the street* into the cultus of the local church.

First, music makes its way into the church both cross-culturally and intraculturally. Songs and *musical innovations* enter the kingdom community through community members. In the cross-cultural context music is *transplanted* and translated to find reasonable fit to the host culture. These translations and transplantations are generally foreign and require substantial teaching as we have seen from the Western hymn. One should not assume that the transplanting of musical elements died with the early missionaries. Each time a church mission group travels to another country, it becomes a carrier of living musical microbes. Some become life-giving, while others become viruses.

Second, once introduced, these musical innovations are *alterated,* depending on the direction of the innovation. When introduced cross-culturally the local community alters the style to fit its own unique musical culture. They may alter the scale, change the harmony, or sing in a different, more appropriate style. When introduced in the local congregation, adjustments or changes are made to clean out elements the local community finds unacceptable to the local church context. This alteration follows a biblical process Hustad calls sanctification, where music is "set apart and brought to the cross of Jesus." Musical elements considered impure, secular, or with evil associations are altered or eliminated.

As music becomes sanctified to the church local community, or accepted in the foreign environment, the existing style begins to be *transformed* to the cultural standards of the community. New styles are transformed to the likeness of Christ within the context of the local community. Often these innovations are mere mimicry of the original introduction, but new and authentic expressions begin to develop.

277

Finally, an *authentic* music expression develops in the form of truly "new songs." An authentic music means that the community can call the music its own. Authentic song comes from within the culture.

There are a number of special problems in cross-cultural music sharing. First, the issue of ownership, especially internationally, is a concern. Until recently, there was little regard for the music of peoples outside the Western capitalist system, which prizes ownership and pays royalties. As an example, several years ago I was preparing an African hymnal. I was going to use a chorus that originated in Africa, but had first been copyrighted in the United States. My publisher insisted that we secure permission before using the song. This still seems wrong to me—that one culture could actually own the music of another and then demand payment from the originator. On the other hand, we find that in many parts of the world, people are too poor, do not have the printing resources, or do not value private ownership, and will copy a single piece of music many times. This "redistribution of wealth" may not be the total answer either. A second problem I have already addressed is that, while many church congregations struggle to find their own authentic voice, others fail to extend their musical repertoire.

Critical Contextualization

Music will find its way into every space, whether the sanctuary of the church or the interior of an automobile. Deciding which music is appropriate takes time, thought, prayer, and biblical standards. We can choose to reject, uncritically use, or modify music for service in the kingdom. We now look first, at a model for decision making, and then conclude with four principles. In the following story from a popular film, we see how music finds its way into a convent and how the sisters responded.

Several years ago, Whoopie Goldberg made a movie called *Sister Act*. In this movie a nightclub singer witnesses her lover commit a murder. Her lover is married to another woman and is involved in the underworld of crime. The singer goes to the police to give evidence and seek vengeance on her married "boyfriend." In order to protect her, the police decide to hide her in a convent, where she is to pose as a nun. The convent is in a run-down and dilapidated neighborhood. Afraid of the streets, the nuns have cloistered themselves behind locked gates and seldom go outside the convent.

It is a tough adjustment for the nightclub singer. She has difficulty following the rules, making it to hourly prayers, eating in silence, and, above all, suffering through the poorly disciplined choir rehearsals. The nuns love to sing; they just don't sing well, so the nightclub singer is persuaded to lead the choir. Under the watchful and skeptical eye of the mother superior, the nightclub singer begins to teach the sisters' choir some of the beats from her own experience. She does more than teach songs. At night she takes the sisters out for a time of dancing in a local bar. Reprimanded, but undaunted, the nightclub singer continues to lead the choir and they begin to sing in Mass. Awakened to a new standard of musical performance and a vision for their ministry, the sisters are now on the streets helping the neighbors and cleaning the outside of the church. The once empty Mass is now crowded with young people who come to hear the music. In the end, the nuns come to the nightclub singer's aid and help catch her former boyfriend. The music of the street challenges the church to make the gospel relevant—not a lofty and fearful religion, but one of incarnation, being with the world in sorrows and problems.

To many, Christian musicians are not trusted if they have come from the "worldly" music scene because it may contaminate the church. And vice versa: Christians who sing secular music have backslidden in the faith.

In the case of *Sister Act*, though fictional, the intentions and results of the nightclub sister were good and right, and the gospel music the sisters sang fit the context. This openly sinful outsider challenged an equally socially sinful congregation to set a new Christian standard. In a movie the artist can play with reality. In many cases, disaster can strike because of the uncritical acceptance of music and all that is associated with it.

Recently, a young music scholar, Mike, was invited to lead a group of musicians in Haiti. The song he selected was from Africa and required the use of drums. His concern, and a legitimate one, was that in teaching a song traditional drums were an important part of the music. However, in Haiti, racine beats and large drums are used in voodoo worship. To many Haitian Christians, these beats and drums are too closely associated with former pagan religious practices to be used in worship. Intuitively, Mike used a process proposed by Paul Hiebert, and adapted here: *critical contextualization* (Hiebert, 1985, p. 188).

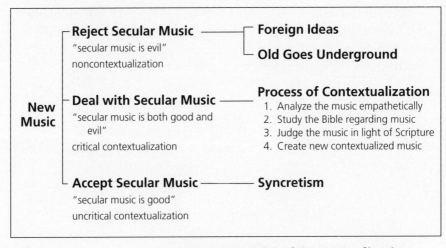

Figure 9.1. Critical Contextualization

It is natural that churches should be cautious about the introduction of new music and vocal styles. As we have seen, every verbal and nonverbal code carries meaning. So how do we decide if it is appropriate for Christian purposes? As you can see in Figure 9.1, we must begin first with the "old music" or secular music style. We must uncover its meaning in the old context before we can effectively introduce it into the new, or Christian, context. There are three approaches.

First, we can reject all new music as basically evil. The result of this approach is that we alienate people because of their music, or they enter into the fellowship but take their music underground, which can create problems later.

A second and equally dangerous approach is to accept all music as good. We uncritically accept this music and the result is a term missiologists call syncretism. Hiebert suggests that we "deal with the new" through critical contextualization. In this third approach, we view music as potentially both good and evil. We analyze the music and discern its meaning within its cultural context. This cannot be done as an outsider, alone. It is difficult for those of us without the knowledge of a people and their culture to know emic or insider meanings. This is best done in dialogue with those who produce the music. An empathetic dialogue treats the musician with respect and seeks to understand from his or her point of view. We ask questions by withholding judgment until an understanding of the meaning is attained. People who sing and perform their music understand the motivations, the context, and the results of their music. Returning to Mike, he did this by discussing the nature of drums and beats with local musicians. He found that only large drums and certain beats seemed to call up the spirits. In other types of music, smaller drums and different rhythms were perfectly acceptable.

A next step is to search Scripture for principles regarding music. This may be the more difficult task because the Christian world is already divided on the place of instruments in the church. Yet, using the psalms, we do find significant evidence that instruments were used in worship. There is no evidence on how the music sounded. Taking this information, Mike discussed with the local people how their music should be judged in light of biblical principles. They were convinced that these nonracine beats and small drums were not in conflict with biblical principles.

The process of contextualization is generally not so methodical or academic. Yet the introduction of new music and singing styles can be conflict-free if a congregation intentionally evaluates the music it is using. Here are some suggestions.

Introducing and Teaching New Songs

It was Solomon who said, "there is nothing new under the sun" (Eccles. 1:9b). Indeed, dramatic innovations in music only occur every few centuries. However, today change cannot be avoided and may be the only constant for the kingdom community. Young people thrive on change and innovation. It is natural that they want the "latest" music and desire to praise God with the music of their street. For adults this can be a frightening experience—so much so, that the first reaction is to prohibit new music and worship styles. So I offer several considerations.

Ride Slow. The introduction of change does not have to be a painful experience. One young calypso drummer described it as "ride slow" meaning to go slowly with innovations. Most mature young people and adults intuitively recognize the process described above. They have learned to evaluate new music and traditions based on the associational elements of the music. To ride slow implies that one takes the time to allow people to adjust and accept the change willingly. C. S. Lewis expressed the feeling of many people who are faced with rapid change by quoting a friend, "I wish they'd remember that the charge to Peter was Feed my sheep; not Try experiments on my rats, or even Teach my performing dogs new tricks" (Lewis, 1984, p. 81).

An effective example comes from the Baptist Church in Yangoon, Myanmar (Burma). For over a hundred years the church has maintained a "high church" Baptist worship with a large choir and congregational singing of hymns. The respectful youth wanted to express themselves through newer contemporary Christian music and praise choruses. After a consultation involving the pastor, church elders, and youth leadership, they decided to hold a youth "talent" afternoon. During this time the young people could enjoy their guitars and other entertainment without offending the congregation.

Lead change. Reaction to change from a congregation who is not interested can be a painful experience. In a word of wisdom regarding worship styles, Marcus Witt comments, "Worship leaders who badger the congregation, trying to make them praise the Lord, miss the point" (Witt, 1998). One cannot force change but must encourage, guide, lead and love in the process. Not all change is good, but how change takes place is as important, or more so, than the change itself. Using congregational committees, consultants, and performers is a good place to start. Planning is a needed element. Once changes have been decided, planning for effective presentation is key. Many times change offends because of one or two stylistic elements. By removing the offensive elements of new music, people can accept the style.

Cooperate and Partner. In the cross-cultural context, missionaries erred when they played a parent role and decided what was best for the local congregation. The situation has not changed. And this does not apply only to Western missionaries. In the "being-with" concept I mentioned in the chapter on healing, the effective change agent is one who is with the local culture, as an example of the mind of Christ.

Do It Well the First Time. When a change is introduced it is generally accepted if it is introduced properly and performed to the highest standards. In my years of experience, the best changes happen when I: (1) involved the congregation and church leadership in the change; (2) announced the change to the congregation, ahead of time; (3) used the resources of the congregation (as the choir, soloists, or other musicians); (4) prepared the best presentation possible; (5) planned the change within an existing structure (worship form) with many familiar elements; and (6) performed the music as a ministry to the congregation and not a show of difference for difference sake.

Introducing New Songs

C. Michael Hawn offers several guidelines for teaching cross-cultural songs in the West. In summary, the basic principles apply in many contexts.

1. Texts

- In addition to the original language of the text, provide a translation so that singers can know the meaning of the song they are singing.
- Provide a pronunciation guide for both the singers and the congregation.

2. Melody

- Try to preserve the original quality of the melody. This can be difficult when singing music from Asia and Africa, but is well worth the effort.

- If the song is originally sung in unison, or without accompaniment, ask the organist to assist with playing the melody, without embellished accompaniment.

3. *Harmony and use of instruments*

- If harmony sounds unusual to local ears, teach this to the choir or music group, before trying it with the congregation.
- Add appropriate instruments using authentic rhythms. For a guitar, try to utilize the original style. For drums and percussion instruments, locate a similar substitute.

4. *Style and movement*

- A recording or videotape is a good way to hear and see music. Most Westerners are concerned about precision and will mimic exactly what they experience. In most non-Western cultures, precision is not as important as the experience, so there is freedom to enjoy the piece of music without emphasis on its "performance standard."
- For many songs, especially from Africa and Latin America, movement is an important part of the musical style. If a congregation is shy about clapping hands and moving to the music, the choir can be an excellent model. Have the choir sing the song through first and through their singing welcome the congregation into participation. Because of the "action potential" of this music, even the most formal congregations will soon join in.

5. *Source and cultural context*

- When introducing the song to the church congregation, give a brief historical and cultural background.
- Since all countries do not share the same standards of ownership, respect the copyright restrictions, and give credit to the composer or community source.

Composing New Songs

One of the tragedies of the late twentieth century and the introduction of technology has been the loss of music making in the community setting. Music making has all but been relegated to a professional class of musical stars delivering music on demand through
an electronic synthesizer, music video, or personal computer. While
many congregations are preparing musical productions on Sunday
mornings, believers are passing the time without a creative outlet.

Fortunately, in many parts of the world, young musicians and
communities still make their own music and want to use their creative gifts for the kingdom. New song workshops are used by a growing number of ethnomusicologists and composers with local musicians to encourage the writing of music for the church. They provide
an excellent resource in both research of local music systems and
can serve as catalysts for music-making. This is not intended as a
substitute for advanced composition or study in music. It does provide an excellent avenue for congregations who have not found an
authentic voice for praise.

Anyone can create a song, though not all songs will find their way
into the congregation or music setting. The process may be as important as the product because music making teaches respect for the
gift of word and music, and gives further practical experience in the
critical thinking skills needed in evaluating song.

New Songs—The Basics

Acceptable songs have three basic characteristics. First, they are
singable. If you were to think of the many songs you enjoy listening
to, you can probably at least hum the melody. Second, appropriate
music is *danceable*. That does not mean that it is used for dancing
(although some congregations enjoy liturgical dance) but that it has
enough rhythm to catch the attention, movement, and structure a
congregation needs to sing together. For example, in the example
of the psalm singing in the case study, while the congregation
seemed to perform it well, it did not keep the attention of my young
friend. Third, appropriate music should have a *meaningful message*

in terms of the language and metaphors that speak to the local congregation. The text should also have a basis in Scripture (Scott, Mbuvi, 1984).

Basic Principles for New Songs

Research the existing forms of music. As we have seen, different cultures have indigenous forms, styles, and methods of composition. Research these ahead of time, preferably with the local people.

Group Writing. Particularly in collective societies, group writing is an excellent process. Instead of a single composer struggling with inspiration and technique, people in groups help each other through the process. An additional benefit is that you have a ready group of musicians to test the song out.

Lead by Example. In my workshops I generally start with a brief introduction, explaining where music comes from using the logogenic and pathogenic models. Often the students will have examples of their own moments of inspiration, whether in spontaneous song or in a dream. I follow with a brief explanation of the elements style, where we have the class analyze songs that they bring to the group. Finally, we compose a simple song together, to see how the process works.

Warming Up the Writing. Many groups are frightened by the thought of writing a completely new song; others are eager. Start by having the group alter an existing and familiar simple composition (like a hymn). They can do this in a number of ways. They can alter the text by writing new words for a specific audience. They can write a new tune, and in a different style, using the old text. Or, they can arrange the song by adding instruments and extending the form with introductions and endings.

Move to Scripture Songs

Scripture songs can be fun to set to music, particularly if they are set in chorus style. Encourage the group to use repetition through cyclical form. Select a passage that is short and without difficult words. The psalms are a good place to start.

Advance to Free Composition. In the next stage we ask the group to compose both text and music in any style they like. These compositions are often very interesting and exciting. At the conclusion of the time of writing, each group should perform the song in front of the main group. The response gives an indication of the "goodness" of the song in the ears and eyes of the local culture.

Share the Music. In the new song workshop the intent is not to make new songs, but to make new songs for a purpose. Generally, the group selects the better songs to share with their local congregations. At the end of a specified time, have the group meet together again and rewrite and revise the songs. If nothing else—and this is just as important—the process of writing encourages creativity and authenticity among God's people.

I'll close this chapter with a story that touched me deeply and that illustrates the importance of sharing our musical heritage wherever the kingdom congregation gathers.

Betty Ann Brigham, Dean of Students at Eastern College, loves singing hymns. She credits her grandfather with instilling this love in her. Growing up in the farming country of Maine, she made regular visits to his house. She vividly recalls his constant singing around the farmyard while feeding the chickens, pigs, and other livestock. "There was not a time when he was not singing, and he knew so many hymns from memory."

One cold winter she visited his farm at Christmas. It was a snowy evening and the bitter cold reached every corner and crack of the house. "I stayed in a room above the furnace. If you've ever been to Maine in the winter you know that it is the only warm place. The heat doesn't quite make it to the rest of the house."

One night, it was unusually cold, so she pulled the blankets from the bed and moved right over the heating vent above the furnace. As she peered down the vent hole, she couldn't see her grandfather, but she could hear him take the shovel and begin shoveling coal into the furnace. He began to sing hymn after hymn. Warmed by his voice and the heat of fresh coal, she fell asleep. To this day she credits his singing example as the foundation for her love of singing hymns of the faith.

Summary

In this chapter we have used the metaphor of an inheritance as a model for understanding and appreciating the vast amount of songs in the present kingdom. We have taken the view that Paul's admonition to the church to sing psalms, hymns, and spiritual songs is a principle for the believer to sing with a purpose, uplifting and building the community of God. The inheritance of kingdom music stretches back into the Old Testament and points to the future in Revelation. In between, we have inherited different musics from the historical church, and inherit today the music of a broad kingdom that includes every race and ethnicity.

We have seen that change is inevitable, but that change does not occur the same in different groups. We can chart this stylistic change through song histories where music is sent from the sanctuary to the street, but musical elements of the street also enter the sanctuary. God's people are given freedom to sing a "new song" as a result of the dynamic blessing in their relationship to Christ. Learning and writing new songs is a way of expressing a renewed and right relationship with God.

Questions for Discussion

1. How has your church traditionally interpreted the passages from Ephesians and Colossians quoted at the beginning of the chapter? Do you agree with their position? Why or why not?
2. Based on your experience, explanation in this chapter, and understanding of Scripture, how would you define a spiritual song?
3. How would you describe your own musical heritage?
4. Does your congregation enjoy the music of other cultures? Why or why not?
5. How do your family, church, and friends respond to new musical innovations?

6. Have you ever composed a song? Was it for personal use or did you share it with others?

7. Have you been a change agent or musical innovator in a setting where your music was either received well, or not received kindly? Explain.

Exercises

1. Many musicians are not aware of the great heritage of songs and hymns they sing every week. For several Sundays (in the sanctuary context), select several favorite CDs or audio and video cassettes, and categorize the music you hear under different stylistic categories. Then, design a music family tree that helps you discover your own music heritage.

2. Hymnologists (those who study hymns) will often compare the number of ethnic hymns in the hymnal to get a picture of how globally aware they are of other world Christians. Take your own church hymnal or songbook (if you have one) and compare it with others from different denominations.

3. This project works well as a class. Over several weeks attend different churches, recording the titles and styles of songs in the church. Then compare.

4. Discuss this statement: Many congregations have hymnals with hundreds of songs, but they insist on singing the favorites.

5. In this chapter we said that every song has a history. There are two histories. The first is a stylistic history that involves musical style. The second history is one of personal testimony regarding its origins. Select a favorite song or hymn. See if you can chart the stylistic history as I have done in the example. Then, using hymn companions, which often have hymn stories, or if you like contemporary Christian music, e-mail the group and ask how the song came about.

6. Select a familiar song, chorus, or hymn. Divide the class into groups and ask each group to modify the basic song into a different style by changing several of the stylistic characteristics suggested in the chapter.

7. Have a writing competition or workshop with the class. Select one verse from the psalms and see how many songs you can compose using the same verse. Select the best one, and introduce it to your chapel or church congregation. Discuss the response.

10

Instruments

Praise the LORD.
Praise God in his sanctuary;
   praise him in his mighty heavens.
Praise him for his acts of power;
   praise him for his surpassing greatness.
Praise him with the sounding of the trumpet,
   praise him with the harp and lyre,
praise him with tambourine and dancing,
   praise him with the strings and flute,
praise him with the clash of cymbals,
   praise him with resounding cymbals.
Let everything that has breath praise the LORD.
Praise the LORD.

(Ps. 150)

In the previous chapter, we talked about a historic kingdom song inheritance. With instruments, the heritage is just as old, the controversies even more fiery. The early church banned instruments because of evil and pagan associations. John Calvin so opposed organs in worship, he burned them. Paternalistic missionaries followed suit, in the Modern Missionary Period, by banning drums and other indigenous instruments. Yet things have changed. Drums are now found in the churches that once condemned them. Gongs and bells, trumpets and trombones, violins and cellos, flutes and oboes ring in many church sanctuaries. Church orchestras, praise bands, gamelan consorts, mbira choirs, and Christian mariachi herald the sound of the harvest.

Musical instruments, like tools, are extensions of the human body. Just as a hammer extends the fist, a drum extends the rhythm of the hands, the trumpet projects the buzz of the lips, and the keyboard manifests the multiple dexterity of fingers. Unlike the voice, however, which is sometimes called an "instrument," crafted musical instruments are once removed from the soul and servant to the body, and therein lies the beginnings of conflict for the Christian community. As musical technology, they can take on a life of their own, overpowering the instrument of the voice. How can they be used in a kingdom that is so centered on the Word?

In this chapter we want to focus on practical considerations of instruments in the church. First, we will discuss the field of organology, or the study of musical instruments. We will then take a brief look at the history of instruments in the Bible and their development in the church context. Finally, we will discuss practical suggestions for use in kingdom ministries.

The Sound of the Harvest . . .

His mother was a devout Methodist. He spent most of his early years attending Sunday school and worship, singing hymns of the Wesleys accompanied by a piano. Like most of his generation, however, Louis loved the sound of the guitar. The gentle strum of folk music transported him to calm, the virtuoso plucking inspired him, and the crashing strokes of new rock 'n' roll expressed his youthful angst. When he approached his mother for lessons she refused with the proverb of the times: "The guitar is the Devil's Ribs. It can only lead to a sinful life."

Undaunted and gently defiant, Louis found a neighbor who owned a guitar and after school began to teach himself. He could not see how something so beautiful could be the embodiment of Satan. It was not long before he showed brilliance and his "secret" virtuosity would become public. He was invited to play in local bands and then made his way to the recording studio.

Like many of his generation, he eventually carried the guitar to church. "God worked through me and my playing. I saw nothing wrong with the music, if the message was good. That was the problem with the church. They focused on the sound, but couldn't hear the message."

...And the Beat of the Street

The old organist was a bit eccentric. Now well into his seventies, he used a golf club for a walking cane and each Sunday made the slow climb to the organ, which was on a raised platform near the pulpit of the church. The church congregation, not wanting the faithful man to lose face, patiently waited for him to climb the steps before each hymn. His hearing and sight loss now prevented accurate worship attention. Occasionally the pastor would yell out instructions from the pulpit, "That's hymn #36, Mr. Wan, *not* #63!" The congregation just kept singing.

This Chinese church rested quietly on the edge of Chinatown until an earthquake rocked it into a crossroads in ministry. After the earthquake, the church had to decide whether to spend $500,000 repairing the building or move to an outlying community where most of the members now lived. There was little parking space at the present church, the younger people were interested in reaching people outside the traditional community, and "Mr. Wan" seemed to be a symbol of a passing worship tradition.

Synthesizer, drums, and guitars were becoming the instruments of the youth church. The church was now faced with two problems: Do we move the church, and what do we do with Mr. Wan?

After many meetings the older members decided to stay where they were. They liked the tradition of the past and the proximity to their cultural roots. The young people decided to plant a church in a new neighborhood, without an organ. However, Mr. Wan was still the present organist. So in a face-saving gesture, the leaders approached him about "training" a new organist. He graciously agreed and gradually a new organist—sixty years old—began to fill in on a more regular basis. One Sunday, Mr. Wan climbed the steps with his golf club, played the three hymns, walked to the traditional lunch in Chinatown with his lifelong friends, and then died following the meal. The youth remembered Mr. Wan, fondly, and the organ he so loved found a place in the new church, in electronic form. Things change.

The Nature of Musical Instruments

When you pick up an instrument, what do you see? What do you call it? What is it made of? Where did it come from? How is it used? These are the first questions an *organologist* asks. An organologist is a person who studies musical instruments. The study of musical instruments is called organology, a term that comes from the Greek term *organon,* meaning a tool or instrument used in some activity or trade. Organologists have several interests. In addition to the basic questions we asked, they also study the historical, social, and cultural significance of the instruments, and the maker and performers of instruments in order to understand the social status the instrument carries. Some study the artwork on the instrument. For example, on the wall of my office is a slit drum (a wooden block of wood hollowed out with a slit on top to produce sound). The ends of the drum have been carved into images of human heads. Just what makes an instrument?

First of all, like the term "music," a musical instrument is defined by culture. Our first categories place music-making tools into two categories: musical instruments and non-musical instruments. Musical instruments are tools brought to musical life. You probably wouldn't consider a handsaw a musical instrument because it is an implement of work for cutting lumber. However, the function often dictates the category, as I can explain using a personal story.

When I was ten I vividly remember my high school band director visiting our church and performing the offertory selection on a handsaw played with a violin bow. He played "Amazing Grace." The handsaw is an oddity or "specialty" instrument—it worked but you wouldn't find it in a church on a regular basis because our culture has not accepted or "ordained" it as a real instrument.

294

In northern Nigeria a group of Christian women organized a pot ensemble to accompany their singing. They used pads to hit the lips of various water pots, creating a lively thumping rhythm. Unlike the handsaw, the pot band was considered more than a musical oddity by the local community.

The body itself can be an instrument. Isaiah (55:12) refers to the trees clapping. While clapping is not a universal expression in all cultures, it is found in many. And the body itself, in dancing, becomes an instrument with a number of biblical references. The most frequently quoted is of David dancing before the Lord when the ark of the covenant was brought to Jerusalem. "David, wearing a linen ephod, danced before the LORD with all his might, while he and the entire house of Israel brought up the ark of the LORD with shouts and the sounds of trumpets" (2 Sam. 6:14). Jesus even quoted a children's song using dance as a metaphor for people's lack of response to his message: "We played the flute for you and you did not dance" (Matt. 11:17).

Another example of the body as instrument comes from deaf culture. In a paper entitled "Development of Deaf Choirs," Vesta D. Bice (1981, p. 1) encourages the deaf to sing (by signing) in choirs through the "art of copying" and "making music visual." Both as visual and physical communication, the body becomes an instrument. "The deaf person is the instrument in which music and the message of the songs must flow" (Bice, 1981).

Sometimes called a dance or movement ministry, many Christian artists draw on the experience of Miriam and her handmaidens who danced before the Lord after the Israelites crossed the Red Sea (Bane, 1991). Movement (dance) is a time of celebration and response to God in worship. As nonverbal forms of communication, bodies "are instruments that are essentially neutral, but they may be used to tell lies or truth, to build up or destroy" (Bane, 1991, p. 44).

Second, any description or classification of instruments must consider the cultural context. For example, the meaning of "guitar" changes both in how it is identified and played, based on the context. It may be called an "axe" in a jazz nightclub, a "box-guitar" on my uncle's front porch, or a "classical guitar" in the concert hall. There may also be modifications to the instrument based on the cultural and acoustical context. Some guitars are amplified. Amplification works very well in large meeting halls; however, in a small room amplification is not necessary.

Third, playing or performance style is equally important. Some church members will applaud a classical guitarist playing a Bach prelude, but be offended by the suggestion that the guitar be amplified to accompany the singing. Technique, or how well the instrument is played, is also important. We appreciate a guitarist who has great command of the instrument more than the musician who can only strum a few chords.

Finally, there is also a social hierarchy of instruments. Many instruments are valued more highly than others, depending on the craftsmanship and materials used to make them, as well as the type of sound desired. A saw is not a violin; it can be purchased in a hardware store. An actual violin may cost hundreds and thousands of dollars. In Thailand, bronze gongs used in meditation are sold by weight. Their sound is not produced for the same musical aesthetic as one might expect in the concert hall. Yet some orchestras will pay great amounts of money for a gong because of the sound it produces.

Classification

Musical classification is based on the production of sound or the material of the instrument. There is not a universal classification of instruments, though organologists apply a basic classification system that I will describe below. Many of the classifications of world instruments are done from an "outsider's" (etic) perspective. To fully understand the instrument one should seek an "insider's" (emic) perspective. In other words, how do local cultures classify their instruments, how do they learn to play them, and which ones do they consider important?

One classification of instruments refers to the materials from which the instrument is made: brass, woodwind, string. More detailed classification systems by musicologists give a general category with scores of subcategories developed first by Hornbostel and Sachs in 1914:

- aerophone: those instruments produced by a stream of air (e.g., trumpets)
- chordophones: instruments in which one or more strings are stretched between fixed points (e.g., violin)
- idiophones: the instrument itself makes the sound when rattled, shaken, rubbed, or struck (e.g., maracas)
- membranophones: sound is produced by a tightly stretched membrane (e.g., drum) (Dournon, 1992)

From the eighth century B.C., the Chinese categorized instruments based on materials that produced sound or contained air: silk, skin, metal, wood, stone, clay, bamboo, and gourd (Dournon, 1992). In India, music was (and is) considered a dramatic art. Their ancient classification system inspired that of the West. They include *tata* (stretched); *susira* (tubular); *avanaddha* (covered); and *ghana* (solid). These terms help us classify and name instruments, but there is deeper cultural meaning to their use.

What social significance do instruments have? Musical instruments are powerful cultural symbols. One cannot think of Africans without the drum, the Scottish without the bagpipes, the Spanish without the guitar, Indonesians without the gamelan, or Southeast Asians without a gong. As icons, our cultural identity is embedded with associations that become sacred to our existence and intensified in the sanctuary.

Musical instruments are powerful ecclesial symbols. We may associate the organ with the Catholics and Anglicans, the tambourine with Pentecostals, and no instruments with the Reformists. We expect to find guitars and drums in a contemporary church and a pipe organ in a traditional church. As religious symbols we may associate the gong and woodblock with Buddhists, or a big drum with voodoo worship.

Musical instruments are also signs and symbols of wealth. There is usually a grand piano in a wealthy urban church, a well-worn piano in an old country church, or the four-string guitar (missing two strings) in the church of the poor. Not only are they symbols, but they reflect a realistic maintenance cost that prohibits the crossover from one class to another.

Musical instruments are also symbols of power. In the past, the Kabaka kings of Uganda would commission drums for new chiefs. The drum became a symbol of power represented in this famous proverb, "The drum beats for the office not the man." Sometimes our use and abuse of instruments have more to do with control than with theology. Early Western missionaries forbade the use of drums in many African churches, and traditional instruments in most other areas of the world. While there may have been some legitimate reasons, and long before the days of contextual theology, local Christians were denied the opportunity for self-discipline under the guidance of the Spirit. In some ways, a change in instruments is a power struggle. Young people want their voice heard, and this is one attraction of modern electronic instruments. There is real power in the ability to overpower a context through sound. Likewise, older established people want to maintain tradition. To change instruments signals a change in theology, or status, but always identity. What guidance does the Bible give?

Biblical Musical Instruments

The Bible speaks much more about singing than instruments. The Bible does include instruments as part of worship and life in biblical cultures although it does not give instructions for their use. As tools, they could be used for glory or for bane, depending on the heart and activity of the person playing them.

There are sixteen instruments mentioned in the Bible. As with cultures today, where instruments are borrowed from and influenced by neighboring cultures, the same would have been the case in ancient Israel. The most frequently mentioned instruments are the following:

String
- *Kathros:* This lyre was used at Nebuchadnezzar's court (Dan. 3:5, 7, 10, 15).
- *Kinnor:* David's lyre (referred to as harp) was a favorite instrument and is mentioned forty-two times in the Bible.

- *Nebel:* This harp is called a psaltery in some translations.

Wind

- *Halil:* This piped instrument was similar to the Greek aulos. It had a shrill sound. Its tone was associated with celebrations as well as mourning (1 Sam. 10:5; Jer. 48:36).

- *Hatzotzrot:* This silver or gold trumpet was about a meter long and had a small bell. This instrument became exclusive to the temple musicians (Num. 10:2).

- *Shophar* (shofar): This instrument is mentioned seventy-two times—more than any other instrument. It is made of a ram's horn. It is still used today in Jewish worship.

- *Ugab:* This is a flutelike instrument (Gen. 4:21; Ps. 150).

Percussion

- *Mena anim:* This loud metal rattle may be like the sistrum found in Egypt and used in the Ethiopian Orthodox church today.

- *Panonim:* These signal bells were attached to the hem of the high priest's garment, both signifying his status and signaling his entry into the sanctuary (Exod. 28:33–34).

- *Toph* (tof): This was a hand drum used primarily by women (Exod. 15:20).

- *Zelzelim:* These were cymbals made of metal (Ps. 150).

Where did all these instruments come from? What was their function? It is doubtful that Adam and Eve played flutes and lyres. It was not until humankind walked the road of development that we first hear of instruments in the Bible because instruments are, as we said earlier, tools. The Hebrew word *kelim* is often used in reference to instruments in the same way as useful things like a kitchen pot. Instruments, in Scripture, were functional tools to be used in worship and the daily activities of life.

The first mention of an instrument occurs in Genesis 4. Biblical accounts suggest the development of two societies from Cain's descendants, Jabal and Jubal, and Tubal-Cain. We can only imagine the instrument development at this point in history. Jabal was the father of tents and livestock, nomadic pastoralists. Jubal, his brother, was the father of the lyre and flute. Useful instruments, flutes and small harps are portable and provide a peaceful and creative way to pass the time while shepherds watch herds graze the countryside. Flutes and small harps are made directly from natural resources. Bamboo easily becomes a flute and branches, animal skins, and sinew are crafted into a lyre.

Tubal-Cain was the father of bronze and metal forging, an activity common to settled communities. Metal forging is a technology from which brass and metal instruments are made. Considerable more effort and craftsmanship are required to make these instruments than a small shepherd's flute. As people leave a more nomadic life to settle into urban areas, instruments gain in sophistication. Instruments are also developed for different cultural functions. The best indication of instrument development in Scripture comes from the use and function within a developing nation. There are a number of functions for instruments in the Old Testament: emotional expression, symbolic representation of power and authority, assembly and war, prophecy and healing, and priestly accompaniment.

Emotional Expression

Did the families of Noah, the city dwellers of Babel and Sodom and Gomorrah, and the nomadic Abraham make music? While surely they did, the Bible does not mention music again until the time of Jacob. For fourteen years Jacob worked for Laban as a "bride-price" for Leah and Rachel. In an attempt to distance himself from Laban after twenty years of indentured service, Jacob gathered his family and flocks and fled. Secretly, Rachel stole the household gods of her father. Three days later Laban heard that Jacob had fled. For seven days Laban the Aramean chased Jacob. And then God visited him in a dream: "Be careful not to say anything to Jacob, either good or bad." So when he caught up to Jacob, Laban said, "Why did you run off secretly and deceive me? Why didn't you tell me, so I could send you away with joy and singing to the music of tambourines and harps?" (Gen. 31:11–27). Music was part of the social structure of

ancient peoples, just as it is today. In this story we find three interesting concepts.

First, the tambourine, a percussive instrument, no doubt was used
for celebrations that included dancing. We find this tradition of tambourines and dancing later in Exodus, when Miriam the prophetess,
Aaron's sister, "took a tambourine in her hand, and all the women
followed her, with tambourines and dancing. Miriam sang to them:
'Sing to the LORD, for he is highly exalted. The horse and its rider he
has hurled into the sea'" (Exod. 15:20–21). Instruments expressed joy
and accompanied dancing. They were also part of a cultural ritual.

Second, greeting and leaving music would have been a way to
show hospitality and express emotion in a functional way. Even
today, some congregations sing a "welcome" song or hymn while
they shake hands and greet one another. Some even greet the pastor to the pulpit with welcome songs. In many worship settings the
benediction is a leaving song. The postlude, or music following the
service accompanies the congregation as they leave the worship
service.

Third, this passage also indicates gender specificity. As we noted
above, contemporary Christian movement ministries draw on this
passage as a biblical precedent for dancing to the Lord. In much of
the Middle East, even today, men and women dance separately. Cou-
ples dancing, as is often found in the West, is not an acceptable standard of social behavior. There is also another distinction which dif-
ferentiates this culture from the modern context. The tambourine,
or hand drum, was played by women. While it is possible that men
played the instrument, in many cultures, certain instruments are
gender-specific. Until recently, for example, the African drum and
mbira (sometimes misnomered a finger piano) were the exclusive
instruments of men.

Power and Authority

If the tambourine was the instrument of joy, it was the trumpet
that symbolized the holy and the authority of God. At Mount Sinai,
God gave directions to Moses: "Only when the ram's horn sounds a

long blast may they go up the mountain." Then, "On the morning of the third day there was thunder and lightening, with a thick cloud over the mountain, and a very loud trumpet blast. . . . The smoke billowed up from it like smoke from a furnace, the whole mountain trembled violently, and the sound of the trumpet grew louder and louder. Then Moses spoke and the voice of God answered him" (Exod. 19).

Symbols are like magnets that attract associations. There is no stronger magnet than the voice of God and a trumpet. Throughout Scripture the trumpet is fused with power and authority. In Revelation, seven angels with seven trumpets unleash the destructive power of God in the day of judgment (Rev. 8). In the same eschatological symbol, the trumpet sound of the Lord will raise the dead (1 Cor. 15:2; 1 Thess. 4:16).

Assembly and War

The blast of a ram's horn or trumpet is a raucous and sometimes frightening sound. The ram's horn, like the conch shell and various other animal horns, is used in societies around the world. It was a signal horn, announcing danger or calling people to assembly. As we described earlier in the chapter on music as prophecy, the ram's horn signaled the year of jubilee. In rebuilding the second temple, Nehemiah (4:17–20) explains the importance of the trumpet being affiliated with power as a voice of authority and as a signaling instrument.

Instruments are also weapons of war. Gideon was a great warrior, but in the face of overwhelming odds he needed a strategy that would thoroughly overcome his enemies. Below his small force of three hundred men, the Midianites and Amelikites settled in the valley "thick as locusts. Their camels could no more be counted than the sand on the seashore." Gideon gave each soldier a trumpet and a torch covered by a clay pot. In the early morning hours the army struck the enemy by surprise. Blowing trumpets and crashing pots, they shouted, "A sword for the LORD and for Gideon." Frightened by the sound, the Midianites turned on themselves in fighting before they realized their situation and fled (Judg. 7).

Prophecy and Healing

As we discussed in detail regarding music as prophecy and healing, in the Old Testament instruments facilitate prophecy and healing. It is quite possible that Old Testament prophets accompanied themselves on the lyre as they prophesied in the city streets. Ezekiel even seems to complain that he is nothing more than an entertainer because people will not listen to his prophecy (Ezek. 33:31–33).

Priestly Accompaniment

Throughout Israel, music was both the tool of common folk for daily activities and for community survival. As the Israelites began to evolve from a nomadic life to a kingly monarchy, worship rituals became formalized. From the days of the tabernacle to the building of the First Temple in Jerusalem, music and musicians were formed into a professional class of musical clergy. Music became an important tool of praise and functioned in the role of accompanying priestly rituals, as we mentioned in Chapter 2. An excellent description of this ritual appears in 2 Chronicles 29, complete with singing and instrumental accompaniment.

This must have been an overwhelming sound and emotional experience because when Solomon earlier brought the ark into the temple, 120 trumpets and singers accompanied the procession in praise until "the temple of the LORD was filled with a cloud, and the priests could not perform their service because of the cloud, for the glory of the LORD filled the temple of God" (2 Chron. 5:13–14). It is this image of worship that so inspires musicians. This formal ritual does not happen accidentally, as David understood. It takes preparation, formal organization, and commitment to the craft.

In 1 Chronicles, David set apart a priestly or professional class of musicians for service to accompany the ark in tabernacle worship.

Of 38,000 Levites, 4,000 were instrumentalists! (1 Chron. 23:5). Singers and instrumentalists were organized much like the musician guilds of neighboring societies. Guilds of musicians were expected to learn specific songs, undertake instruction, and rehearse. In Mesopotamia, as early as 4000 B.C., cuneiform tablets have revealed contracts for singers to perform psalm singing in Sumerian temples (Malm, 1995, p. 97). Set apart for temple service, David's musicians at a professional class would virtually thrive until sometime before the destruction of the temple in A.D. 70.

It was then that the worship patterns changed from a system of sacrifice in the temple to one of public worship and instruction in the synagogue. Synagogue worship and instruction involved elements of praise, prayer, and instruction through the reading of Scripture and exposition (Martin, 1975, p. 24). Instruments of sacrifice gave way to the intonation and chanting of Scripture. It is from the later practice that the New Testament church inherits its form, while Old Testament metaphors inform its language.

The New Testament and Instruments

The Old Testament was the instrumentalist's dream. It was noisy, flashy, prophetic, loud, and exciting. It was a world of music, in which you sang while you worked, tapped on a drum and danced around when you felt happy, or mourned in sadness with the gentle strum of strings. Then we enter the New Testament era. It sounds and reads like one of silence. Are we to put our instruments down? Is there some direction for instruments in the kingdom?

Musical life didn't stop for New Testament people; it just changed in many ways. In the day-to-day routine mothers still sang lullabies, field workers and sailors sang songs, and portable instruments like the flute and lyre hung from the belts of young shepherds who played them in the heat of the day to pass the time. What did change was the religious life.

Slowly at first, and then in waves, it became a time of persecution. Early believers attended the synagogue, but as Greeks, Romans, and Samaritans began to follow in the Way of what would become

Social and Cultural Use
Signal, Symbol, Accompaniment

Emotional Expression Enjoyment	Assembly, Pronouncement, and War	Praise and Worship	Prophecy and Healing
References and Events			
Gen. 4:19 Origins	Exod. 19:13 Assembly	Exod. 15:20 Joyous praise	1 Sam. 10:5–7 Prophecy and Saul
Gen. 31:27 Joyous event	Lev. 25:9 Call to justice (Jubilee)	Exod. 19:19 Symbol of God's power	1 Sam. 16:23 Healing
1 Kings 1:40 Rejoicing with Solomon	Num. 29 Feast of Trumpets, sacrifice	Exod. 20:18 Presence of God	2 Kings 3:15 Prophecy of Elisha
Job 21:12 Making merry	Josh. 6 To accompany the ark in war—Jericho	2 Sam. 6:14 Sound of the ark and David dancing	1 Chron. 15:16 The ark is brought to Jerusalem
Job 30:31 Mourning	Judg. 7:22 300 trumpets in war	1 Chron. 15:16 The ark is brought to Jerusalem (bronze)	1 Chron. 25:1 Set apart for prophecy
Dan. 3:5 Instrument of Nebuchadnezzar	2 Sam. 2:28 War signal	2 Chron. 5:11–14 Overwhelming temple music	2 Chron. 5:11–14 Overwhelming temple music
Matt. 11:17 Mourning	1 Chron. 15:16 The ark is brought to Jerusalem	2 Chron. 29:25–30 Temple worship	Isa. 5:12 Music in disregard of God
Matt. 9:23 Jesus dismisses the flute players	2 Chron. 13:12 Battle cry	Ps. 150:4 Praise	Isa. 23:16 History
	Ezra 3:10–12 Return from exile and rebuilding the temple	Isa. 24:8 Silence as judgment	Isa. 24:8 Silence as judgment
	Neh. 4:18 Trumpet as signal	Ezra 3:10–12 Return from exile and rebuilding the temple	Jer. 4:19–21 Call to prophecy
	Dan. 3:5 Instrument of Nebuchadnezzar	Isa. 38:20 Eternal praise	Amos 5:23 Unheard
	Hos. 8:1 Call to action		1 Cor. 14:7 Metaphor
	Joel 2:1, 15 Call to sacred assembly		
	Rev. 8–11 Seven trumpets of angels		

Figure 10.1. Biblical Instruments

Christianity, worship began to take on a new form. Lines began to be drawn between who belonged to which group. Where did their loyalties and allegiance lie? It is hard to know what people think and believe, so outward expression becomes important. And instruments can be a concrete symbol of allegiance.

Christians lived in and between worlds of religious thought and music. Both Greek and Roman cultures had highly developed music systems that accompanied religious rituals, sporting events, and social occasions. Because music was so closely associated with religious ceremonies, most Christians maintained a separation from rites that were in direct contradiction to a godly lifestyle. The conflict and controversy is well documented for the Corinthian church. Lawsuits, sexual immorality, food sacrificed to the idols of other religions, and conflict in worship styles caused tremendous division among a body of believers, finding their way in the practice of faith. For many it was easier to draw lines than to deal with the basic principles of the faith.

Aside from the heritage of synagogue worship, which had no instruments, save possibly for the sounding of the shofar to call the assembly, there was not a tradition of instruments to build on. Because believers met in homes, often in secret, instruments were no longer needed for war and sacrifice. When the Greeks, Romans, and other nationalities joined the movement, they faced a dilemma similar to that modern-day instrumentalists face. Can the same tools be used in a new context? Because the Greek lyre and aulos were used in the cult of the gods Apollo and Dionysus, and especially with many Roman ceremonies that were quite offensive, the answer was no. As in every Christian age to follow, there would have been a concern for the harvest and skepticism about the beat of the street.

Prelude to the Modern Era

Early Christian communities faced three hundred years of sporadic persecution. With the Roman Empire in decline and the sacking of Rome by barbarians, it was not until Constantine converted to Christianity in 393 that some organization and peace came to the Christian movement. With the blessing of Constantine, the Roman authority began to codify. First, there was the development of a church cantor. In monasteries, the cantor took on more responsibilities than singing, including certain administrative acts of maintaining libraries and directing the liturgy. By the eighth century there existed a Schola Cantorum, a singing school for a clergy guild of musicians in the image of Old Testament Levites. From this time, musical instruments slowly returned to the liturgical context from outside the church, primarily to accompany singing.

306

Instruments for Worship

Because of pagan associations with Greek and Roman culture, the church for many centuries did not allow instruments within the liturgy of the church. We can imagine that there was an instrumental dualism: instruments were not used in worship, but could be enjoyed outside the church. This is certainly the case in Islam, where the incantation of prayer is for worship, while Arab culture outside the mosque breathes with music informed by Islam.

In Figure 10.2, you can see how instruments are viewed in the kingdom. In the circle, and outside the box, are the churches that use no instruments in worship. Today these are primarily Orthodox traditions. Both John Calvin and Ulrich Zwingli (1484–1531) prohibited instruments in church worship, including "humanly composed" songs. This tradition continues today as stated in the Constitution of the Reformed Presbyterian Church of North America:

> The singing of praise is an ordinance of worship and is expressed in words set to music. The Psalms of the Bible, by reason of their excellence and their Divine inspiration and appointment are to be sung in the worship of God, to the exclusion of all songs and hymns of human composure. They are to be sung without the accompaniment of instruments, inasmuch as these are not authorized in the New Testament. (RFCNA, 1970, p. 307)

For these parts of the kingdom, which have taken a more dogmatic and bounded-set view of Scripture, the discussion of instruments is a mute point. Because they were not authorized in the New Testament, they may be enjoyed only outside the "sacred" city. They will not be heard in praise of God again until the establishment of the future City of God. On one level I can appreciate this pietistic approach to worship. As we saw in the discussion on the voice, the human voice provides a meditative and soulful connection to the Word that can be difficult to find in contemporary and secularized musical styles and idioms. The noninstrumental worship experience, especially in the quiet of seclusion, provides a setting for innermost contemplation and communion with God. It takes training and focus to really appreciate the music and worship experience of these traditions.

In the circle within the box are the many churches through history which have used instruments of all kinds. By far, the majority of Christians accept and use instruments, though they vary in which kind and for what purpose.

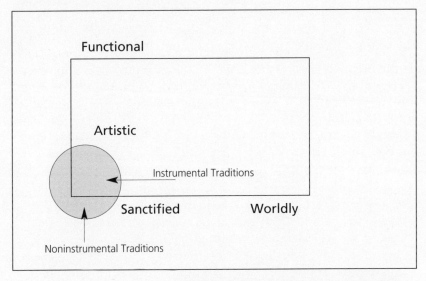

Figure 10.2. Instruments in Worship

For those who have taken a more centered-set and less dogmatic approach to Scripture, the choice of instruments requires careful adaptation. In this matrix are the changes that often occur as instruments are adopted and introduced into the Christian context. The process is similar to the one I described in the previous chapter regarding acceptance of worldly music styles. There are three variables that determine the use of instruments: context, functional-artistic continuum, and worldly-sanctified continuum.

Context. The first consideration in the use of an instrument begins with the historical and cultural context. Early church worship excluded instruments from worship. To the best of my knowledge. there has not been an instrument created specifically for the church, although many developments have occurred for church purposes.

A case in point is the organ. First invented by the Greeks about the third century B.C., the *hydraulis* used water as a way of producing sound. In a long and more technical process, the organ appeared in the courts of royalty, until sometime in the tenth century, when it made an appearance in a cathedral in France. This introduction had to do with more than its availability. Larger buildings means more acoustical space to fill. It is the same principle that necessitates public address systems in large buildings. It takes more sound to fill the room. The development of the keyboard also provided a practical way for one person to play all the notes of a four-part composition. As the organ became "sanctified" for church purposes and music was composed for the organ and its use in accompaniment, other modifications became available, such as the reed organ around 1850 (Hustad, 1993).

Functional-Artistic Continuum. Any instrument in the kingdom can be evaluated on the functional-artistic continuum. A functional instrument is practical, portable, and relatively inexpensive and requires a minimum of effort to utilize in music-making. Drums and tambourines, even guitars, are excellent examples of this end of the continuum. They also represent instruments available for a holistic church. In the case of the reed organ, these instruments were never considered "artistic" (though they may have been played with artistry) and remained functional in the accompaniment of choirs and facilitation of liturgy. Eventually, with the introduction of the piano by Charles Alexander in the evangelistic revivals of the early twentieth century and the development of the Hammond organ in 1935, the reed organ fell into disuse (Hustad, 1993).

At the other end of the continuum, the pipe organ is an artistic instrument requiring great expense and technical expertise. Many compositions have been written specifically for the pipe organ, and it takes sophisticated technical skill to play one well. They are also very expensive to purchase and maintain. It may be the most artistic (in these characteristics) of all instruments used in the church.

The Salvation Army is a good example of the integration of the functional and the artistic. William Booth (1829–1912) began to work with the poor of London in 1865. A Methodist minister, he resigned his pastorate to reach to common laborers who enjoyed bar tunes more than church songs. Starting with two converted members of a local band, Booth saw the attraction of music. "Music would not be an end in itself but a means to an end, the 'salvation of souls.'" In his words, "We want to use our instruments to blow salvation into the sinner" (Smith, 1986, p. 279). Booth even prohibited the use of harmoniums because of their association with the organized church! Marching into the streets the bands played popular tunes. Not only were "souls" added to the kingdom, but many fine Salvation Army bands still exist. The Salvation Army has cultivated a very high standard of artistry in their music, and the musicians regularly perform the "classics" and their own composed music in the concert halls around the world (Miller, 1993).

Worldly-Sanctified Continuum. Christians live in the world and express their human gifts and emotions with "worldly" instruments. Because the New Testament did not specifically instruct the use of instruments, Calvin and Zwingli considered them inappropriate for worship. They were "worldly." Salvation Army founder William Booth took "worldly" instruments and sanctified them for kingdom use. This "worldly" designation, like the early church, has to do with the pagan and immoral associations that attach themselves to the instrumental tool. As they are "sanctified" or set aside for kingdom functions they make their way into the worship context as well.

For example, you may remember the African lyre player from the chapter on worship. He was a *litunguu* (lyre) player among the Bukusu people of western Kenya. Traditionally, the *litunguu* player was considered a prophet, in that he would sing songs during important events, recount history, and even foretell the future based on current events and trends. When the lyre player became a Christian, he brought the instrument into his small church and began using it for "sanctified" purposes. When I asked him how he could take an instrument that was sometimes played in places that were non-Christian, he merely commented, "When I was baptized, my instrument was baptized also."

Sacred Instruments. In spite of our theological justifications for positions, it is the symbolic nature of instruments that creates so much controversy. Instruments are "sacred" to our identity as persons, cultures, and churches. To change facilitates a reordering of our worldview and resulting ecology of theological practice. As unlikely as this is to our closed canon of Scripture, and with no disrespect intended, what if biblical archaeologists discovered a missing manuscript of the apostle Peter? In this manuscript, he outlines the teachings of Jesus on the practice of music in the church. In this "parable of song," Jesus describes the importance of a "holy dance" before prayer, accompanied by a lyre and a drum. Prayer is to be intoned in the key of "F" and following the prayer, the faithful are to sing in unison Psalm 150 accompanied by every instrument mentioned in the psalm. How might you have to change your worship practice? Some of us would have to learn how to dance! Others might demythologize this as an uninterpreted parable on the eschatological nature of the sonic order of the kingdom. Still others might hold this up as a justification for the dancing and drumming they already enjoy. The point is this: while we do know that Jesus enjoyed music, though not in English or using Western scales, his concern was for our hearts in relation to God and each other. Our practice, the musical tools we use, the language we speak, the musical styles with which we express ourselves must always conform to kingdom will. Our present practice is as much determined by historical and cultural tradition as by biblical commands.

So as our technology changes the instruments we use, our culture incorporates our technologies and theologians seek to interpret the Scripture in our contemporary world. Young people learn to play new instruments because they spark the creative impulse. Old organists die, and with them the organ morphs into an electronic keyboard. How, then, do we use instruments in the kingdom?

An Instrumental Ministry

When selected and used with grace, instruments provide cultural identity, aesthetic enjoyment, and the musical foundation to enhance both corporate worship and private experience. Universally, and when culturally appropriate, instruments directly support ministry in eight basic ways.

1. Melodic reinforcement to aid in singing. Instruments provide excellent melodic support for both congregation and choir. Especially in the singing of new hymns, where the melody is unfamiliar, or with a young and inexperienced choir, melodic instruments reinforce, support, and encourage the human voice.

2. Melodic associations for contemplation and prayer. In times of prayer and contemplation instrumental music helps focus thoughts. Because of the associational character of melodies, instrumental music helps in recall of personal spiritual moments. It also creates a spiritual mood, where the music corresponds to cultural standards.

3. Harmonic undergirding and support. Whether organ, piano, keyboard, guitar, or instrumental group, the harmonic nature of chordal music provides a fullness and support to singing. While there are times when either the solo voice or unison singing is desirable and preferred in some contexts, the harmonic style of music can support the inner voices of a choir or congregation.

4. Rhythmic-driven accompaniment for singing and movement. Both rhythm instruments and the rhythm of music itself provide structure, forward motion, and energy to singing. In consort with dancing or liturgical movement, it sets the mood and gives the movement direction by providing the structure.

5. Timbre or color to singing and worship. Each instrument, and various combinations of instruments, have unique timbre or sounds. It is these sounds that set the mood of music and may even contribute to the healing function. Their meaning determined by culture, these musical colors help create moods. For example, to me a brass choir is bold, a string ensemble is soothing, a single flute can be light and lift my spirit.

6. Amplification of sound. Instruments extend sound beyond the human voice; in the contemporary context amplifiers often become instruments. Brass, percussion, and organ fill a room with a great sound. So do the bagpipe (a great instrument for some worship experiences) and huge, thumping drums.

7. A creative outlet for instrumental talent. The use of instruments provides a creative outlet for many gifted and talented musicians who might not use their talents elsewhere.

8. A learning aid. Research shows that children who learn to play instruments not only gain self-confidence and self-esteem, but they learn self-discipline that carries over into other parts of their lives.

Instruments from different cultures also provide a window on other cultures.

Instrumental music provides many benefits for the local community in a holistic ministry of the music. Not all instrumental music is effective, however. When played without preparation, proper maintenance, instruction, and guidance, instruments can be a distraction.

Principles for Effective Instrument Music Making

When instruments are tuned, in good condition, prepared for service, and dedicated to ministry, they are a blessing to God and the kingdom. However, when things go wrong they can become a nuisance and distraction. So below are suggestions for instrument ministry. These apply whether playing for church worship, for evangelistic meetings, or in the recording studio.

Dedication to God's Purposes. Like the *litunguu* player who baptized his instrument, musicians should dedicate themselves and their instrument to God's service. This does not mean that they only play in church! It means that their lives and instruments come under the lordship of Christ, whether it be in sanctuary, on the street or even the "secular" marketplace of academia, concert hall, recording studio, or entertainment arena. They perform a holistic ministry in God's world. Part of this dedication has to do with commitment to the highest standards within one's abilities, whether it be in practice or performance.

Not all instruments are beneficial to a particular service or ministry. Understanding the cultural appropriateness and spiritual timeliness, whether intraculturally (within one's own culture) or cross-culturally, is part of dedication. It often takes time and research to understand this need.

Support of the Text. When accompanying singers or congregations, the primary message is in the text. Care should be taken to avoid distraction from this purpose, whether it be from excessive volume or an excessive ego that draws attention away from the message. This implies that instrumentalists should be both sensitive and submissive to leaders of the service, who may perceive the need for a balance the performer does not.

Quality Instruments. Instruments are expensive, and no one should be ashamed of a used guitar, horn, organ, drum, *litunguu,* or gamelan consort. Some used instruments may be of better quality than new ones. The principle is to purchase the best you can afford. If you are not sure, seek the advice of good performers. They have experience to back up their opinions.

Rehearsal. There is no substitute for rehearsal and practice. More so than with the voice, it shows when an instrumentalist doesn't practice. In the group context, ensemble suffers. Congregations and audiences, particularly in the present day where standards of excellence in performance come from the studio, have higher expectations than ever before. However, no group should be subjected to professional standards that are impossible to meet. The important issue is to enjoy playing and to both offer and receive the music as a gift to the best of one's ability. Congregations and audiences can be especially forgiving and appreciative when the music comes from their own kingdom community. Rehearse!

Well-Tuned for Worship. This implies more than tuning the instrument; it means being in tune with others and the guidance of the Spirit. When improperly tuned, singers lose pitch. When too loud, the message is lost. When played with prideful intention, music shifts focus from God to player. Instruments should introduce and place the text in a context.

Summary

In this chapter we have discussed instruments in and for kingdom service. The basic principle is that all of the instruments in God's world are possible for the service of ministry. However, we have discovered that not all of God's people view instruments the same way. First, we looked at the instrument from the organologist point of view. Second, we considered the names, origins, and purposes of biblical instruments, including a short discussion on how different Christians have interpreted their application in the local church. We saw that there are two dimensions in the choice of an instrument: its functionality and its worldliness. Functional instruments are very portable and practical for a holistic ministry. We saw how worldly instruments can be sanctified for kingdom ministry. Finally, we looked at both principles and practices for planning an instrumental ministry.

Questions for Consideration

1. What instrument seems to cause the most conflict in your church or culture? Why?
2. Would you agree that the body is an instrument?
3. Can you think of noninstruments (like the saw) that have been used for musical worship?
4. Using the discussion of biblical instrument functions, what do instruments symbolize in your church or community?
5. Does your church have both functional and artistic instruments? Have you ever sanctified a worldly instrument?
6. Using the lists for an instrumental ministry, which of these could be improved in your home church, chapel, or community worship?

Exercises

1. Plan a service for the dedication of a new instrument. In your service, weave in passages of Scripture mentioned in the text.
2. Design and conduct a survey of your congregation regarding instruments in the church. Specifically ask what instrument they believe is "sacred."
3. Interview a believer who uses his or her instrument in service for the kingdom. Ask about his or her call, preparation for serv-

ice, practice habits, and attitude toward the worship, evangelism, and healing potential of instruments.

4. Divide into groups. As a class project, trace the history of the instruments most frequently used in your church's worship.

5. Using the instrument classification system mentioned in the chapter, how many different instrument classes are used in your home, church, school, and community?

11

Musicians

These are the men David put in charge of the music in the house of the LORD after the ark came to rest there. They ministered with music before the tabernacle, the Tent of Meeting, until Solomon built the temple of the LORD in Jerusalem. They performed their duties according to the regulations laid down for them.

(1 Chron. 6:31–33)

I also learned that the portions assigned to the Levites had not been given to them, and that all the Levites and singers had gone back to their own fields.

(Neh. 13:10)

The trumpeters and singers joined in unison, as with one voice, to give praise and thanks to the LORD.

(2 Chron. 5:13)

So far, we have seen that a ministry of music is holistic ministry. Music expresses a unity of praise and worship. It calls the kingdom to righteousness and justice. Music proclaims a saving message of God and facilitates healing of body, mind, soul, and community. Reflecting the different voices who sing about God, it teaches knowledge, wisdom, and truth. We have also learned about the voice, songs, and instruments of the kingdom. Who performs this ministry of service? Musicians.

In this chapter, we discover the nature and character of the kingdom musician. First, we will explore the call, gifting, and affirmation of the musician. Second, we will discuss the role and status musicians have within culture and the church. Third, we will consider how musicians are trained in their craft. Finally, I will propose a comprehensive model for kingdom music education and training.

The Sound of the Harvest . . .

His trumpeting voice was loud and raspy. He swung his hips in an awkward movement while making large, swooping motions to clap his hands. When open, his mouth was a full eight inches in diameter, exposing a huge dental whiteness in the moonlight. Drenched in sweat, tattered clothes hung from his clothesline frame in a soggy mass.

He was not pretty to look at, but he could sing! Not only could he sing, but he had the charisma and vocal power to wake up sleeping children and their grandmothers to join in an all-night worship service. With every musical phrase he commanded a response. Each verbal phrase was turned with Scripture, local proverbs, urban slang, and rural metaphors. Within minutes, the congregation was alive with jubilant singing.

. . . And the Beat of the Street

"It's the mixolydian mode! It's the mixolydian mode!" His jubilant voice barely carried across the room over scores of dancing seminar participants. Jay had traveled halfway around the world to share his musical talents with a hundred eager musicians who had gathered from all over the country. For a week they attended classes in music theory, worship leadership, Bible study, and musical composition. As musical leaders in their respective communities, they

318

sought the spiritual and technical skills needed for effective ministry to their growing congregations.

Jay was especially suited to this cross-cultural service. A professional musician, composer, and professor, he had many gifts at his disposal. One gift suited the situation well. He could improvise. A jazz pianist, he had composed songs for television commercials and conducted his own jazz band. He managed to balance the demands of ministry in his local church and a professional music vocation. As a theory teacher, he studied ancient church modes and modern scales. It was on the last night of the workshop that he discovered the character of local traditions. Up to this point, the students learned about Western music. When a call came for a local talent show, they began to reveal their hearts and cultures. A young woman stood to lead the group in a local Christian chorus and the group responded with enthusiasm. It was then that Jay, improvising at the keyboard, discovered a link between African traditional music and American jazz.

The Call to Make Music

Will future generations make music? An old man, who for nearly sixty years faithfully played his trumpet, said about his grandchildren, "They only want to play the computer and turn on MTV. They are not interested in learning to play an instrument." Indeed, technology has made it easy for us to relegate our music creativity to a machine. A young person described "house music" as music designed on a computer in someone's basement, for the purpose of escape. A college student enjoys composing music on his computer for personal consumption. The church is not without a similar loss of community music making. Over the past several years I have attended Bible studies, Christian conferences, and meetings in which no one present could play an instrument, nor seemed the slightest bit concerned that singing was not part of the experience.

While the Bible does not predict the coming of technology nor outlines principles for its application, it does speak very clearly about music in ancient Israel and the New Testament church. Before we can begin to answer the question regarding the future of the place of musicians in the contemporary church, we may do well to review the historical place of music.

Kingdom citizens are to sing and make music. In the Old Testament, music was an accepted and expected part of community life and worship. Everyone made music for life: to mourn, to make war, to celebrate, and to praise God. Music was prescribed, especially for the high moments of worship. Music in this ancient culture maintained an identity, provided for group cohesion, and served as a worship expression.

In temple worship, music was designated and commanded for "the ministry at the house of God." David along with the commanders of his army set aside some four thousand musicians "for the ministry of prophesying, accompanied by harps, lyres and cymbals" (1 Chron. 25:1). These musicians "were under the supervision of their fathers for the music of the temple of the LORD, with cymbals, lyres and harps, for the ministry at the house of God" (1 Chron. 25:6).

New Testament times provided completely different circumstances. The temple was destroyed, and the new place of worship was no longer a physical space but a spiritual place of "spirit and truth" (John 4). Early Christians, faced with the demands of urban life and often under persecution, were prohibited from gathering in a single location for orthodox and formalized worship. However, music making was not eliminated from worship—only adapted to the context. Blasting trumpets and noisy cymbals were less suited for the house than the temple. The church grew too fast for a professional musical clergy who could minister to diverse congregations. So the ministry of music became a congregational expression. Everyone sang, or had a song.

The writer of James seemed to understand this need and encouraged a singing church: "Is there any one of you in trouble? He should pray. Is anyone happy? Let him sings songs of praise" (James 5:13). The apostle Paul equally understood the relevance and importance of music in building the kingdom community. He encouraged the faithful to "Speak to one another with psalms, hymns and spiritual songs. Sing and make music in your heart to the Lord, always giving thanks to God the Father for everything, in the name of our Lord

Jesus Christ" (Eph. 5:19–21). In Revelation, one reads that at the end of time, all living creatures will sing, "Then I looked and heard the voice of many angels, numbering thousands upon thousands, and ten thousand times ten thousand. They encircled the throne and the living creatures and the elders. In a loud voice they sang" (Rev. 5:11–13).

With all this biblical music history, why isn't there more instruction on who these musicians are, and how they should apply their craft? As instruments are tools, musicians are carpenters. The Bible gives no more instruction on how to make a good cabinet, build a house, or dig a well. The Bible is a spiritual guide with instructions for a spiritual kingdom in a world of cultures. The emphasis is on spiritual gifts applied within cultural standards. All people are called to make music, all are gifted for spiritual service, though some are more musically talented than others. The Old Testament gives several pictures of the requirements and the basis for a musical call.

First is the picture of the young shepherd and warrior David, called to be the king of Israel. In 1 Samuel 16:18, we read that David was called to the service of Saul because of his musical ability: "I have seen a son of Jesse of Bethlehem who knows how to play the harp. He is a brave man and a warrior. He speaks well and is a fine-looking man. And the LORD is with him." Certainly the model musician, David was skillful on his instrument. His character was above reproach, and he had a spiritual relationship with God. Yet, he also had two other qualities often found in good musicians today.

First, he knew how to use language, to speak, and possibly sing, with words that communicated beautifully to life's circumstances. If his psalms are any indication, we can attest to the timeless value of his poetry. Second, while we may not like the implications in an image-driven technological society, David was good-looking (by whatever cultural standard). Not only was he pleasing to listen to, but also to look at. Both of these aesthetic qualities have positive and negative implications.

Another picture of the musical call comes from those of the temple clergy, the Levites. In 1 Chronicles 25:7, we read that the temple musicians were both trained and skilled in their musical craft. Their music was so pleasing to God that in the dedication of the ark of the covenant, "the temple of the LORD was filled with a cloud, and the priests could not perform their service because of the cloud, for the glory of the LORD filled the temple of God" (2 Chron. 5:13–14). And in at least one case, the levitical musicians had so consecrated themselves for worship that the Bible says they "had been more conscientious in consecrating themselves than the priests had been" (2 Chron. 29:34).

The Gift of Music

What is a musical gift? How do we know if someone is gifted? How does this gift of music minister? We need to make several distinctions for this discussion. First, the gift of music includes talent. Talent is what Gardner (1993) defines as a music intelligence. Second, even with a talent for music, a person exhibits an interest and enthusiasm for it. Without enthusiasm and interest, the gift is never developed through self-motivation and disciplined practice. Third, a person may exhibit a number of musical gifts. In my experience, there are, within the church context, at least seven classes of musical gifts. Some musicians have only one, some more than one, and a rare few, all seven.

Leader of Musical Groups. Like the temple musician Asaph, those with the gift of musical leadership have organizational ability. While some musical ability is necessary, good musical leaders, conductors, and organizers have the ability to conceptualize the end performance and gather people together for that purpose. Leading a musical rehearsal has more to do with guiding parts into a whole than with singing or technically playing an instrument. True, some organist/choirmasters have the wonderful gift of playing the organ well and conducting from the instrument. However, the skills of leadership are motivating musicians, negotiating conflicting sounds as well as conflicting egos, managing people, and organizing the details of performance. While these can be learned, the gift of organization and leadership is a natural ability, and, as we will discuss below, a spiritual gift of service for the kingdom.

Maker of Singing. Commonly referred to as leading singing, charismatic song leaders cause people to sing, as in the first case study. While studying church musicians on the coast of Kenya I learned a wonderful word for this gift: *mwimbishaji*. Taken from the root verb *kuimba*, "to sing," this causative verb literally means "to make to sing." Makers of singing "heat up" a group until everyone wants to enter into the singing. With or without an instrument, their charismatic personality and enthusiastic singing/leading instill trust, which allows them to introduce the song with the same charisma. This gift is not often witnessed in mainline churches, where congregational singing is led from an organ. However, in many charismatic churches with contemporary worship teams and congregational singing traditions, one can appreciate the infectious ability of a gifted person who induces people to sing by inviting them into the musical event. It is little wonder that this gift is easily transferred to the pulpit. Sometimes the ability to lead people through text and melody is a test of leadership for the pastorate. And, many pastors are excellent song leaders.

Maker of Songs. In the Native American tradition of the Navaho and Cheyenne, people who create new music are called "makers of songs." The gift of musical composition is the creative ability to make a tangible song out of available resources. Composers are thinkers in sound. Sometimes this is done through dreams or visions. Sometimes, as in the case of Esther, it is a gift of the Spirit; more often, it is crafting a composition. While some composers craft a melody and then write a text, many compose the text and create a melody that closely follows the linguistic curve. A song, however, is not born until it is actually sung or brought to life by a singing congregation or performing musician. So the true test of a maker of songs is the life of the song within his or her community.

Singer of Songs. The most prominent gift to the church is the singing of songs. Given to all, all do not exhibit the gift equally. The gift of singing is most evidenced in the use of the human voice in a culturally appropriate and acceptable manner. Cultures set their own standards for "good" vocal production. These are the ability to pronounce text, sustain a breath adequate to produce a clear tone, and express the meaning of the text in an emotional manner. Most often known as soloists, these gifted singers provide a model and example for the best in a culture's ideal of music.

Amnon Shiloah (1997) provides an interesting model derived from a study of Jewish and Muslim musicians of the Mediterranean. In the Mediterranean, there is a difference between utilitarian (functional) music and artistic music. Poet-singers are concerned with the function of their singing in community. They narrate and articulate the moods, values, and aspirations of the community. They do this through an excellent memory, a pleasing and clear voice, and dramatic (and charismatic) expression. This description is an excellent one for the solo singers of the kingdom, who inspire congregations to worship. Though the quality of "a pleasing voice" varies from culture to culture, a clear voice, excellent memory, and dramatic expression are found in many of the kingdom's singers.

Players of Instruments. Playing an instrument requires technical skill, a good ear, finger dexterity, and a sense of rhythm more acute than that demanded by singing. Anyone who has ever tried to play a drum set, finger a violin without frets, or play a Bach fugue on the piano will appreciate this gift. While a naturally gifted singer can often sing music without a rehearsed and developed voice, instrumentalists cannot easily do so. Deficiencies in technical abilities are quickly noticed. As we noted in the previous chapter, instruments are the extensions of the body. The technical ability to play certain instruments may correspond to physical characteristics and talents.

Teachers of Music. There is an old expression which states, "If you can't perform, you teach." This implies that teachers teach because they do not possess a performance ability to sustain a living through music. Contrarily, teaching is a spiritual gift "to prepare God's people for works of service, so that the body of Christ may be built up until we all reach unity in the faith and in the knowledge of the Son of God and become mature, attaining to the whole measure of the fullness of Christ" (Eph. 4:12–13).

Excellent teachers bring people from what they know into a higher and more complete holistic musicianship. This involves skill development, culturally appropriate artistic expression, critical listening, and historical understanding. Kingdom teachers also integrate their faith in learning, nurturing, and mentoring musicians into a fuller knowledge of the faith. Ask almost any musician and they will confirm that it was a special teacher who not only helped them improve their craft, but nurtured them spiritually and equipped them for ministry.

Common Singing. A final gift, given freely to all, is the ability to sing. It is this common ability on which the music of the church is given—congregational singing. Some congregations have learned to sing in parts, others enjoy the unison of plain chant or the solo-response style of the chorus. While there are a few who may have "crossed-ears" and be what is commonly referred to as "tone-deaf," where they have never learned to match pitches, no one should ever be discouraged from lifting his or her voice in song. They may never express that gift in a choir of trained musicians, yet their singing is a blessing. Related to this gift are those with the gift of hearing—listening, appreciating, understanding and growing in response to the ministry of music.

The Evidence of the Gift

Unless someone expresses a gift, we don't know he or she has one. First, a person with a musical gift, like Jeremiah, cannot hold it in (Jer. 20:9). It is an enthusiastic "fire in the bones" flaming out into sonic expression. But even more than expressing music, gifted musicians thirst for musical knowledge.

Second, those with the gift actively seek more information and training to improve on the gift they have. They seek to develop their gift. This is, as we will discover later, undertaken within the cultural structures of society, whether under the tutelage of a mentor or in a school of music.

Third, the gifted musician shows growth in technical ability. A guitar player who never progresses past three chords, a conductor who uses the same rehearsal techniques, or a vocalist with a two-song repertoire all may love music, but the potential of their gift remains limited.

Fourth, a good ear is essential. The ability to match pitches provides for a pleasing sound in solo singing and playing, but also allows harmonious consort with other musicians. This ear for music, combined with technical ability and emotional expression, gives the instrumentalist or singer the ability to move and inspire the audience. All of these gifts remain latent unless there is the audience. It is in public performance that musicians receive the affirmation of their gifts.

Affirmation of Gifts

Like the messenger who presented David to Saul, or David who later appointed the temple musicians, musical ability is affirmed by others. Many times this is indirectly. Tthere is negative affirmation through nonverbal and indirect messages. A soloist receives little applause. An instrumentalist is not invited to return for another performance. An audience refuses or is reluctant to join in singing. These nonverbal and indirect messages give negative signals about the absence of a musical gift, just as we give positive affirmation of a gift.

Immediate applause gives affirmation, as do positive comments. In Nigeria, a musician is "sprayed" by placing money on his or her forehead. Street musicians in many urban subways place a guitar case or box in the pathway for passersby to throw in their coins of appreciation and affirmation. We also have more formal ways of recognizing giftedness through diplomas and awards that set cultural standards for musical performance. While congregations may applaud and provide encouraging comments, there are more substantial methods for affirmation. Kingdom communities can affirm and encourage musicians in at least four ways.

Provide a Vision for Development. A vision is a model of perfection that individuals or groups aspire to reach. Many choirs and music groups emulate professional models. These musicians, who strive for excellence, provide both a standard and a vision for others. There are two ways this is done. First, younger and inexperienced musicians learn from the performance of others. This is the real value in choir music festivals and traveling concert groups. I have witnessed, many times, the change in young groups who began to see and hear how music could be performed through the example or modeling of more proficient musicians.

Second, it is important to see one's potential in those with similar life circumstances. In an interview with Marlene Dell-Lindo of the Caribbean Theological Center in Limon, Costa Rica, we discussed a vision for the Jamaican-descent churches of this coastal town. "We must see something that is a model for us to attain. In the past, we have had many good models from the United States, but they were not the best models, though their music was excellent. We need to see models that look like us." She, of course, was referring to the ethnicity of the performers.

Set a Standard for Development. A standard for development is an expectation of excellence. Churches can and should expect the absolute best that a musician has to offer. This is different than a standard for performance. Churches that expect musicians and their music to sound like concert pianists or recording musicians will always be disappointed and looking outside their congregations for music. At the same time, an unrealistic standard is not part of a functional ministry, but professional artistic spheres. For example, until very recently, in my thirty years of conducting choirs and instrumental groups, I have never excluded a singer or player from being part of the group because he or she "could not sing" or play an instrument. It became a challenge to expect and nurture the best from each person. This often meant confronting individuals with their deficiencies and helping them to improve the standard of the group.

A standard for development also includes improvement through continuous teaching and development. This can include participation in music festivals, church music institutes, advanced training, and opportunities for private lessons. (These we will discuss at the conclusion of the chapter.)

Give Support for Development. Should musicians be paid? Many pastors complain that their musicians leave the church and play in secular jobs to earn a living. "Our musicians are now in the business of making money," a long-time Salvation Army band member complained. Some churches hold that musicians, like many craftsmen, should give their talent to the Lord and volunteer for service. Other churches with huge resources pay a salary and even ordain ministers of music as associate pastors of churches. Regardless of whether a church has the resources to pay salaries, churches can provide different kinds of support. First, congregations and their leadership

327

can pray, not only that God will raise up and anoint gifted musicians for the church, but that the musicians could serve in effective ministry to the congregation. Second, churches can provide scholarships for private instruction and education. Finally, congregations can make a place for musicians by enlisting musicians to use gifts in ministry through teaching and performance. In this process of support, churches may have unrealistic expectations.

Show a Tolerance for Growth. Musicians, and artists in general, are a creative lot and seek to exercise their creativity in the service of God. Just as some guidelines are needed, some tolerance for growth and experimentation is also important. For example, occasionally my church invites the children's choir or youth handbell choir to share in the worship event. They are not perfect, but their sincere offering is often a touching experience. At the same time, there is some tolerance for an overenthusiastic young guitarist who has yet to learn the appropriate context for his expressive rock style playing. Nurturing congregations recognize that without a place to express youthful exuberance in the sanctuary, young people may seek unhealthy environments, outside the safety of a loving and healthy, nurturing family.

The Role of Musicians

Just as the definition of music is determined by society, so is the class of "musician." A musician is defined in terms of the ability to sing, play, compose, and lead music for the purposes of community expression in song. Most societies have a special class for musicians, just as they would classify craftsmen, doctors, or clergy. This class has certain behavioral expectations, purposes within the society, and ascribed or achieved status. With the status come certain rewards and limitations.

Just as we saw a priestly class of musicians in the culture of the Old Testament, many societies have a professional class. Achieved through excellence in performance rather than ascribed through inheritance of position, these musicians choose music as a vocation. Many people pursue music as an avocation, however, and perform on an unpaid or voluntary basis.

With the advent of technology, we see the commercialization of music and the possibility for musicians to earn enough money from recording sales to support their work. By and large, however, most musicians are avocational. Musicians in many societies work at regular jobs and perform their music as a secondary activity. Their role is definitely important to the society but their status is not very high. For example, while most congregations recognize the importance of music in the church, music and musicians remain secondary to other ministries. Recently, musicians have been elevated in status because of such strong emphasis as worship leaders in "praise and worship." There may be a correlation to the commercialization of music through the music industry.

Along with this class and status are a number of expectations for performance and behavior, some deserved and others incorrectly generalized. Musicians in most societies entertain and provide accompaniment to high cultural events at court, political events, and social functions. These entertainment and accompaniment functions often free the musician from the same behavioral expectations of people of a higher status. People expect musicians to excite and invigorate, even manipulate or evoke emotions. As part of the "special" class, society members often tolerate musicians' behavior, in a way they would not with other members. They expect that musicians are prone to inappropriate behavior with drugs, sex, and other lifestyle issues (Merriam, 1964). These same expectations and tolerance are often carried into the church and present a snare in ministry.

In an honest appraisal, musicians for the kingdom face certain dangers in ministry. There are four great personal temptations to musicians.

First, is pride. Proverbs teaches that pride goes before a fall. Confidence in one's ability is a necessary quality for the musician. It takes courage and confidence to stand before others. However, when confidence turns to overconfidence, musicians place themselves in tempting situations.

Second, pride often is the result of power. For a few minutes in Sunday worship, during a concert on stage, or in the control room of a modern studio, the musician often wields the same power as any benevolent dictator. The musician has emotional control over an audience. This power to uplift at best, and manipulate at worst, can become an addiction when ministry is focused on audience approval.

A third area is immoral behavior. Music evokes the emotions of people. When these emotions become attached to an individual they can be misdirected. Music is also a very sensual art. Plato, knowing this emotional and sensual power, was careful to prescribe which scales could be performed. The great fear of parents is that of watching their children pulled into a performance based on the strong rhythm of rock music. Even within the highly kinetic and movement-oriented cultures of Africa, Christians have determined which movements lead to sensual desires and which are appropriate for worship.

For example, the descendants of African slaves, the Gulla people of South Carolina, danced in their Christian worship in what is known as "ring-shouts." However, they were not allowed to cross their feet in dancing because of its "sinful" associations.

A final temptation is that of selfish ambition. In interviews with contemporary Christian musicians—Big Tent Revival, The Waiting, and Jars of Clay—I asked the same question, "What motivates your music?" Immediately all three responded, "The money!" They were joking, of course, and explained that that is the stereotype many people have of Christian recording artists. Many of these artists live a meager life in order to share their faith through music. Though not limited to the entertainment arena of commercial music, the temptation of some Christian musicians is to obtain a lucrative recording contract. The more recordings they sell, the more money they make. This temptation can also lead to another, and that is to compromise the message in order to sell more recordings (or have more people in attendance at a concert, for that matter). However, we should not confuse compromise with contextualization. There is a difference. In the former, one hides or omits the truth; in the latter, one tries to make the truth relevant to an unbelieving audience bridging from one culture to another.

A Ministry of Music

Musicians, like other ministers and leaders of the church, should be held accountable for their lives and work. This may be the problem. Musicians are not held accountable because they are marginalized, sometimes as a special class, and therefore, do not serve on committees, participate in Bible study, or join in other growth opportunities. As a young music educator, I was encouraged and mentored by a local pastor who saw in me a gift for the church I could not or would not see. Over a period of four years, he nurtured me, informally, into a ministry that has lasted to this day.

Both church leaders and young musicians can take heart in Paul's letters to Timothy. Left alone in a growing church congregation with numerous problems, Timothy seemed to internalize the stress of his assignment and faced stomach and other ailments. As a young leader, he was faced with the complaints of widows, demands of authoritarian elders, the sexual temptations of younger widows, and the allure of wealth. Timothy was to be diligent in watching both his life and doctrinal belief (1 Tim. 4:15–16). This took the direct advice to be confident in the face of elders who would use his youth against him, to be self-disciplined in his personal life, and to remain pure of the desires of youth, money, and sex. He was not to rely only on youthful energy, but train for future ministry. Paul also knew that Timothy could be pulled into useless arguments. By focusing on his ministry—"keep your head in all situations, endure hardships, do the work of an evangelist, discharge all the duties of your ministry" (2 Tim. 4:5)—Timothy could look forward to a long and productive ministry.

Following the example of Paul and Timothy churches can minister to the musicians who minister to them. Within the church congregation musicians should be encouraged to fulfill their own role of ministry as persons of prayer. Congregations sense when musicians have an inauthentic faith. When undergirded with prayer musicians are prophet/performers who see the needs of the congregation and with the Spirit's gift of music, lead, encourage, and guide the body in praise and prayer. They then help unify music expression as servants to the kingdom. This special role is one that is a spir-

331

itual gift of service for ministry. Based on the gifting of the church in Ephesians 4:11–12, music is the tool for fulfilling gifts of a holistic ministry, outlined in the first part of this book as musical priest, prophet, proclaimer, healer, preacher, and teacher. Without both spiritual and musical training, however, the kingdom may be left without an expressive voice.

The Training of Musicians for Ministry

Music is a gift to the kingdom. Because of its importance, music demands encouragement and training. This training seeks the goals of biblical understanding, Christian ministry, and musical competence within the context of a dynamic culture. It is a continual process of training and retraining as generations grow in faith, worship, and service.

Musicians learn their craft through two principal methods: imitation and directed learning. Merriam (1964) explains that early music training comes through enculturation. First, through imitation children learn the musical values of a culture through songs and games. Today much of the music enculturation of our children comes from television. Traditional music is dying out because traditional musicians, and the events that require their service, are becoming part of the past. In the congregational setting, children learn the value and enjoyment of music when the congregation expresses music in worship and education.

Second, musicians are educated through directed learning. The training of musicians can take different forms, depending on cultural tradition. In the Western literate context formal schooling and private instruction are important. Teachers may give private instruction, or in the school context a large number of students are trained through music classes, choirs, and instrumental groups. However, this is not the case in many other cultures, where a special bond or relationship develops between the teacher and student, often called a master/student or mentor-based training. An interesting example comes from India, which has a long history of classical Indian music.

Paul Warnock, a multilingual musician and professor, explained his revelation through learning to play the sitar. There are two concepts for learning Indian music: *riaz* (discipline) and the *guru-shishya parampara* (relationship of the master and the disciple). These Indian masters of music would practice twelve to sixteen hours a day. Ustad Allaudin Khan would "attach his hair to a chord attached to a rafter" so that if he nodded to sleep during his practice he would be jerked back to practice.

Warnock's guru's musical ancestry stretched back for eleven generations. In order for the tradition to pass on, a teacher needed a disciple. Warnock learned living music from the master, who allowed the student to memorize basic *ragas* (scales) and then develop his own individual style, though stamped with the imprint of the master, as he progressed in discipline. At the same time the depth of the relationship grew as the guru saw the development of the student. "None of this is possible without a teacher. You need someone who knows the way. Without a relationship with a sitar teacher my ability to learn sitar would be nonexistent." One can understand how Warnock could better experience and understand the spiritual reality underlying life—particularly his relationship with Christ (Warnock, 1996).

Twelve Principles for Music Training

The teaching of music is a holistic process. Were one to teach only musicians, there would be a wide gap in the appreciation of music and its role in the church. This is demonstrated in Figure 11.1.

Diverse segments of the congregation need to know about music and its function in the life of the kingdom community. This is taught, or rather experienced, on an informal basis through sermons, hymns, and musical concerts. As Michael Hawn suggested in correspondence, "I think the one thing that we can learn from world music makers is that the voice of the congregation is the most important in the church and the rest derives its significance, in part, because it helps sustain the [sounds of the harvests]." This does not make noncongregational music unimportant or irrelevant but places emphasis on the foundational support of the community.

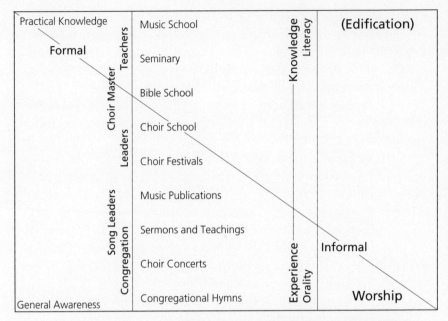

Figure 11.1. Holistic Music Education

As the gifts and practice of music become more specific, so is the need for formal instruction. In other words, while a congregation has a general awareness of the purpose of a music ministry, gifted musicians require specific training in improving their craft for ministry. This training takes place on different levels. For example, music workshops give encouragement to growing leaders. These yearly experiences, however, do not provide the training needed for advanced learning. Music education by extension, local music schools, college and seminary music programs equip a growing number of vocational and avocational musicians around the world. The following principles guide the holistic training of music ministers. The local community, students, and instructors work together for the betterment of the whole community.

Community Participation

Principle 1. The community recognizes the need and has a vision for education and training. Whether mission organization, national convention or union, or local church body, leaders recognize the need and provide encouragement, resources, and personnel for training.

Principle 2. Music education and training involve the whole kingdom community. Education should be broad-based to bring the body into understanding the function music fulfills in the kingdom. Not only should the community be aware of the functions of music, but it should participate in planning and support. For example, the Caribbean Theological Center in Limon, Costa Rica, involved ten churches with a need for music training. Cooperatively they were able to plan and implement a program a single church would be unable to do.

Principle 3. Goals are based on community and societal needs. The ultimate goal of training is to serve the community. Like individuals, communities have musical and spiritual needs and cultural traditions. Planning takes these into consideration. For example, teaching musicians where unemployment is very high may need to be coupled with job skill training.

Principle 4. Training takes place within the context of a holistic view of the kingdom of God. Musicians who submit to a calling of ministry need more than technical musical training. First, there should be a balanced study of biblical knowledge, music as it has developed in the salvation history of the church, and music within the context of contemporary and historical culture. Second, methods of training consider and respect local cultural traditions. For example, one of my best music classes was a group of African students in a diploma program. For three years, these twelve students and I lived and learned together often in the local community. We traveled to traditional events learning about culture and organizing music events for local congregations. When final examination time came one student failed miserably. The class virtually refused to accept the results and negotiated a solution whereby they could all pass together. In their tradition, all rites of passage, of which they considered this one, were completed in an age-set group.

Principle 5. The local church participates in the selection, guidance, and training of the musician. Musicians are called and affirmed from a community. It is this community that supports the student through prayer and financially, if possible. They provide a community of accountability. For example, in one final examination students were given their oral exams in front of their home congregation. While it produced some anxiety, the church responded with appreciation.

Training

Principle 6. There is a balance between skill acquisition and ministry awareness. Students understandably want to learn how to make music. While these skills are essential, without understanding, personal vision, and commitment to the holistic ministry of music, the skills become an end to themselves.

Principle 7. Training of musicians is residential, locally based, and ministry-continuous. Even with the highly specialized need for training musical professors and scholars, musicians benefit from an ongoing relationship and ministry with a local congregation. This ministry focus helps the student put theoretical learning into immediate practice.

The Students

Principle 8. Students should be multiply gifted, affirmed by their congregation, self-supporting, and ministry-reproductive. Following the principles outlined at the beginning of the chapter, music leaders are multiply gifted with spiritual and musical gifts. These are best recognized and affirmed by their congregation. A simple test of service is how well the student has effectively trained others under his or her ministry in the local context.

The Teachers

Principle 9. The effective teacher is musically competent and multimusical. Teachers require a level of musicianship that transfers across cultures. In most cases this means being multimusical with a practical performance ability in the music of several cultures. Particularly in the mission context, but in the urban setting as well, future kingdom musicians will minister to multiethnic congregations with different musical expressions. Brian E. Schrag (1989) has suggested this as an essential skill for cross-cultural musicians who become what ethnomusicologist Mantle Hood termed "bi-musical," by learning and becoming fluent in other musical systems.

Principle 10. Teachers use the local community as a classroom. Music as an art can afford the privilege of the gallery. Music as a function requires a community. There is a wealth of music in the local community that serves as a learning resource for teachers and students. Whether learning about worship rituals by attending a local service, testing the functions of music on the streets, or interviewing a local musician about technique, the local community is a classroom that cannot be replicated in a textbook or videocassette.

Principle 11. Teachers train no more students than they can personally guide through life participation. In an age of mass production, the first impulse is to train large numbers of students. The resulting problem is that the greater the student-to-teacher ratio the less time there is for meaningful interaction. The kingdom needs more mentor/teachers.

After the Training

Principle 12. One final principle may be the most important. Sometimes after musicians finish a course or graduate from a program of study, they are left as islands to discover fellowship and encouragement. Like ancient organized guilds, modern music associations provide excellent opportunities for spiritual and professional support. Today, many musicians maintain support through Internet newsgroups.

Summary and Conclusion

In this concluding chapter we considered the musical servants of the kingdom. Gifted, talented, and equipped for service they inspire us to a vision of the Celestial City depicted in Revelation. With a rich inheritance, as old as David and his temple musicians, contemporary musical priests, prophets, poets and teachers serve a holistic body called to witness in the streets. Where do they go? What lies ahead for a holistic music ministry? As a summary and conclusion I'll draw on several recent experiences.

The first comes from a memorable experience in Vietnam. Literally holding on for my life on the back of a motorcycle taxi, we sped down Hoa Binh Street on the outskirts of Ho Chi Minh City. I vividly recall the acrid smell of boiling pig blood and intestines (a favorite food) intermingled with the dust and fumes of hundreds of bicycles and motorscooters competing for every available road space. I was in search of the ancient Vietnamese Water Puppets, a unique puppet show that developed from rural Vietnamese rice culture. Earlier in the day, while visiting The Museum of Vietnamese History, I met a young college student on an outing with her brother and sister who wanted to practice their English. In the course of our conversation she told me of one of the few remaining places that still performed the ancient music.

Entering Dam Sen Park I found the Water Puppet show, and much more. Like most every city in the world, Vietnamese people tenuously hold on to tradition and eagerly grasp for innovation. Inside the walls of a small pavilion, a large group of children watched puppets appear from beneath the water. Puppet dragons breathed fire, acrobats twirled, and royalty processed, as the children marveled at how puppets could be controlled under the water. However, the real show was outside the pavilion. A military style marching band paraded about the grounds, while Hoa dancers performed a lion dance in a nearby walk-way. In a park with literally thousands of Saturday guests, I still wondered where all the people could be. In the distance the driving beat and squealing guitar of rock music drew me forward. I heard no cheers or screams like you hear at most rock concerts. Into a small park, I was greeted by thousands of Vietnamese standing in appreciative silence as young leather-clad artists danced, sang, and played Western-style rock. I came to see "Vietnamese" culture and I found it, a blend of old and new on the streets of a park. There was a place here for a kingdom musician. But it takes a specially gifted one.

In a recent Oakland, California controversy, one school board made a public statement that goes something like this: because African languages are genetically based, ebonics is a valid language and should be supported as part of the educational instruction. While they later recanted the statement, it did reveal the belief held by many people. Black (or any culture) people sing black music because they are genetically programmed to do so. Therefore, they cannot or should not sing other types of music. It crosses a musical color line that blurs the boundaries of our musical boxes of identity.

During the Angels of Harmony tour of Africa, which I described in the introduction, one choir director even verbalized the question most people were thinking: "How do you get white kids to sing like that?" Our capacity for music is infinite, our exposure to music is fluid, our selection is both personally and culturally determined. We are all bound together in forces that are greater than ourselves—change.

Change is driven by the migration and travel that brings people together in a common market. In this age of mobility—spurned by technology—change is inevitable. It is our response that impacts our music making. In some cases, our musical face is forced, as in the previously mentioned example of Cambodia, or the hegemonic demands of a sending church in "foreign lands." Sometimes the change is protected. Communities encapsulate their music to foster a strong group identity. Or, we may see the need to imprison a culture in its music by protecting people from the "outside" world. However, slowly and surely, with each new contact between cultures, as we adapt to new environments of sound and space, our identity changes and is reflected in the music we choose to express ourselves.

One can see the face blending in Nairobi, Mexico City, Ho Chi Minh City, or St. Davids, Pennsylvania (my present community). Centuries of mobility, migration, and developing communication technology drive cultures toward the top of a Babelonian pyramid. Round music is squared, square music is rounded. Young musicians may yet be born who will write a global song. Musical faces kaleidoscope and dynamically converge in search of a kingdom identity, while the soul yearns for effective service.

Determining the face of music is difficult enough in this pluralistic and global age. What may be as difficult, yet more important, is understanding the function and role music holds for Christians in this age. Can music serve the kingdom as a whole when the parts seem so different?

James Banks defined a final identity. *Globally competent* people have a concern and empathy for issues affecting all people, and while maintaining their own autonomy, seek to uphold universal concerns. Musically, we can strive for a balance between "global music expression," which implies a common language, and respect the "heart music" of people in a diverse world, while ministering in a holistic manner.

But is there yet a further identity that moves beyond our concepts of space. Can a music that holistically ministers and serves the God of earth, sky, and sea also serve in a kingdom that includes the God of cyberspace? What does the future hold for this part of the kingdom? If we could peer into the future, we might find this scenario.

In the cyber world of the future we see a lone person immersed in a computer screen, with a desire for community. Physically ill and incapable of human contact, she is searching for God and his people. Such a person is Zani.

Zani is alone. In the quiet of her bedroom, she logs on to a computer. A sole lamp lights the room. She plugs in her electrical guitar to the audio input of her computer, adjusts the video camera toward her face that will send digital signals over the Internet, and waits to participate in a global simultaneous worship service. Why worship on the Internet?

"I can attend public worship," she says. "Many Christians are repulsed by the physical disfigurements of my disease."

One day Zani, a gifted guitarist, was "surfing" the Internet and discovered a cyberchurch. The visual symbols, music, and participant comments attracted her. Through initial discussions "on line," Zani discovered people who shared similar life experiences and tastes in music—but who also reached out to her. While some had disabilities that prohibited physical worship, others were simply turned off by the music and worship of local congregations. These cyber Christians were uncritical of her appearance. Nurtured by the pastor and members of this cyberchurch, Zani was invited to participate in the weekly cyber-service.

Zani fidgets with chords and melodies until 3:00 A.M. Her computer screen lights up. The conductor appears on-screen and counts out, "1-2-3-4. . . ." Zani, along with instrumentalists around the world, join in an introduction with exhilarating drive. Global Christians blend their voices as they sing, together, in the world of cyberspace—declaring the glory of God.

While this scenario may be difficult to understand, or accept, for those of us with limited computer knowledge and skills, it is beginning to happen. There is a call for kingdom musicians in this world as well. In the final analysis, God has given individuals and cultures the gift of music and the capacity to respond to music, wherever they are. This musical response to a relationship with a living God and an expressive offering to the Giver of this blessing, is a means of acknowledging Christ's lordship over our lives and declaring God's glory and salvation. Because of this gifting, we are individually and collectively accountable to God in a vast kingdom, deep in tradition and wide in cultural diversity, and beyond the limitations of physical space.

Christians must embrace a holistic ministry that includes music making at every level of life experience, including places outside the church sanctuary. Music making is not a secondary activity and ministry for Christians. Nor does a holistic music ministry make music making a utilitarian tool for manipulating people into conforming to our purposes. While I have focused on the functions of music within a few recognizable categories, and reported what I see happening in the kingdom, God is not bound by our categories. The Spirit of God can lift the human spirit, convict of transgression, or heal the grieving soul through any music, in any context.

This does not mean, however, that we should uncritically go willynilly about the world believing that music has no meaning, or that our own expressions of faith will speak to others. Music is as much about people who participate, as the music itself. Christians of every gifting, social class, race, and ethnicity are called to be faithful to God; and communicate, by expressing their own spiritual harvest in the beats of the streets, expanding and growing in the fullness of a kingdom still to come.

Exercises

1. Interview several musicians, both expert professionals and avocational (volunteer) musicians. Using themes from the chapter, discuss with them their gifting, training, and ministry of music.
2. Have a class discussion about the spiritual difficulties for musicians. In what ways can musicians minister and mentor each other? In what way should the church minister to musicians?
3. Using the figure regarding a holistic music education, survey your church to see which of these activities are already being done. In what ways could your church improve the ministry of music through education and training?
4. Design a church music newsletter that would assist musicians in gaining a fuller understanding of their ministry.
5. Debate the role of a music ministry for cyberspace of the Internet. If available, have a computer expert who is interested in music visit your class and discuss the ways in which music is now being used on the Internet, and the potential for Christian musicians.

References

Adeney, Bernard T. 1995. *Strange Virtues: Ethics in a Multicultural World*. Downers Grove: InterVarsity.

Afagbegee, Gabby-Lio Kagiso. 1984. Inculturation: Drums Are Not Enough. *The African Ecclesial Review* 26, Number 6: 369–71.

Aldrich, Joseph C. 1981. *Life-Style Evangelism: Crossing Traditional Boundaries to Reach the Unbelieving World*. Portland: Multnomah.

Allen, K., and J. Blascovich. 1994. Effects of Music on Cardiovascular Reactivity among Surgeons. *JAMA* 272: 882–84.

AMTA homepage. American Music Therapy Association <http://www.namt.com> 8455 Colesville Road, Suite 1000, Silver Spring, Maryland 20910, USA (301) 589–3300, Fax: (310) 589–5175.

Baert, María Luisa Santillán. 1992. The Church and Liberation. In *Voces*, pp. 68–71.

Bailey, Albert Edward. 1950. *The Gospel in Hymns: Backgrounds and Interpretations*. New York: Charles Scribner's Sons.

Balisky, Lila W. 1997. Theology in Song: Ethiopia's Tesfaye Gabbiso. *Missiology: An international Review*, Vol. 35, No. 4, October 1997: 447–456

Bane, Randall. 1991. Dancing before the Lord. *Ministries Today*. May/June.

Banks, James A. 1988. *Multiethnic Education: Theory and Practice*. 2nd ed. Boston: Allyn & Bacon.

Barrett, David B., editor. 1971. *African Initiatives in Religion*. Nairobi: East African Publishing House.

Bebey, Francis. 1975. *African Music: A People's Art*. Translated by Josephine Bennett. Westport: Lawrence Hill & Company.

Becker, Gaven de. 1997. *The Gift of Fear*. New York: Little, Brown.

Berger, Joy S. January 5, 1997. Personal conversation.

———. 1998. Personal conversations and correspondence. See also Joy S. Berger, Music As a Catalyst for Pastoral Care within the Remembering Tasks of Grief. DMA dissertation. Louisville: The Southern Baptist Theological Seminary, 1993.

Best, Harold M. 1993. *Music through the Eyes of Faith*. San Francisco, Calif.: Harper.

Bice, Vesta D. March 23, 1981. *Development of Deaf Choirs*. Training manual.

Blacking, John. 1973. *How Musical Is Man?* Seattle: University of Washington Press.

Blue, Ken. 1987. *Authority to Heal*. Downers Grove: InterVarsity.

Bosch, David J. 1991. *Transforming Mission*. Maryknoll: Orbis.

Candeliaria, Michael. 1992. Justice: Extrapolations from the Concept Mishpat in the Book of Micah. In *Voces*, pp. 40–45.

Castuera, Ignacio. 1992. Justo L. González, ed., The Best Administrator Is A Poet. In *Voces: Voices from the Hispanic Church*. Nashville: Abingdon, pp. 128–36.

(The) Catholic Encyclopedia. www.knight.org.

Chen Zemin. 1996. Recent Developments in Congregational Singing in Mainland China. *1996 Annual Conference of the Hymn Society in the United States and Canada*. Oberlin, Ohio.

Chernoff, John Miller. 1985. Africa Come Back. *Repercussions: A Celebration of Africa-American Music*. Edited by Geoffrey Haydon. London: Century.

Cone, James H. 1991. *The Spirituals and the Blues*. Maryknoll: Orbis.

Corbitt, J. Nathan. 1988. Congregational Songs of the Harvest. *The Hymn* 39, no. 2: 24–25.

———. 1994. Dynamism in African Christian Music: The Search for Identity and Self-Expression. *Black Sacred Music* 8, Number 2: 1–29.

———. 1993. Music as Prophecy in the African Church. *Christian Media* 7.

Costas, Orlando E. 1982. *Christ outside the Gate: Mission beyond Christendom*. Maryknoll: Orbis.

———. 1992. Evangelism from the Periphery: The Universality of Galilee. In *Voces*, pp. 16–23.

Costello, Mark, and David Foster Wallace. 1990. *Signifying Rappers*. Hopewell, N.J.: Ecco.

Costen, Melva Wilson. 1993. *African American Christian Worship*. Nashville: Abingdon.

Cox, Harvey. 1984. *Religion in the Secular City*. New York: Simon & Schuster.

Daney, Rev. Hershell, and Rev. Bill Thompson. 1998. January 10. Tulsa, Okla.: personal interview.

DeMoss, Robert G., Jr. 1992. *Learn to Discern*. Grand Rapids: Zondervan.

Dictionary of the Ecumenical Movement. 1991. Geneva: WCC Publications.

DiSabatino, Dave. 1996. History of the Jesus Movement. Thesis at McMaster Divinity College, McMaster University, Ontario, Canada. [cited June 15, 1997]: <http://www.best.com/~dolphin/jpindex.shtml>.

Doran, Carol, and Thomas H. Troeger. 1992. *Trouble at the Table: Gathering the Tribes for Worship*. Nashville: Abingdon.

Dournon, Geneviève. 1992. Organology. In *Ethnomusicology: An Introduction*, edited by Helen Myers. New York: Norton, pp. 245–300.

Driver, Tom F. 1993. *The Magic of Ritual: Our Need for Liberating Rites That Transform Our Lives and Our Communities*. San Francisco: HarperCollins.

Dyson, Michael Eric. 1996. *Between God and Gangsta Rap: Bearing Witness to Black Culture*. New York: Oxford University Press.

Ellis, Carl. 1982. Jazz Theology: Black Music Can Teach Us How to Talk about God. *His*. February.

Ellul, Jacques. 1970. *The Meaning of the City*. Grand Rapids: Eerdmans.

Elwell, Walter A., ed. 1988. *Baker Encyclopedia of the Bible*. Grand Rapids: Baker.

Erickson, Millard J. 1992. *Introducing Christian Doctrine*. Grand Rapids: Baker.

Foley, Edward. 1996. *Foundations of Christian Music: The Music of Pre-Constantinian Christianity*. Collegeville: Liturgical.

Fonesca, Isabel. 1995. *Bury Me Standing*. New York: Vintage Departures.

Foster, Richard J. 1992. *Prayer: Finding the Heart's True Home*. San Francisco: Harper.

Fraser, David. 1995. *The Meaning of the Kingdom of God*. Monograph. Personal conversation.

Gardner, Howard. 1993. *Multiple Intelligences: The Theory in Practice*. New York: Basic.

Gaston, E. Thayer, editor. 1968. *Music in Therapy*. New York: Macmillan.

Geertz, Clifford. 1973. *The Interpretation of Cultures.* New York: Basic Books.

Green, Joel B. 1995. Healing and Health in the Ministry of Jesus. *Radix* 28.

González, Justo L., editor. 1996. ¡*Alabandle! Hispanic Christian Worship.* Nashville: Abingdon.

———. 1992. *Voices: Voices from the Hispanic Church.* Nashville: Abingdon.

Goodman, Felicitas D. 1988a. *How about Demons? Possession and Exorcism in the Modern World.* Bloomington: Indiana University Press.

———. 1988b. *Ecstasy, Ritual and Alternate Reality: Religion in a Pluralistic World.* Bloomington: Indiana University Press.

Graber, David. 1990. Experiencing Native American Music: Living with Cheyenne and Crow Indians. *Mission Focus.*

Grout, Donald J., and Claude V. Palisca. 1988. *A History of Western Music.* 4th ed. New York: W. W. Norton.

Guilbault, Jocylne. October 1991. Ethnomusicology and the Study of Music in the Caribbean. *Studies in Third World Societies,* Number 45.

Gutiérres-Achón, Raquel. 1996. An Introduction to Hispanic Hymnody. In Justo L. González, ed. *!Alabadle! Hispanic Christian Worship.* Nashville: Abingdon, pp. 101–10.

Haik-Vantoura, Suzanne; John Wheeler (ed.); Dennis Weber (transl.). 1991. *The Music of the Bible Revealed: Deciphering of a Millenary Notation.* Bibla Press.

Harper, Michael. 1986. *The Healings of Jesus.* Downers Grove. InterVarsity.

Hauerwas, Stanley, and William H. Willimon. 1989. *Resident Aliens: Life in the Christian Colony.* Nashville: Abingdon.

Hawn, C. Michael. 1996. The Consultation on Ecumenical Hymnody. *The Hymn* 47, no. 2: 26–37.

———. 1990. Hymnody and Christian Education: The Hymnal as a Teaching Resource for Children. *Review and Expositor* 87: 43–58.

The Healing Power of Music. *Health News and Review,* Spring, 1995, p. 23.

Hiebert, Paul G. 1985. *Anthropological Insights for Missionaries.* Grand Rapids: Baker.

———. 1983. *Cultural Anthropology.* 2nd ed. Grand Rapids: Baker.

———. 1976. Culture and Cross-Cultural Differences. In *Crucial Dimensions in World Evangelization.* Arthur F. Glasser, et al. editors. Pasadena: William Carey Library.

Hiebert, Paul G., and Eloise Hiebert Meneses. 1995. *Incarnational Ministry: Planting Churches in Band, Tribal, Peasant, and Urban Societies.* Grand Rapids: Baker.

Hudson, Phil. 1990. The Church and Worship Formats. *Afri-Com* 3, no. 3: 6–12.

Hunt, T. W. 1987. *Music in Missions: Discipling through Music.* Nashville: Broadman.

Hustad, Donald P. 1993. *Jubilate II: Church Music in Worship and Renewal.* Carol Stream: Hope.

Joncas, Jan Michael. 1997. *From Sacred Song to Ritual Music.* Collegeville: Liturgical.

Jourdain, Robert. 1997. *Music, the Brain, and Ecstasy: How Music Captures Our Imagination.* New York: Morrow.

Katra, William H. January 1987. A Mexican Hymnal and the Struggle for Justice. *Theology Today* 43, no. 4: 524–51.

Keller, W. Phillip. 1979. *Taming Tension.* Grand Rapids: Baker.

Kelly, Curtis. 1997. David Kolb, The Theory of Experiential Learning and ESL. URL. http://sol.brunel.ac.uk/bs_project/level2/textmbs200/textbs200_asscrit.html.

King, Roberta Rose. 1989. Pathways in Christian Music Communication: The Case of the Senufo of Cote. D'Ivoire. Ph.D. Dissertation. Fuller Theological Seminary, School of World Mission.

Klem, Herbert V. 1982. *Oral Communication of the Scripture: Insights from African Oral Art.* Pasadena: William Carey Library.

Kline, Chris. August 3, 1997. Preaching violence, Mexican rap group makes waves. *CNNInteractive*<cnn.com>

Knoke, William. 1996. *Bold New World: The Essential Road Map to the Twenty-First Century.* New York: Kodansha America.

Koenig, John. 1997. *Healing in Practicing Our Faith: A Way of Life for a Searching People.* Dorothy C. Bass, editor. San Francisco: Jossey-Bass.

Kraft, Charles H. 1991. *Comminication Theory for Christian Witness.* Nashville, Tenn.: Abingdon.

Kraybill, Donald B. 1978. *The Upside-Down Kingdom.* Scottdale: Herald.

Land, Mitchell. 1989. Communication: Our Old View Demands a New Look. *Evangelical Missions Quarterly* 25, no. 4: 410–17.

Leaver, Robin A. 1987. Theological Dimensions of Mission Hymnody: The Counterpoint of Cult and Culture. Paper presented to the 1987 meeting of International Association of Hymnody.

Lewis, C. S. 1952. *Mere Christianity.* New York: Macmillan.

Lewis, C. S. 1984. *The Joyful Christian.* New York: Macmillan Publishing Co., Inc.

Liesch, Barry. 1996. *The New Worship.* Grand Rapids: Baker.

Lingenfelter, Sherwood G., and Marvin K. Mayers. 1986. *Ministering Cross-Culturally.* Grand Rapids: Baker.

Lomax, Alan. 1976. *Cantometrics.* Berkeley: University of California Press.

Lowell, Charlie. 1997. Telephone interview with Keyboardist for Jars of Clay. 11-21-97.

Lundström, Karl-Johan, Donald K. Smith, Samuel Kenyi, and Jonathan Frerichs. 1990. *Communicating for Development: A Practical Guide.* Lutheran World Federation.

McElrath, Hugh T. 1990. The Hymnal as Compendium of Theology. *Review and Expositor* 87: 11–32.

McLuhan, Marshall, and Bruce R. Powers. 1989. *The Global Village: Transformations in World Life and Media in the 21st Century.* New York: Oxford University Press.

McLuhan, Marshall, and Quentin Fiore. 1967. *The Medium Is the Massage.* New York: Bantam.

Magesa, Laurenti. 1975. Young People and Liturgy. *The African Ecclesial Review* 17 no. 4: 206–11.

Malm, William P. 1995. *Music Cultures of the Pacific, the Near East, and Asia.* Englewood Cliffs, N.J.: Prentice-Hall.

Mapson, J. Wendell, Jr. 1984. *The Ministry of Music in the Black Church.* Valley Forge: Judson.

Martin, Ralph P. 1975. *Worship in the Early Church.* Grand Rapids: Eerdmans.

———. 1982. *The Worship of God.* Grand Rapids: Eerdmans.

Mazie, David M. August 1992. Music's Surprising Power to Heal. *Reader's Digest* (Reprint).

Mazrui, Ali A. 1986. *The Africans: A Triple Heritage.* London: BBC Publications.

Mbiti, John S. 1986. *Bible and Theology in African Christianity.* Nairobi: Oxford University Press.

Merriam, Alan P. 1964. *The Anthropology of Music.* Evanston: Northwestern University Press.

Miller, Keith. 1973. *The Becomers.* Waco: Word.

Miller, Steve. 1993. *The Contemporary Christian Music Debate: Worldy Compromise or Agent of Renewal.* Wheaton: Tyndale House.

Morgenthaler, Sally. 1995. *Worship Evangelism: Inviting Unbelievers into the Presence of God.* Grand Rapids: Zondervan.

Myers, Bryant L. 1996. *The New Context of World Mission.* Monrovia: Marc.

Munson, Marty, with Rosemary Iconis. July 1995. Plugged-In Preemies. *Prevention* 47, Issue 7: 42.

Music and Medicine: Deforia Lane's Life of Music, Healing, and Faith. 1994. Videocassette. Zondervan.

Netland, Harold A. 1991. *Dissonant Voices: Religious Pluralism and the Question of Truth.* Grand Rapids: Eerdmans.

Nettl, Bruno. 1983. *The Study of Ethnomusicology: Twenty-nine Issues and Concepts.* Urbana: University of Illinois Press.

Njoku, Jak. July 9, 1990. Personal conversation. Harare, Zimbabwe.

Nketia, J. H. Kwabena. 1974. *The Music of Africa.* New York: W. W. Norton.

Nouwen, Henri J. M. 1972. *The Wounded Healer.* New York: Doubleday.

Ong, Walter J. 1982. *Orality and Literacy.* New York: Routledge.

Paz, Octavio. 1985. *The Labyrinth of Solitude.* New York: Grove Press.

Peacock, Charlie. CCM Update-Industry News. <http://www.ccmcom.com/ccmupdate/97_09_15/news.html>

Perkins, John M. 1993. *Beyond Charity: The Call to Christian Community Development.* Grand Rapids: Baker.

———. 1982. *With Churches for All.* Ventura: Regal.

Postman, Neil. 1993. *Technopoly: The Surrender of Culture to Technology.* New York: Vintage.

Rosado, Caleb. 1992. The Church, the City, and the Compassionate Christ. In *Voces,* pp. 72–80.

Real, Michael R. 1989. *Super Media: A Cultural Studies Approach.* Beverly Hills: Sage.

Reynolds, William J., and Milburn Price. 1978. *A Joyful Sound.* New York: Holt, Rinehart & Winston.

Samovar, Larry A., Richard E. Porter, and Lisa A. Stefani. 1998. *Communication between Cultures.* Belmont, Calif.: Wadsworth.

Saurman, Mary E. August 1995. The Effect of Music on Blood Pressure and Heart Rate. *EMNews* 4, no. 3: 1.

Schrag, Brian E. 1989. Becoming Bi-Musical: The Importance and Possibility of Missionary Involvement in Music. *Missiology: In International Review,* 17, Number 3, July 1989: 311–19.

Schreiter, Robert J. 1990 Mission into the Third Millennium. *Missiology* 18, no. 1: 3–12.

Scott, Joyce, and Steve Evans. July 17, 1990. Personal correspondence.

Scott, Joyce, and Pastor David Mbuvi. 1984. *Composing Songs from Scripture.* Teaching Manual. Nairobi: African Inland Church.

Shelemay, Kay Kaufman. 1982. Zema: A Concept of Sacred Music in Ethiopia. *The World of Music* 24, Number 3: 52–64.

Shiloah, Amnon. On Jewish and Muslim Musicians of the Mediterranean. *Ethnomusicology Online* 9/10/97. Http://research.umbc.edu/eol

Shimron, Yonat. 1997. Orthodox Christianity on the Rise in the South. *Spartanburg Herald-Journal,* November 16: B5.

Shorter, Aylard, editor. 1978. *African Christian Spirituality.* London: Geoffrey Chapman.

Singing in the Pain. *Men's Health,* July/August, 1995, vol. 10, Issue 6, p. 98.

Small, Christopher. 1977. *Music, Society, and Education: An Examination of the Function of Music in Western and African Cultures with Its Impact on Society and Its Use in Education.* New York: Schirmer.

Smith, Donald. 1992. *Creating Understanding: A Handbook for Christian Communication across Cultural Landscapes.* Grand Rapids: Zondervan.

Smith, G. Douglas. 1986. The British Brass Band and the American Churchestra. *Review and Expositor* 83, no. 2: 275–87.

Spencer, Jon Michael. 1990. *Protest and Praise; Sacred Music of Black Religion.* Minneapolis: Fortress.

———. 1991. *Theological Music: Introduction to Theomusicology.* New York: Greenwood.

———. 1989. The Theology of American Popular Music. *Black Sacred Music* 3, no. 2: 7.

Starosta, William J. 1984. Qualitative Content Analysis: A Burkeian Perspective. In *Methods for Intercultural Communication Research.* William B. Gudykunst and Young Yun Kim, editors. Beverly Hills: Sage.

Storr, Anthony. 1992. *Music and the Mind.* New York: Random House.

The Story of Taizé. 1997. Ateliers et Presses de Taizé.

Stott, John R. W. 1975. *Christian Mission in the Modern World.* Downers Grove: InterVarsity.

Sum, Thang Cin. 1995. The Mourning Songs of the Zomi People of Myanmar. Student Research Paper.

Taylor, Jim, and Watts Wacker with Howard Means. 1997. *The 500-Delta: What Happens after What Comes Next.* New York: HarperBusiness.

Tippett, A. R. 1967. *Solomon Islands Christianity: A Study in Growth and Obstruction.* New York: Friendship.

Titon, Jeff Todd, editor. 1996. *World's of Music: An Introduction to the Music of the World's Peoples.* 3rd ed. New York: Schirmer.

Volbrecht, Terry. 1991. *Songsources: Using Popular Music in the Teaching of English.* Cape Town: Buchu.

Wahby, Wafeek Samuel. 1992. Congregational Singing: A Dual Blessing. *Orientation Express.* J. Nathan Corbitt, editor. Nairobi: Communication Press.

Wan, Dr. William. February 29, 1996. Interview. Eastern College.

Warnock. Paul. July 1996. Riaz and the Guru-Shishya Parampara. Personal correspondence.

Webber, Robert E. 1985. *Worship Is a Verb.* Dallas: Word.

Wenger, Malcolm. 1990. Sing to the Lord a New Song. *Mission Focus.*

West, Cornell. 1993. *Prophetic Reflections: Notes on Race and Power in America.* Monroe: Common Courage.

Whelan, Thomas. 1983. Liturgical Music and Ethnomusicology. *The African Ecclesial Review* 25, no. 3: 172–82.

The Willowbank Report. 1978. Report on a Consultation on GOSPEL AND CULTURE. Wheaton: Lausaunne Committee for World Evangelization.

Witt, Marcus. 1996. Leaders Don't Push. Strange Communications. <http://www.strang.com/mt/stories.mfl97101.htm>

Wolterstorff, Nicholas. 1983. *Until Justice and Peace Embrace.* Grand Rapids: Eerdmans.

World Heath Report 1997-Executive Summery. http://www.who.ch/whr/1997/exsum97e.htm#the_state_of_world_health

Yoder, John Howard. 1972. *The Politics of Jesus.* Grand Rapids: Eerdmans.

York, Terry W. 1996. Psalms, Hymns, and Spiritual Songs: Is There a Difference? *Southern Baptist Church Music Conference Proceedings* 13: 64–67.

Index